KT-485-911

Passionate Enquiry and School Development:
A Story About Teacher Action Research

Marion Dadds

The Falmer Press
(A member of the Taylor & Francis Group)
London • Washington, D.C.

UK   The Falmer Press, 4 John Street, London WC1N 2ET
USA   The Falmer Press, Taylor & Francis Inc., 1900 Frost Road, Suite 101,
       Bristol, PA 19007

© M. Dadds, 1995

All rights reserved. No part of this publication may be reproduced, stored in a retrieval system, or transmitted in any form or by any means, electronic, mechanical, photocopying, recording or otherwise, without permission in writing from the Publisher.

First published in 1995

A catalogue record for this book is available from the British Library

Library of Congress Cataloging-in-Publication Data are available on request

ISBN 0 7507 0432 2 cased
ISBN 0 7507 0433 0 paper

Jacket design by Caroline Archer

Typeset in 10/11.5pt Bembo by
Graphicraft Typesetters Ltd., Hong Kong.

Printed in Great Britain by Burgess Science Press, Basingstoke on paper which has a specified pH value on final paper manufacture of not less than 7.5 and is therefore 'acid free'.

Contents

Acknowledgments

One never achieves solely by one's own efforts. There are many friends and colleagues who have made invaluable and invisible contributions to the development of this work.

Prime thanks go to Vicki, to her school colleagues and to her teacher colleagues on the Advanced Diploma course. Their willingness to give freely of their time and privacy can never be repaid. Thanks are also offered to Pauline Minnis who worked extraordinarily hard in her part-time role in the early stages of fieldwork. Her contribution added scope and insight to the research.

John Elliott and Colin Conner gave invaluable advice and feedback on earlier drafts and versions of this work. Marion Blake, Alister Fraser, Susan Hart and Peter Ovens have listened to ideas in the making and this listening has helped to take my thinking further. Geoff Southworth provided the final spur to publication.

My administrative colleagues at the University of Cambridge Institute of Education have given unstinting support; John Child and, after his retirement, Gillian Morley and Barbara Shannon. Rita Harvey has suffered endless drafts and frustrations at the word-processor, keeping her counsel under the most demanding of circumstances. Mavis Robinson and Rachael Oubridge have offered many hands.

To them all I offer sincere thanks.

Preface

'The point of a story is to present itself momentarily as complete, so that it can be said: it does for now, it will do; it is an account that will last a while. Its point is briefly to make an audience connive in the telling, so that they might say: yes, that's how it was; or, that's how it could have been.' (Steedman, 1986, p. 22)

Introduction

This book is the most readable, thoughtful, and detailed study of the potential of action-research in professional education that I have read. At its heart is the case story of Vicki, a primary school teacher on a part-time course in 'Applied Research in Education' leading to a Masters Degree award. It depicts her use of action research, through a series of school-based assignments, to improve her teaching and to develop herself as a person and a professional. It also depicts her use of action research to change the curriculum and culture of the schools she worked in over the period of the course to make them more consistent with her personal and professional values.

This portrayal of a single teacher is remarkable for the extent to which it identifies and explores the relationship between the complex factors operating in the context of Vicki's work as a teacher to reveal not only the constraints on her freedom of action and judgement but the opportunities for enhancing her practice, developing herself as a person and a professional, and changing the culture of schooling. With great skill Marion Dadds renders Vicki's work as a teacher-researcher intelligible in the light of the complex interactions between her biographical context, the organisational climate and culture of the schools she worked in, and the personal qualities she brought to her professional role.

The story of Vicki testifies to the potential of action research-based professional education in Higher Education Institutions at a time in the UK, and indeed many other countries, when the role of Higher Education as an agent of professional development has been called into question, and not without some justification. Academic cultures still continue, although less than politicians and the public often think, to reproduce and model a view of the relationship between theory and practice which has demonstrably not worked; namely, that academic institutions transmit theoretical principles which can subsequently be applied to the work situation by practitioners. Such principles are largely derived from research carried out by specialist researchers operating from the academy within the framework of their discipline.

Marion Dadds case story depicts a teacher constructing her own practical theories of the situations she confronts in her classrooms and schools and testing them in action. In establishing an interactive relationship between her search for understanding and her practice Vicki displays considerable methodological creativity. As Marion Dadds portrayal reveals Vicki begins to construct a methodology of insider educational inquiry which strongly contrasts with the methodologies of research promoted within the traditional academic culture. Objectivity is reconciled with a passionate commitment to values, research methods are created to enhance rather than constrain the practical usefulness of research, and the concept of validity is redefined in terms of practical and developmental criteria. From this study of a single case Marion Dadds provides the reader with some highly generalisable insights into the potential of action research to fuse theory with practice in a form which renders it a powerful process for improving teaching and schooling.

I hope that this book will not only be read by practitioners and academics, but also by politicians, administrators, and the parents of children in our schools. It is readable stuff.

This book gives us grounds for optimism about the power of individuals to effect significant change in the work-place and its organisational context. Following the centralisation or curriculum policy-making in the UK over the past 6 years, it is now fashionable for some educational researchers in the academy to sneer at the idea of teachers undertaking innovative curriculum experiments in their classrooms and schools through the use of action research. They argue that this idea, emanating from the 1960s and 1970s, is now redundant and where it persists constitutes pure fantasy. These researchers argue for a focus on policy-making and implementation processes, and their research either aspires to become an instrument of state power or to adopt a more 'stand-offish' critical stance.

This book may just persuade the academics I have alluded to, who now call themselves 'education policy researchers' to think again about the experimental innovation tradition of curriculum inquiry which stemmed from the seminal work of Lawrence Stenhouse over twenty-five years ago. The context of Vicki's work is the course that he originally developed at CARE in the early 1970s and which was subsequently located both in Norwich and Cambridge. Stenhouse not only initiated a support for teacher-researchers through this course, but encouraged all the tutors involved with it to become researchers into their own practices as professional educators. This book exemplifies the kind of second-order action research Stenhouse encouraged in Higher Education. If more of us followed Marion Dadds' example, we might see a considerable transformation in the culture of academic institutions. Already in some the transformation process is well under way.

John Elliott
Centre for Applied Research in Education
University of East Anglia, UK

Chapter 1

Introduction

Face to face with her was an education
Of the sort you got across a well-braced gate —
One of those lean, clean, iron, roadside ones
Between two whitewashed pillars, where you could see
Deeper into the country than you expected
And discovered that the field behind the hedge
Grew more distinctly strange as you kept standing
Focused and drawn in by what barred the way. (Heaney, 1991, p. 22)

The journey metaphor is well used. Some would say that it is over used. Yet I can think of no better way to describe the learning of the two action researchers in this story.

Vicki and I began our separate travels at about the same time. She started a two-year part-time Advanced Diploma course for primary and middle school teachers. This was a major professional, in-service undertaking for her. Action research was at the heart of her work on the course. For me, coordinating and tutoring this course at the Cambridge Institute of Education was at the heart of my work. I decided to undertake some research with the teachers to improve my understanding of their learning. Action research, thus, became integral to my work for the next few years. During my action research, I asked questions of Vicki's. I needed to know how I could improve the course to support the teachers' research. Before I could do this, I needed to know what it meant for them to do action research, how it impacted on classroom practice, how it worked in the school, or not, as the case may be.

We may never fully understand what brings anyone to a major learning project. Each of the twenty-seven teacher researchers in Vicki's Advanced Diploma group would have a different story to tell. For myself, I suspect, the reasons were like the layers of the ancient landscape, or the telling of history, each reason on the surface masking a deeper and different one below. On the outer, visible layer there were identifiable professional motivations; an endless fascination with the nature of learning, for example, and with the singularity of each unique learner's experience. This had been no less interesting in my years of working with mature primary and middle school teachers in in-service education (INSET) than in my twelve previous years with primary children. Surfaces usually mask a world of underlying complexity and intricacy (Gleick, 1987). The visible world of the learner or the classroom which the busy teacher apprehends may be but an illusion or a distortion of the life beneath. As we look more closely at the seething complexity, all is not what it seems. As we take off the outer layer of perception, there are worlds to discover below.

Nor can I resist the pleasure of seeing the rewards that learning can bring, rewards that seem even greater in the face of the difficulties and struggles which have, usually, to be surmounted.

On the other hand, I regret that I also harbour an unshakeable attachment to the protestant ethic, a result, no doubt, of my working class origins. Endeavour has to be for something beyond itself. It has to justify its utilitarian value to the world. Nothing can be wasted. I struggle constantly with this and have made progress over the years, but our work and our learning must also make a small contribution to the human condition; otherwise relaxation and peace of mind are denied. Education solely for its own sake is the privilege of the leisured classes, a luxury the workers could never afford.

These fragments of personal history made it inevitable, then, that I would find a ready identity in the action research work which was thriving at the Cambridge Institute of Education when I joined the staff in 1981. The Schools' Council project (1983) found me a home as consultant. Here, I was invited to offer critical friendship support to a small group of teacher action researchers in one primary school. The experience taught me much about the possibilities and difficulties which faced teachers as they sought to study their classrooms and as a consequence create even better opportunities for children to learn. The Masters' Degree in Applied Research offered me a team teaching role. As I worked with colleagues in this context, I encountered the ideas of Stenhouse (1975), Polanyi (1958), Schon (1983) and Elliott (1981), amongst others. Here was encouragement to think seriously about the validity of personal theorizing and to see its manifestation in practice. There were collaborative field-work seminars, for example, in which teacher researchers' own knowledge and experience were valued, and, indeed, considered necessary as a resource for the development of practical theory. These evolving practical theories were also resourced by informal lectures and workshops; by ideas from other writers and researchers in the field. In addition, my parallel Advanced Diploma in Educational Studies gave me all the scope I needed to develop a pedagogy for action research with teachers of children aged three to thirteen.

In all these activities at Cambridge, the value placed on teachers' own experience and knowledge was heartening. As a primary teacher in the past I had seen myself for many years as a member of an often scorned theoretical underclass. Educational theory was a commodity made by experts in other, higher order institutions. It was difficult. It was exclusive. It was superior. Its creation and purpose were disconnected from the earthly thoughts, practices and experiences of people like myself in schools. After 1981 my professional engagement with the ideas and practice of action research restored the voice of the knower for me. Subjectivity and practitioner reflection were legalized in the making of theory. So too was the practical usefulness of theory in improving education for children. I felt I had found the holy grail.

Yet all was not settled. Glad though I was to find that theory had been located in its human and practical origins by Stenhouse, Polanyi and Schon, their perspectives were essentially cognitivist. Something was missing from the views of subjectivity which I was meeting; some deeper parts of being. There were, also, gaps in the action research literature at the time, I felt, even though the major texts were illuminating and educative in many ways and had been an invaluable resource for my learning. The seemingly tidy and logical shapes of the action research process (Kemmis and Mc Taggart, 1981; Elliott, 1981) did not appear to match adequately the experience of the teachers with whom I was working, as they struggled, persisted and endured from week to week on their research projects in schools. The teachers' descriptions and accounts of their work bore little resemblance to the tidiness of the action research models. Their research stopped, started, lurched forwards, regressed, travelled blind alleys, reached peaks. Good research planning sometimes failed. Serendipity often prospered. The teachers fretted, declared, delighted, cried, argued with colleagues, suppressed frustrations with their word processors and caretakers, left their wives and husbands in the pursuit of development and practical theories. Affective views of subjectivity were missing from my reading but not from the teachers' experiences. Affective dimensions of the action research process were missing from the neat models but not from the teachers' untidy lived realities. I had a daily urge to lift the flaps and corners of the action research arrows, spirals and boxes; to take a closer look at the embroiled underworlds below the clean theoretical diagrams. I had a need of additional and different action research discourses.

Also, the protestant ethic had become double-edged, for conscience saw me encouraging others to do what I was failing to do adequately myself. If action research was such an eminently valuable way of improving one's work and if I was persuading my in-service teachers that this was so, why was I not doing anything substantial myself? The only significant action research I had undertaken had been completed several years before as a primary school teacher (Dadds, 1978), though I had not known it as action research at the time. Since then I had only been skirting around the edges of enquiry into my practice. Credibility was becoming an issue for my conscience. I was teaching what I seemed not to know substantially from personal knowledge. There was a need to improve the professional capital of my inner world as a basis for teaching. When I searched for a focus for a substantial action research project, therefore, the possibilities were endless. There was much I did not understand about most of my in-service action research work. The main difficulty lay in limiting the choice.

The focus fell upon the in-service Advanced Diploma course. Like many other courses at the Cambridge Institute, this one sought to help teachers to relate their in-service (INSET) learning to practical classroom and school developments. The action research projects were promoted to help this. Also, many teachers before Vicki had been keen to share their learning with school colleagues, for many wanted to benefit the school in practical ways in return for the privilege, as they saw it, of day release for their attendance on the course. Some were successful in this. Others were less so and I was curious to understand what made the difference. From discussions with teachers on previous courses, several hypotheses were raised which caused me to make changes. First, I encouraged the practice of 'negotiated' research (Dadds, 1986a) between the in-service teacher and her school colleagues in anticipation that this would foster more collegial involvement and ownership and, as a consequence, help the research to find its practical value in school. The course had previously operated on a more individual mode of development, promoting more 'idiosyncratic' or individualistic research (Dadds, 1986a). Research which arose from the interests of the individual, rather than the group would, I hypothesized, be less likely to serve the needs of the school. It would be less effective in supporting practical developments beyond the teacher researcher's own classroom.

I also started to think more seriously about the role of the academic text in dissemination of research within the school. The texts which teachers were creating for the purpose of assessment for the academy might not be the most helpful for school audiences and for the development of practice. The requirements of the awarding academy might, thus, be in conflict with the needs of the school (Holly, 1984). So I suggested a range of alternative forms in which the students might present their research. These went beyond the more traditional research report to incorporate school discussion documents, school policy documents, audio-visual presentations, in-service or teaching materials. I hypothesized that this might encourage teachers to construct texts for school purposes and school audiences, texts that might be more user-friendly and oriented to practical development work. These alternative texts should, nevertheless, emerge from the systematic enquiry, analysis and reflection of the research process.

As part of my action research, I wanted to learn something of how these new features of the course were operating. I also wanted to gain deeper understanding of how in-service (INSET), teacher development and school development linked. The teachers' experiences presented something of a black box which I needed to look inside if I were to understand these matters further.

Enthusiastic beyond belief, I jumped into this bottomless research pond — and almost immediately drowned because all twenty-seven teachers on the course were willing to respond to the innumerable questions I wanted to ask in questionnaires and interviews. No one declined in the preliminary stage, contrary to my expectations. Here was my first lesson in time management within part time, no-budget action research.

In the second stage, some did decline. Now I wanted to gain perspectives from the teachers' school colleagues. I wanted to triangulate the teachers' data. So I developed questionnaires, with the possibility of follow up interviews, for the headteacher and another school colleague. Six teachers on the course acknowledged that they would feel uncomfortable with this. The other twenty-one gave me permission to go ahead. This did little to improve my time management problem. The Institute generously made available the help of Pauline Minnis as part-time research assistant for a short time to help with the interviews. The puritan boundaries of the no-budget action research creed were broken for a while. Relief and data overload set in.

In the third stage, Jo, Christopher and Vicki agreed to be the subjects of case studies. So did their school colleagues. The database was extended to include in-depth interviews with Jo, Christopher and Vicki; interviews with other school colleagues; interviews with pupils; analysis of the teachers' action research reports submitted for assessment. Jo agreed to be 'shadowed' on several occasions after return to school from the course.

From these three, Vicki's was the case story which, almost pragmatically, had the full run of my pen before the others. First I started writing the story of Jo but hesitated in the presence of sensitive and highly personalized data. Jo's story was telling of a new and undiscovered 'self' that had emerged through the research and in-service process. It was a 'self' that propelled both her research and her career forward in a strong and positive way. She found new confidence and positive self-esteem. But these also propelled her into a passionate love affair and temporary breakdown of a seemingly stable and comfortable marriage. Jo gave full clearance on the data and I started writing the story in a partially fictionalized form to disguise sensitive issues. Yet the delicacy of her story and the curious, uncomfortable prospect of committing it to permanent research text caused me many months of anxiety, inhibition and hesitation.

In the hesitation I considered beginning to write Christopher's story, but there were difficult data there, too, and difficult ethical challenges. The data were showing Christopher's as a divided school. Everyone in the field gave clearance but exposure of those controversial data in the written case story could have been harmful and hurtful to some. I hesitated over constructing a text which could reflect back that divided reality to participants. Whose responsibility would it be if the text caused further divisions and hostilities? Were some hoping that the research text would be the channel through which controversies and differences would be spoken in a way that had not happened face-to-face in the school? Was I, in that sense, being manipulated as research agent to speak publicly of others' unspoken hostilities? These were difficult research questions which inhibited me from telling the second story, despite all the many interesting and illuminating insights it raised about my areas of enquiry.

So into both these ethical chasms, Vicki's story stepped, unique in its case, as all cases are, different in many ways from the other two, yet bearing many similarities to them, and to some of the stories emerging from other teachers on the course. Vicki and Springfield School took over my pen.

To preserve anonymity as far as possible, many details about Springfield have remained invisible. Only those which arise naturally in the data or which are essential to understanding the case are revealed. Suffice it to say, here, that Springfield was a large urban school, drawing upon a varied catchment area. Many families were depressingly poor. Many led a comfortable material existence. Most parents were keenly interested in their children's education. Relationships with the community were open. The school was well resourced in comparison to many others in which course members worked.

As the reader may eventually conclude, this was a more than comfortable case to write. Most of the data was ethically unproblematic to use. Indeed, had I not had the parallel case experience of Jo and Christopher, with all their dilemmas and discomforts, I might have been more than suspicious of the positive tenor of the Springfield School material. The methodological problem of my triple role with the teachers was evident. At one and the same time I was the tutor and examiner as well as the researcher. As the tutor I would make judgments about the teachers' work in the awarding process. In offering accounts of their learning and its impact on practice to me, I often wondered if the teachers would, thus, be motivated, consciously or otherwise, to portray themselves in a favourable light. I wondered if they, and their colleagues, would only tell me what they wanted me to know, using the research to foster positive images for the purposes of assessment. There was good reason why they should. This is not to question the integrity of the teachers and their school colleagues. Rather, it is to acknowledge the difficulty all researchers have in fully believing in their data. The doubts and role conflict are exacerbated for insider researchers studying their own practice. This overlay of role relationships and role conflict are not ideal conditions for the ideal research speech situation (Dadds, 1991), for many unknowable motivations and stories may lie beneath the spoken words and deeds of field participants (Stronach, 1989). We do well to remember this when we are creating our theories. We can develop our methodologies in response but ultimately, we have to live with our inevitable doubts. To this end, one measure I employed was to invite uncomfortable and critical data about the effects of the course on teachers and practice at several points in the research. Some such uncomfortable data were forthcoming in the Springfield case. These spoke of the disruption to the smooth running of staffing arrangements and to the management of Vicki's class caused by her day release. A supply teacher was required one day weekly to release Vicki to attend the course. Extra planning, preparation and co-ordination were therefore required of Vicki, the supply teacher and senior management to optimize teaching continuity. There was, however, added pressure and disruption on Vicki, her colleagues and her pupils. Vicki's school colleague, Jeff, spoke assertively of this and of the added stress on Vicki from doing the course; of her tiredness as a result. Vicki spoke openly, too, of difficulties in her own learning.

Disconcerting though some of these data were to me as course tutor, they helped to provide some reassurance; they helped me to place more faith in the constantly 'comfortable' data, for I had evidence that Springfield participants were not reticent in feeding back 'uncomfortable' perspectives. Also, the openness of the Springfield teachers and headteacher seemed in itself to be evidence of the integrity of the data. Pauline and I were free to observe whatever we wished, speak to whoever we chose, ask questions we desired. So, in its entirety there was nothing in any of the full case data which I felt nervous about using and I felt able to make thorough use of the material without fear of damage or retribution.

During the research my thinking underwent a major shift in focus, reinforced and consolidated by Vicki's case. From looking at her story as one which taught me lessons about the links between action research and school development, I also started to ask questions about validity of teacher action research. The reasons for this change of focus and question are discussed more fully in chapter 7. Suffice it to say here, in the way of introduction, that Vicki's case caused me to see in greater detail the value that this work has for teachers and children. As a consequence, it caused me to think about the discourses which might be developed in order to enable constructive debate about the value of small scale teacher action research. The thoughts which emerged from this are elaborated in chapters 7–13. These chapters also make manifest the learning which emerged for me as a result of my engagement with Vicki's case story and can be read as an account of my thinking at a particular point in my intellectual life. This learning has not been terminal and new questions arose which led to further small scale research (Dadds, 1994c and 1995).

The selected layers of my history told here have, no doubt, helped to shape my desire to pursue this research and to argue that the teacher action researcher's voice and work be given due recognition. Through my research I have come to see more clearly the validity of such teacher action research and I have also grown to admire the unassuming, significant achievements of teachers such as Vicki by studying her learning in this way. I have also come to understand that developing theory and practice through action research is not simply a matter for the intellect. There are many forces embedded within our histories and emotional lives that are brought to bear. Vicki's action research was a form of passionate enquiry. It was informed as much by her past as her present; as much by her feelings as her thoughts.

One must resist the trap of generalizing too far beyond the particularities of the case. Yet in many ways, Vicki is herself and she is an archetype. In her story lies the landscape of many untold others. Thus there is an educational story to tell worth the telling, particular in its focus, more general in its issue.

My thinking and practice keep moving as teachers like Vicki generously share their worlds with me. Such stories provide a basis for my professional development. Witnessing the teachers' hard earned and well fought positive achievements also adds much needed enlightenment and joy to the educational scene in its more seemingly hopeless moments. Vicki's story held my attention and imagination for many years. I hope that it may hold the reader's attention for the few hours needed to investigate change and development through passionate teacher action research. If time is short, all is summarized in chapter 14.

HAROLD BRIDGES LIBRARY
S. MARTIN'S COLLEGE
LANCASTER

Chapter 2

Vicki: Teacher Action Researcher

To be an agent is to have the capability of making a difference; of intervening in the world so as to influence events which occur in that world. To be a human agent is to be a highly knowledgeable and skilled individual, who applies that knowledgeability in securing autonomy of action in the course of day-to-day life. (Giddens, 1982, p. 212)

Biographical Glimpses

Vicki started her teaching career in the late 1960s. Her first post lasted for three years in a primary school for children 5 –9-years-old. In her second post she taught for two years in a middle school for children 9–13. A full-time domestic life as wife and mother of two young children consumed her for the next seven years before she returned to teaching. Now she took up a full-time post at Springfield School where she had full class teaching responsibilities. She was also Coordinator of the Humanities Curriculum throughout the school. During her fifth year at Springfield she applied successfully for a place on the in-service Advanced Diploma course at the Cambridge Institute of Education.

An autobiographical introduction to her third and final action research report on gender in education gives a partial, but illuminating, glimpse into her past. Here was a woman from an intelligent but educationally underdeveloped respectable middle class background. Her parents were aware of, but unable to utilize, the benefits of formal education and professional development. Vicki wrote,

My father's own education and ambition was very much affected by pressures from home, social conditions and the implications of war. Although he achieved success in his chosen career, the lack of opportunity for further education was a source of deep disappointment to him.

Similarly, Vicki's mother suffered from lack of educational opportunities, a deprivation which was prevalent amongst women of her generation. Of her mother, Vicki wrote,

My mother, by the very nature of her sex and her position in society, had little education and that which she had was abruptly ended at 12 when she became a shop assistant to help alleviate the financial pressures my grandparents were suffering.

Her mother took the traditional domestic path as Vicki was to do a generation later. Unlike Vicki, this was to be the predominant pattern of her mother's life. Vicki wrote,

A career of marriage and motherhood was only briefly interrupted by a short spell of war work in a factory, an environment so alien to her as to make 'outside' work never a feasible alternative again. She is an intelligent self-educated lady whose true educational potential has never been realized.

In her mother, then, Vicki had, for better or worse a traditional domestic role model but she also experienced non-traditional parental expectations. These were patterned into Vicki's young life. Vicki believed that two factors were important in her development. First, along with her three brothers, Vicki was given educational encouragement from her parents. The children 'were always encouraged from an early age to work hard and progress', though Vicki did 'not believe (her) father transferred his own frustrated ambitions on to his children'. Second, despite being the only girl amongst four children, Vicki had no recollection of differential or unequal treatment from her parents. She wrote,

I cannot recall during my childhood and adolescence any differences in attitude or any injustices that separated me from my brothers.

Responsibilities were shared and shared fairly.

I am not aware of being given 'female' jobs. I know I brought in the coal . . . I had a much younger brother but caring for him did not fall specifically to me. The allocation of chores was scrupulously fair and the only restrictions I experienced were those that would have been labelled 'moral protection' and were those my brothers were not subjected to.

If anything, Vicki was the subject of a certain positive discrimination by her father.

Opportunities and expectations in education were no different for any of us. If anything, I was perhaps given more attention than the boys. My father was aware that 'a bit extra' was needed if you were to succeed when only a girl.

This enlightened socialization seems, however, not to have been without its problems. Vicki believed that the parity of treatment may have raised parental expectations which she failed to fulfil in choosing teaching as a career. She felt that she had failed her father. She wrote,

> He was disappointed that I chose a 'female' teaching job.

Furthermore, these experiences in the microcosm of her family culture did not fit Vicki for all she was to meet as an adult. Her parents had given Vicki every encouragement to develop multiple, rather than narrow, roles. Such encouragement was not mirrored in the world at large. Vicki suggested,

> On reflection perhaps (my father) was trying to fit me into a male framework and this liberal attitude perhaps was one of the factors that ill-prepared me for the world outside and the prejudices I was to meet.

These prejudices were to rear themselves within the early stages of marriage and motherhood. The marriage was a meeting of contrary beliefs, attitudes, expectations and life experiences.

> Marriage was the greatest shock. I had been an independent if some-what naive being. My husband had come straight from home, from a mother who diligently waited on her last fledgling. I was shocked at the role I was expected to adopt as he was equally shocked that I was not prepared or even able to take on that role; that of stepping into his mother's shoes or the housewife role.

Bringing those two sets of beliefs, attitudes and world views together may have been a painful, traumatic transition. The problem was compounded by the romantic and misleading models of love and marriage which these two young people had encountered. Vicki wrote,

> Adjusting and compromise played a great part in the first years of our marriage as the dream that had been sold to us became a reality.

Between the confidence of childhood and the disillusion of marriage, Vicki had continued to have relatively liberating and fulfilling experiences at school and college so it was little wonder that these marriage problems came as a shock. In her third successful year at secondary modern school, Vicki transferred to grammar school. She was unhappy in her final year and this led to early leaving at the end of the lower sixth and acceptance to 'teacher training college on just my "0" levels'. College more than compensated for a year of unhappiness. Vicki studied at a women's college where her year group became 'autonomous, self-reliant and confident'. As young adults, Vicki and her peers learnt to manipulate 'some rather restrictive rules' but experienced a 'freedom that perhaps women in mixed colleges had not'. The absence of men may have been a deprivation of sorts but it had a bearing on the growth of positive self-images, self-esteem and confidence. She recalled,

We were not in competition with men. We deferred to no-one in our day to day lives. We were not subject to male attitudes and prejudices apart from the odd lecturer who foolhardily tried to bring elements of sexism into seminars and lectures.

This may, then, have been another important time of socialization for Vicki in which she acquired the norms, expectations, attitudes and values of a feminist culture. Like the family culture, this did not reflect the prejudices and stereotypes of a wider world which Vicki was to meet later. Whilst contributing to the growth of confidence and self-esteem, therefore, it may have failed to provide the personal resources which Vicki needed to deal with contrary and challenging perspectives on women's roles and relationships.

The 'world of work' made that challenge a reality along with the shock of marriage, for 'leaving college, marriage and starting work all came within eight weeks'. She explained that, on leaving college,

With this euphoric and pioneering spirit, we entered the world of work. Some of us, as I had, had worked to earn money during the holidays, and were aware that 'factory or shop' workers who were female suffered some inequalities. As an assembly worker in a radio crystals firm, I remember how appalled I was that the student next to me, doing exactly the same job as I was doing, got a substantially higher wage. His only extra qualification was that he was a male.

Prejudice and discrimination in the workplace were to recur. Several years later, as the mother of two children who were now 'less demanding', Vicki 'contemplated and took up supply teaching'. In doing so, she was to meet societal prejudice and discouragement once more. She applied for a post as headteacher's relief at a primary school. The courteous, solicitous but, for Vicki, stinging letter of rejection read,

I regret to inform you that you have been unsuccessful in your application for the above post.
    I thank you for your interest, it was an extremely difficult choice, the fact that your own children are still rather young was a factor that had to be taken into consideration.
    I wish you every success in your quest for a permanent post and feel sure you will be successful in the near future.

Vicki was angered that she 'was not treated as a serious professional individual but, rather, caste in the "stereotype mother role"'. This event took place in 1979 and much has changed since then. But the experience had a bearing on Vicki's long term feelings, attitudes and preoccupations, all of which would become manifest in the final year of the Advanced Diploma. The occasion was so significant that Vicki kept the letter for several years. It became background data for her action research.
    The dilemma between education and motherhood, between personal

maternal fulfilment and professional development was strong. Vicki expressed it thus,

> In my darkest moments my cry was they educate us but they don't take away our maternal instincts!

Nor was full time motherhood the dream she had expected, no more than marriage was the garden of Eden so many believe it may be. She wrote,

> The next myth to be overturned was the motherhood myth. One child still afforded some measure of independence and was no great shock, but two!

Vicki experienced a loss of self-esteem. 'The job I was actually doing held little status in the eyes of a society . . . which has persuaded us to see it as a caring but unimportant role', she wrote.

She also suffered guilt and isolation as a result of being unable to feel satisfied with her situation. She wrote,

> The middle class wife/mother who has two healthy children, a lovely home and a caring husband who is economically and emotionally supporting her, should not feel unhappy.

Yet she had to face 'the horrific fact, that life at home is dull, and often unrewarding and unfulfilling'.

The contrast is stark between the confident images we have of her childhood and adolescence, and these negating adult experiences. Here is evidence that a difficult and painful process of challenge and confrontation took place in her early adult life, a process that gave rise to anger, frustration, self-doubt. But it was a process which, as we shall see later, was to bear professional fruit for herself and many others who came within her orbit. Vicki's history determined her learning path during the Advanced Diploma.

First Impressions from the Advanced Diploma Interview

I remember little of the selection interview with her on 10 June, in the year the course began, though I still retain images of a quiet, unassuming but questioning woman with a puzzled, confused frown across her brow. She was modestly and casually dressed with a warm, comfortable, womanly but unsettled presence. My file notes from the interview reminded me that it took some time to move from descriptive conversation to the analytical. When we did, Vicki displayed a 'deep reflective style'. She was prepared to follow her thinking into new and deeper levels. The interview felt comfortable because of Vicki's 'pleasant, easy manner', though she 'fielded some tough questions on professionalism and accountability'.

We talked about her classroom practice, about her educational beliefs and her professional aspirations. We discussed points from her letter of application. More than anything, she seemed to want the course to be a stimulus to the intellectualization and development of her practice. To this end she was keen 'to keep up to date with research and innovations' and 'was interested to share ideas and opinions of other course members'.

I gained a strong sense of a new or latent Vicki waiting behind her spoken and written words of application. She saw the course as a potential catalyst. She hoped it would be 'a stimulus to bring out of myself . . . new ideas, new approaches' as well as 'reaffirming already held beliefs'.

There was strong consideration for her school too. She could already see a role for the action research projects here. They 'might reveal areas of the curriculum or school life . . . that need rethinking or revitalizing'. They might also 'bring to light certain strengths that may have been missed or (are) not being exploited to their fullest extent'. Vicki expressed a sense of obligation in this, a certain altruism, for she felt that her action research assignments 'could possibly help the school, if only in a small way, to grow and develop'.

When final selection came, I was glad to offer her a place on the course, because of her open mindedness, her willingness to entertain complexity and uncertainty, her readiness to see questions as opportunities for exploration, rather than necessities for closure. She would also be an asset to the course because it spanned the 3–13 age range across which Vicki had taught. She had valuable experience to offer.

Early Beginnings and Insecurities

Vicki's frown was, for me, to remain one of her prominent characteristics for some time in the early part of the course. She looked troubled, confused, insecure and I often wondered what lay behind it, especially as she spoke out seldom in the full course group.

The group was large, too large, twenty-seven. Like a number of other teachers, this bothered and inhibited Vicki. Several weeks into the course she came to talk to me about her sense of inadequacy, her feeling of failure in not making spoken contributions in the plenary sessions. Like many in such circumstances, she felt that others in the group had 'got it all together' and that this highlighted her own failure, lack of skills, low level of knowledge. I told her that others before her had felt this way and that I feared this was an unfortunate by-product of learning in such a large group. We compared her feelings in the small group work. Yes, life was better for her here. She felt she had something to offer, that making a contribution to debate was far easier and more purposeful.

Plenaries certainly did not suit Vicki's preferred style and context, whatever they were. And throughout the course, we both failed to release her from these inhibitions. Perhaps it was neither necessary nor desirable to do so. Her sense of self-esteem was at stake.

Her frown continued to puzzle me for some time. I often wondered if she felt as harassed as she looked and whether it had become habitual over the years of domesticity and full-time teaching. Despite her sense of inadequacy, she often raised potent questions and unassuming insights in small groups. This occasionally happened in the large group, on the few occasions when she gathered the courage to speak. The questions were, perhaps, indicative of her genuine unknowingness and confusion. One could interpret the frown as a manifestation of that and I often did. But in their effect, her questions often became a source of valuable challenge in the group. For me, these questions showed capacity for seeing into the heart of many issues, though Vicki claimed later that she did not see herself in this way.

As the course progressed through its first year, Vicki's self-confidence, like that of most of her course colleagues, developed though she never over-came her dislike of the large plenary group. I fear my unconscious expectations may have added to her problem from the outset. Vicki said, in a research interview during the second year of the course,

> I find large groups extremely difficult. I find it very difficult to offer anything in large groups. The small group work I have appreciated a lot . . . but when I went for my interview, you did say that you were looking for people who would contribute and wouldn't just soak up and wouldn't actually contribute a lot.

This expectation caused apprehension which may have posed something of a weekly torment. 'I thought after that you might get me to talk but you haven't done that, which has relaxed me more'.

Part of her development on the course was a growing ability to work more comfortably and harmoniously with a range of people, though the con-text remained important to the comfort. In her second year Vicki explained,

> We've got to the stage now when it doesn't matter what group we're in. I could work with any of the twenty-seven and be happy to say anything; it's just *en masse* that I've found difficulty. But on looking round there are four of us who are the same, as I'm not the only one.

Perhaps this compensated for her negative self-reckoning, knowing that others, too, experienced the same problem. There was a small but significant reference group with whom she could share a common, if troubled, identity.

Alec Sees a Different Person

When I test my own perceptions and memories of Vicki in the early months of the course, I find them tenuous at least. She did not stand out prominently from the full teacher group, only in as much as I worried about the seeming distance and puzzlement which I read into her frown. She made few obvious demands on me and as a result received less attention than others. Perhaps Vicki preferred it that way.

I remember the clash of perceptions on reading the first notes from her research supervisor. Alec was supporting Vicki's first action research study. His report, towards the end of the first term, the autumn, offered Vicki to me as 'a bright and lively student'. I felt guilty and confused. This was distinctly not the Vicki of the large plenary group, nor the one I had, by then, come to know through the small group work. Jealousy and a certain sense of professional inadequacy set in. How had Alec, her supervisor, been successful in drawing out a persona which I had failed to elicit?

Alec also told me that Vicki was 'already well involved in her study, has given some interesting accounts of her progress. It should be good. I look forward to reading it'.

Despite my transitory sense of failure, my professional spirits were warmed and raised by this short account, encouraged to know, again, that the teachers' progress did not stand nor fall by my own, lone efforts. Slightly comforted by my own lack of omnipotence, I think I remember relaxing my mind a little about Vicki for a while. Whatever Alec's secrets were, I was glad to be lifted of one small but significant worry.

Adding to Early Insecurities

Vicki's own account of her early course experience contradicted Alec's image. By her own admission she was starting from a recognizable base of insecurity, one experienced by many other married women who have spoken of similar feelings and who experience difficulty keeping abreast of professional developments. These insecurities provided a shaky foundation for Vicki's learning in the beginning. After the course she admitted,

> I'd been back (in teaching) five years. I know it sounds a long time but I still felt (that I missed a lot) while I was out. And when you get back you don't like to ask. Things go on around you and you can't ask all the time 'what does that mean?'

Relatively rapid and complex changes had taken place which she found confusing and unmanageable. She remembered,

> The GRIST and the TRIST — all these projects. And if you don't ask, you don't know them, so I suppose the course came at the right time for me. I was ready for something to happen.

But the first term on the course only added to Vicki's lack of self-confidence. 'The first term was awful', she said. 'I hated the first term. I loathed it.'

'Did you? Why?' I asked.

'I couldn't cope', she replied honestly. 'It was about infants and I had very little infant experience. I had nothing to offer at all really.'

In retrospect, I felt guilty and sad that a woman who had successfully nurtured two young children from the womb to the state system should have felt this way about her own knowledge and experience; should have been caused to believe that she 'had very little infant experience'. Here was a gap between my professional rhetoric and pedagogical reality. The value and necessity of personal knowledge had somehow slipped the net. This added to her low self-esteem. Yet Vicki admitted that her lack of self-confidence was endemic. 'I don't think (self-confidence) was ever particularly there', she claimed. 'I was never particularly confident all the way through.'

She also had difficulty in judging her own professional success, despite the views of colleagues. 'I knew I was reasonably successful in teaching because people told me I was', she said. 'But it's not easy to see that you're succeeding in teaching. It's one of those things that's so intangible.'

Fortunately, things improved after this difficult beginning. I was relieved to hear her say, in a post-course interview, 'But then when we got into the second term when it came into my age range, it took off.'

This seemed to start the gradual journey into improved confidence and a changing view of herself which was helped by the interest and involvement she invested in her action research projects. But more of that later.

A Second Supervisor Remembers Vicki as Colleague and Student

Harry took over from Alec as Vicki's research supervisor mid-way through the course. He had been one of Vicki's school colleagues several years previously. Now, as her guide and supporter on the course he had a new professional relationship with her. As he shared his perception of Vicki he, too, spoke of the insecurity. 'When I first knew her she was quite insecure about things, particularly about work at school', he said. He paused — then,

> She was not on a full-time contract. Because she didn't have that security it made her — kind of

Again, he paused and I waited —

> kind of almost — fretful, I guess.

The word 'fretful' caused me to think of Vicki's frown.
Harry continued,

> I think also at that time, she was almost distant — she never seemed to smile a lot.

We might congratulate Alec for his interpersonal success in finding the liveliness in Vicki so early in the course. I was to see much more smiling from Vicki as the two years of the course progressed. But Harry's testimony confirmed my early perceptions of Vicki as a worrier, as anxious, as preoccupied for I do not remember much smiling in that first term. Harry said,

And later on, when I regained contact with her on the course, well, she never seemed to smile much even then. She just seemed to be carrying around this concern and worry with her all the time.

As a colleague years previously, Harry had found her congenial and communicative, despite her insecurity. With his chin in his cupped hands, his elbows propped on the table, his head five or six years a way in the past, he reflected,

> It's actually quite difficult to remember back to that, but she was one of the few people in the school I could talk to. She was quite open.

This period in their past professional lives which they held in common was marked by an inadequate management structure within the school. Harry was pleased, eventually, to achieve promotion from his position of responsibility away to another school. He had not wanted to be linked professionally much longer with a school that was acquiring a worrying reputation.

In time, Vicki saw this headteacher leave and a new one begin. This was coincidental with the beginning of the Advanced Diploma but we will consider this change and its consequences later. Back in those times of shared dissatisfaction, Vicki proved to be a perceptive colleague.

> She was also quite aware of the shortcomings in that school and some of the people in it. I felt there was a kind of tacit understanding there. She knew that I knew what the problems were. She also knew that I was limited in what I could do about it.

It seems that Harry may have found Vicki to be a supportive colleague at that time. But her low esteem caused her to deny her right to challenge and judge. Harry said,

> She was very supportive, but I very definitely felt that she was in this frame of mind of, well, I'm coming back into teaching, and I know my place.

It was also important to her that what she valued should also be valued by others. As Harry shifted his chin and turned towards me, his eyes still fixed in the past, he said,

> And I also think she was very concerned about what her colleagues thought about her, so it was very important that the work she was doing should be taken seriously somewhere along the line.

Harry's view of her as 'intense' reinforced my own emerging perspective. He saw this as a productive, creative kind of intensity which meshed with personal integrity in the face of her beliefs and values. He saw her as 'committed and sincere in what she's doing'.

Academically, Harry thought well of her work. In fact, 'the work she did was more than adequate, much more than that', he said. This confirmed my own view of her learning, a view that was endorsed by the course external examiner who saw two of her three research studies. He was impressed by the deep and exploratory nature of her thinking and by her willingness to take risks. I had expected that her early sense of inadequacy might manifest itself in depressed academic attainment. Not so. Uncluttered by the social pressures of the plenary group context, her ability became apparent in her first action research study. After the success of this work in the first term, and Alec's report, my view of Vicki was irreversibly changed.

Thinking of my impressions of her in the selection interview, of my view of her as an open-minded, exploratory thinker and of those deep-seeing, searching questions she occasionally contributed to the world of the plenary group, I said to Harry, 'What about her mind?'

There was, he felt, a close link between her search for new understanding and a process of self-discovery. He said,

> I felt that she was very much in the process of discovering something in herself. So I always got the feeling that she would make an observation on herself, about herself, or about her understanding of something, and then that would lead on to another layer below that.

This matched my first perceptions of Vicki and gave me a sense of something absolute, eternal almost, as though Harry had taken out of my head some words, ideas of truths which I had fostered of Vicki. Those early glimpses of her thinking style which had fleeted across the selection interview unrolled across time and experience. Harry continued,

> She would always go on finding a little bit more and a little bit more.
> So there's a kind of persistence there.

As she found her way, thus, into new and deeper understandings she evolved a new idea of herself as a creator of knowledge. She seems to have developed a new view of the nature of knowledge, too; of knowledge as evolutionary, rather than fixed. Answers were no longer simply out there to be given, acquired, injected, absorbed. Knowledge, she learnt, could be created from an active process of self-creation. Harry said,

> Also, what came out, right towards the end of the course, and it showed in her attitude towards that last research project, was the sudden realization that there are no experts, there are no final answers.

Harry 'felt this to be the most important side' of her development. As such, he noted a significant change, for he 'always felt, in the early days, that she was deferring to an authority that existed somewhere out there'.

This newly evolved view of knowledge and expertise, which allowed a more positive sense of self-worth, may have been inseparable from a newly evolving confidence. She may have felt stronger about, more accepting of, herself as she came to value her own views of the world. Harry remarked,

> She also took on a more confident air about her I guess — particularly leading up to her final research assignment.

At this point, we see evidence of the shift from deference to what was outside herself, to something like pride and belief in what was inside herself. For Harry, the evidence was clear. He went on,

> I just got the feeling that it wasn't so much — (He paused to rethink, to re-shape, to formulate.) — before that she was always trying to please me with the work. But with that final research assignment — it was more a matter of, well, here it is whether you like it or not.

There had been a shift over the two years of the course from outside expertise to inner belief.

The Vicki that Two Fellow Course Colleagues Saw and Remembered

Having obtained Vicki's permission to seek views from within the teacher group, I had to decide where to locate those from a diverse group of twenty-seven.

Sue was central to the socio-network as course representative so I had expected that she would have given clear impressions of Vicki. This was not to be so. And what she did say surprised me at first, for she saw Vicki as someone who 'seemed to have her act together pretty well'.

This is not the Vicki we saw at the beginning of the course though it was more descriptive of the latter day Vicki. Sue was sharing retrospective impressions after the end of the course. And maybe, as she looked back over the shoulder of time down the tunnel of the two years just passed, her inner eye fell on the latter image of the changed, more confident, more self-believing Vicki. (It is, thus, foolish to interpret data independently of the context of time and circumstances from which they were created.) Indeed, of the three colleagues about whom Sue spoke, Jo, Christopher and Vicki, she 'saw Vicki as a person who got her act far more together than the others, to be quite honest'.

Sue had developed a closer relationship with Jo and Christopher. She engaged more with them; she felt she knew and understood them better. 'With Chris and Jo I got into in-depth discussions about their work, about various ups and downs at work and that sort of thing', Sue reported.

She had shared professional chit-chat with Vicki. 'There was perhaps more superficial chat with Vicki', she explained, 'about, how are you getting on, what are you doing and she would probably say, I've applied for such and such a job'. The talk was light and amicable, 'and she was always a generally friendly person rather than seeming to be heavily involved in chat', Sue said.

They shared little of themselves that was personal and they did not single each other out. 'I remember talking to her a lot', Sue said. 'It was usually with other people and it was usually about school and jobs and things, rather than more personal life.'

There is evidence of Vicki's tendency to stay near the margins of central action and interaction on the course. We saw it in her struggle to participate in large plenary groups. We can see it in a comment Harry made about her place in his small supervision group of three teachers for he observed,

> When she was (studying) at the Institute, I never felt that she was part of the little group I had. I always felt she was very much on the outside of that.

We can see it in Sue's perceptions. 'Vicki was like some other people on the course, people who seemed to be part of the course, but a distant part.'

Sue had a sense of Vicki being peripheral to the hub of debate and socializing that went on. Indeed, she did not know of any network of relationships within which Vicki operated and she could not 'remember who Vicki particularly related to off hand'.

Sue harboured the impression that no-one 'knew Vicki particularly well'. That, of course, may not have been the case. From the centre of the informal course structure that Sue dominated, it may have been difficult to see the outskirts clearly. It does not follow that such an attempt at long-sightedness renders an accurate image — just an interesting one that is worthy of consideration. Sue herself admitted that Vicki may, indeed, have operated more actively in a sub-group away from the central action, that 'she may have got involved elsewhere'. She felt that Vicki's active presence was underrepresented in the informal life of the course. The informal course life was characterized by powerful learning, talk and socializing and it was often manifest around coffee and cigarettes. Sue tried to explain,

> Well, possibly as a tutor you wouldn't have felt it quite the same as course members, but a lot of the valuable things that came out of our discussion, our visits, talks, your talks with us and the videos we watched, anything we did, a lot of the valuable stuff wasn't only during the time we spent with you, but was the discussion that went on afterwards. And when you really know people on the course, and people are being honest and really putting their feelings in, and there are lots of arguments and things going on afterwards, there is often much more deep thought posed than actually at the time when you'd had to soak it up in the course. I think Vicki was very much a course

member during lecture times or whatever you like to call it, but I think there was an awful lot of sitting outside the library and drinking coffee and those things. And we really did talk and discuss and get into debates — I mean that William Tyndale thing, and progressivism, we couldn't leave it alone.

Sue suggested that Vicki did not play a high profile role in this deferred and informal learning even though 'she no doubt had her own reasons for that'.

Neither did I have any clear memories of Vicki being centrally engaged in the language, life and laughter outside the library where the teachers gathered in the easy chairs around the coffee tables. When cigarettes, coffee and enlightenment were being put to good effect, I was usually offering supervisions or solace to course members elsewhere. I made it my business to wander around the edges of the informal processes at the beginning of the day, and when I could at the end of the day, coffee breaks and lunchtimes as the teachers gathered outside the library. But there were often a myriad diversions that prevented me from doing this often. Nor was formal data gathering a conscious part of my purpose when I did have a chance to wander. Such are our missed research opportunities.

My memory, however, retains strong images of Vicki's central role in one important small course group in the fourth term of the course. And from this, as we shall see in time, she did not withhold commitment, passion, intellect, even though these qualities were not very evident in the formal full plenary groups, nor the relatively full and, probably demanding, hurly burly of the informal course life.

Steven was the second course member who shared his perceptions of Vicki. He worked closely with her in term four in the small group and he also worked with her as a school colleague 'in the same middle school in the days when (he) was a peripatetic person'. How long ago that was, his data do not say but we were told that they 'got along fairly well as people.' He spoke of her qualities. 'From what I remember of her at school and on the course', he said, 'she seemed to be consistent. There weren't any real inconsistencies'.

This consistency was accompanied by 'fairly definite views', Steven continued, 'and I think at the end of the day she was going to let you know what those views were. You knew where you stood'.

This was consistent with Harry's testimony of her as a person of commitment and persistence.

Steven also spoke of a further dimension to the commitment that manifest itself in professional care, concern and engagement with the needs and welfare of others. He described her as a 'very caring person, very concerned for the best possible education for her pupils'.

It was a two-fold professional caring in that 'she wanted to do the best for people, certainly her pupils', and also 'in the sense that she really cared about what happened to them, and wanted to give them the best possible education, the best of herself'. This care was related to her sense of commitment and persistence of which we have already spoken. 'When I say caring I don't mean that she was soft', he explained, 'because I think if she felt something should be pursued, she would do it'.

Her moods, like those of most of us, seemed to vary. And despite his comments about consistency over the years of knowing her, Steven observed Vicki's mood swings 'because some days she would be quite jolly and outgoing and other days she seemed to be more inward looking, quiet'.

Steven saw her as a sociable person who 'seemed able to relate to both male and female equally well', but he didn't really recollect her being at the centre of anything'. Rather, any social roots she had in the course were within less 'high profile groups, and some of her relationships were ephemeral'. 'There are some people, in a group of that size, who seem to know everybody', he said, 'what they are doing, who their friends are, little lines going back and forth between these people. I don't think Vicki was like that', he observed. 'There were little groups that she got on fairly well with and nodding acquaintance with others.' Vicki agreed that this was so.

More particularly, her deepest social roots on the course may have been with old acquaintances. 'She was more comfortable with people that she knew', he explained, 'because she knew Christopher fairly well, they had worked together'.

Steven also felt her social roots lay deeper with those of like mind, heart, and beliefs, 'whose ideas she felt touched her own'. So her reference groups were, to some extent, developed through ideological matching. Vicki later confirmed this to be so. She had developed a close friendship with Joan, a nursery teacher. Vicki's child-oriented views of the curriculum were congruent with Joan's. Vicki enjoyed their discussions and mutual visits. The integrated work of the nursery teacher and the strong caring nursery ethic interested Vicki and she felt she could learn much from Joan. Their friendship continued after the course.

We should not be astonished at the difference between Sue's and Steven's views, given the nature of perception. We perceive, to a great extent, what we are. Our images are contextualized by our personalized schemas and inner eyes (Abercrombie, 1960). These comparisons show how the situational context drew in, or drew out, different parts of Vicki's persona. There was passion, commitment, intellect, in some corner of Vicki's inner experience that was manifest in some situations. There was also worry, anxiety, inadequacy at certain times and in certain circumstances. These may have been well hidden from some but not from others. None of these latter characteristics were seen by Sue. On the contrary, Sue saw Vicki as 'mature, knew what she was at, what she was about', a perspective which does not match the Vicki of the early course days and which surprised Vicki herself. Sue's perspective may have done better justice to the later images we shall soon see. Vicki seemed to present or project different parts of herself at different points in her development and change. She did not feel to be the confident, all-together person Sue saw her to be, even though she confirmed the growth in self-confidence which others saw over time. She found it strange and curious that others should construct her in this way from outer appearances, when her inner life felt otherwise.

Views from the School

We have a brief glimpse of Vicki from the perspective of Sandra, a school colleague. Sandra was working in Vicki's year team and under Vicki's leadership as Humanities Coordinator.

We are introduced to a seemingly more relaxed person in this context. As Humanities Coordinator Vicki provided a working structure, which also offered flexibility for individual differences and preferences. Sandra told us that 'Vicki's a *laissez-faire* sort of person. Providing you're doing something within the rough parameter of what she's said, she'll leave you to get on with it.'

We shall see, later, through the medium of Vicki's first action research study, the sense of responsibility she brought to her leadership and development role. Here, we can note her effectiveness in supporting the curriculum and teaching of her team. We can see how this gained her the professional respect which emerges later in other contexts. We hear from Sandra that,

> She's very good at providing the resources and the back up. So if you need something, she'll sort it out in that respect.

Here is Vicki solving problems for, and with, others; supporting them, helping.

An even briefer view from school came from two girls who were pupils in Vicki's class. From an interview designed to elicit pupils' views of Vicki's course, Wendy and Karen claimed that Vicki went along to the course to find out about 'the best ways to teach'. When asked to elaborate, Karen asserted, loyally, 'I think she's alright as she is', followed immediately by, 'she doesn't think she is'.

One wonders if Karen had seen straight to the heart of Vicki's earlier sense of inadequacy, doubt and dissatisfaction with herself. Who can say what depths of understanding move beneath the shallows of a child's words and innocent gaze.

Trying to Focus the Lights: A Transitory Summary

Here, then, are some of the many sides of the prism making the changing light of Vicki's persona, some of her own making, some reflecting the lights in the eyes of others around her. It is little use pretending that we 'know' Vicki through these partial, selected, fragments of the kaleidoscope. The best we can say is that we have been treated to some glances, through some windows, looking onto a person whose presence is common to the lives of the onlookers. That is all. No more. No less. So let us attempt, before moving along, to summarize what we might confidently claim to see in this many sided prism.

We see a woman who has encountered, from childhood through to motherhood, some contradictory socializing experiences. The liberal encouragement which her parents and her college offered to her gender role development was in sharp conflict with experiences in marriage and the workplace. She has gone through some pain and struggle in the face of the challenges to her views of self. These, as we shall come to see, contributed to the driving force behind some of Vicki's more passionate pursuits in her action research. The difficulties encountered at a deep personal and domestic level were later to be transformed into a professional mission. We shall see more of how that happened, what it looked like and how it impacted on others. Now, we will simply allude to this interweaving of the personal and domestic self with the professional self; this carrying of Vicki's experience of the past into new historical moments of the present.

We also see a woman who, despite appearing to project different parts of her self to different people, and in different contexts, nevertheless shows to all a strong sense of commitment to her ideas and beliefs. Each viewer gave testimony to this. A capacity for persistence drives her where she feels commitment.

There was also common agreement about Vicki's intellectual capabilities and about her questing nature. The searching, questioning quality of her mind was evident from the early days of the Advanced Diploma. We also know that through contradictory gender socializing experiences, there was an inherent refusal to accept norms and stereotypes which were not conducive to her growth. She has questioned others' definitions in the past and she has also questioned herself. Evidence of historical self-doubt is there.

Nor was she an intellectually complacent and accepting woman. Rather, she pushed at the boundaries of understanding and perception, almost as a matter of course. Steven once said that whenever he had clarified his thinking, Vicki would raise a question or statement that challenged him, made him rethink.

She seemed able to tolerate, even feel comfortable with, the ambiguities and uncertainties of this questioning. This was complemented by other intellectual qualities for there was evidence of certainty, definite views, firm beliefs. We have hints of the strong person-centred nature of these in the care and concern that Vicki expressed for her pupils' development and well being; in the values she shared with Joan. The questing and the certainty were not incompatible. They existed productively side by side.

It is no great surprise that we each saw Vicki in slightly different ways despite areas of common perceptions. Each viewer used a unique pair of eyes and we each shared a different role relationship with Vicki. Our differences in perception may, thus, have been as much a feature of our different 'selves' as of Vicki's changing and multiple being. Together, we saw a woman responding with a range of moods to the problems and satisfactions of different learning and social contexts. That is no great surprise. We saw a person with an easy, comfortable and sociable manner who participated well on the fringes of the social action but did not become active at the heart of it. Her reference groups on the course were various. There is evidence that she identified with those with a similar sense of inadequacy in plenary sessions; that she mixed more easily and comfortably with acquaintances from the past; that she mixed more with those whose beliefs she shared. Thus, she related to others through her sense of learning, her history and her ideology. There was a multiple matching of self-identity in the relationships she had on the course.

We also saw a woman who, over the period of the course, came to believe in herself and her perspective in a new way. This made her less dependent on significant others and external expertise. There was a growing confidence in internal expertise as she came to accord status and value to self-created knowledge.

There was a dip at the start of the learning curve which spanned the course. If this was anything to do with the insecurities which she brought to the course, it was also reinforced by course content and pedagogy which partly overlooked Vicki's own experience and personal knowledge. Vicki's self-confidence fell further into this pedagogical void. Only later did self-confidence grow as the course started to draw more successfully upon her pool of personal knowing. Vicki gradually found her own biography represented in the course and was able to draw upon it in the learning process.

Chapter 3

Seeing Changes and Development

There is no doubt that Vicki experienced significant and readily visible changes during the two years. From Harry, we have already heard of the multilayered mining into 'self' which he witnessed in year 2 of the course, and of Vicki's changing attitude to the authority of external knowledge and inner experience. Other people bore witness to other changes and Vicki herself gave clear accounts.

Evidence from School Colleagues

Let us look, first of all, at the changes which Vicki's school colleagues saw. Mid-way through the course, Richard, Vicki's headteacher was unequivocal. 'There is evidence of much greater confidence, stemming from a clearer sense of purpose', he wrote.

This improved clarity, he believed, was accompanied by a more focussed understanding of classroom practice. Vicki had developed a stronger intellectual basis for practical decision making. 'Classroom practice is underpinned by a constructively critical and analytical approach', he claimed.

Richard felt there had also been changes in Vicki's school contribution. Inner changes were manifest in a more assertive involvement in the professional discussions leading to policy formulation and practical implementation. He had noticed, 'a marked increase in awareness and confidence with regard to discussion and implementation of school policies'. This increased surety, confidence and involvement seemed to be related to reduced tension, worry and anxiety; 'whilst Vicki has developed a more assertive manner, she is also more relaxed and sociable'. This letting go, this relaxing, this development in social, professional ease, may have been a by-product of developing confidence. As Vicki became more comfortable with, and sure of, herself so, perhaps, she relaxed more with herself and with others.

In the final term of the course, Richard's testimony was expressed even more forcefully; Vicki's professional drive was more evident in action. He had noticed Vicki's commitment, her involvement and her willingness to try to make something happen as a result of the time she had spent on her studies. Vicki was no longer peripheral to change and growth within the school. She was less passive, less self-effacing. She had become an important part of the machinery of change, a contributor to its dynamic. 'She's developed as a person, as a force in the school; she's a much more confident, powerful thinking force in the school than she certainly was two years ago', he observed. 'And certainly her contribution to planning groups and working parties is much more evident now.'

There were, the Head felt, three factors operating to enable this new force to be effective. There was the course, the school and Vicki herself. He felt, firstly, 'that's very largely due to the course'; secondly, 'also to her willingness and keenness to bring some of that back into the school'; thirdly, 'the space that it's been given in the school to flourish'. We shall return later, to a closer exploration of this triad and the way in which the three strands plaited themselves together in the cause of change and development.

Jeff worked closely with Vicki at Springfield. He was supportive of her ideas, professional development and in-service work. They shared an educational philosophy and several years of common professional experience. Jeff admitted that 'she's been very valuable as somebody who has similar ideas to myself'. Thus, he admitted that 'the things that I've said about Vicki are very positive because she now has the sort of views I hold — probably always did have. We agree with each other a lot about things'.

As a close working colleague, Jeff had been in a good position to notice these practical changes. In the previous year he 'was her year leader and consequently had more to do with her teaching and her class'. Because he did not have full class teaching responsibility himself, 'he was able to be in other people's classes . . . and so was actually able to observe the sorts of things that she did more often than usual'.

First, he saw changes as the course progressed in her curriculum organization, pedagogy and planning. Vicki's development had impacted on her teaching, her classroom practice. Jeff wrote, 'there seems to be a greater sense of integration of various subjects and approaches in her teaching and planning'.

Jeff also commented on the developing intellectualization of practice. A broadened mind was associated with sharpened practice. 'An increased breadth of vision and depth of theory has made her work and thinking feel tighter and more well grounded.' There was more higher order questioning of practice, he suggested, as Vicki sought a rationale for her teaching. The 'why' question was more pressing.

In the second year of Vicki's course, Jeff coordinated a different year group. His new role involved 'revamping the first year curriculum' and this necessitated close liaison with Vicki in her role as Humanities Co-ordinator. From this position, he observed the influence of Vicki's first action research study on the humanities curriculum. He saw the effect which her developing thought about cross-curricular matters exerted on her practice and on the way she conducted her management coordinating role. Jeff had, thus, seen changes in both Vicki's classroom and management practice.

Like the Head, Jeff had also noticed that 'her level of confidence has increased' and that this new force was finding productive outlets in the professional life of the staff group. It was contributing to and influencing the intellectual journeys of other colleagues. 'This has resulted in a more forthright involvement in the overall thinking of the school.'

Jeff said 'forthright'; Richard said 'assertive'; I said 'sure'. All these words point in the same direction; imply the same processes happening inside Vicki. We also begin to glimpse how Vicki's changes were evolving in the fertile school context; how they were becoming manifest in the thought and work of the full staff group.

Vicki's Own Reflections on Change

We know already that Vicki started from a position of low self-esteem, feelings of inadequacy and an inability to contribute subtantially in a large group. We remember that she hated the first term and that this did nothing to improve the fragile view she held of herself. We also know that things improved in term 2 when the course related more closely to her own professional experience. Almost three terms later there were marked changes and Vicki acknowledged, 'there's no doubt that I've developed a lot over the last couple of years'.

In her classroom, she developed a greater willingness to experiment, and to take risks. 'I'm more prepared to try out new ideas, fresh approaches', she said. At times, the course acted as a catalyst. 'Several times during the course I went back to experiment with ideas and approaches that we had discussed', she added. This experimental, risk-taking side of Vicki became manifest later in her second action research study.

She had been particularly influenced by work on teachers' classroom language and by the concept of 'wait-time'. Here, she had thought deeply about the role of 'enabling silences' in the learning process. 'So, it's being aware of things like that, being aware that kids need time', she explained.

Her focus of attention had moved from what she taught, to what the children were learning; from attention upon the curriculum, to attention upon the learners. She said, 'I'm now thinking of the children more than the curriculum. I've always been against (views of) curriculum that have been opposed to views of children any way'.

Also, Vicki referred to a greater awareness of children's needs. This had been brought about by her second action research study. New awareness and new knowledge had, she felt, influenced practice. 'Being more aware helped the way I taught and handled the children', she claimed. The new knowledge, awareness and practice were outcomes of the enquiry process underpinning the action research assignments. 'Deep investigation and involvement by its very nature has made me more aware of the needs and expectations of the children', she wrote.

Observation work had been a valuable part of the research and learning process. More looking had led to more seeing. More seeing had led to more understanding and to changes in professional perception. 'I've learnt observation techniques', she said. 'I now stand back and observe the children, myself and other staff. I see more and understand more.'

These enquiry processes had also emancipated her from the unreflective mechanisms of practice. 'Previously I feel I was swept along, caught up in everyday bustle. Now I am aware of the "overall" view.' Classroom enquiry work had also given her a new way to study, to reflect upon and to evaluate her work. It was raising professional self-awareness. 'This observation has made me more aware of my own teaching, good and bad', she said. 'I am more able to analyze my successes and failures.'

There were other changes which affected her professional life. She alluded primarily to the development of confidence, completing the triangle Jeff and Richard had started. 'I have become far more confident', she acclaimed. Nor, she felt, was it groundless. It had its roots in increased knowledge. Its source lay in being 'more knowledgeable on educational matters' and, as a result 'being able to converse more effectively with other educationalists'. The knowledge had given her confidence. The confidence had underpinned improved professional communications. This improved capability as a professional communicator fed upon itself and generated other cycles of confidence. 'This has given me more confidence in my job and this has spilled over into my personal development', Vicki claimed.

These links between relevant professional knowledge, communication skills and confidence had given rise to the changes which Richard and Jeff had seen in Vicki's school contribution. Vicki implied that there were also accompanying attitudes to develop in order to put this change to good collegial use. Confidence alone was not enough. Sensitivities and personal understanding were also necessary. 'I have changed my attitude to other people', she asserted. 'I now argue more relevantly and am able to listen and understand more sympathetically.'

Challenge and debate in small group work on the course helped to develop these personal and interpersonal qualities. 'It has also made me understand myself', she believed. Perhaps this new self-understanding fostered greater understanding of others.

Of her developing communicative confidence, she wrote, 'I can now swop jargon, with the best of them, which I couldn't do when I started the course', though she admitted that 'it sounds the wrong reasons' for making claims to development. She was more pleased that, as a result of developing professional language, she found she could now 'talk at a level'. Her developing language was indicative of the new ideas and understandings of which she spoke. Talk was an integral part of her self-confessed new confidence, a confidence that bore fruit in both classroom and collegial practices. 'I'm far more confident in talking to any educationalist than I probably would have been before, because I've focussed and I've thought and developed', she said. A clearer professional rationale was emerging. 'It's made me think more carefully about the teaching I want to do and the way I want to approach it.' There was a clearer sense of her own development and of her children's. 'I can now see myself developing as well as teaching — not just me but the children as well — which I couldn't see so clearly before.'

Lest it be thought, mistakenly, that this well grounded confidence burst through every previous insecurity or inadequacy, it is well to remember the continuing dislike which Vicki harboured for work in the large group. She did not overcome these inhibitions. They survived the life of the course and well beyond and at the end of the course she wrote, 'I thought as I grew more confident I would be able to add more to the big group. I haven't.'

What Vicki did lose, however, was the sense of inadequacy which matched these inhibitions. She had come to recognize her problems in the large group as part of the way she was. She also came to accept this without undue critique and dissatisfaction. 'I now know that is me', she reflected. 'It's not simply lack of confidence, it's my character. I can now accept that. I understand it in myself.' Simply understanding the problem did not help Vicki to change her group behaviour. Rather, the outcome of her self-reflection and self-understanding was inner wisdom and acceptance rather than overt change. She came to change the way she perceived herself in the world, rather than change the way in which she acted in it.

In Vicki's self reflections, then, we have evidence of a variety of changes taking place. There were practical, visible changes to aspects of classroom practice. There were changes to the nature of professional reflection which she brought to her work, as intuition was increasingly laid bare for intellectualization. In this process, self-evaluation and classroom observation became a more common and regular feature of professional thought.

Beyond the classroom, her contribution to collegial work changed, too. Interpersonal confidence improved as she made a significantly greater contribution to school and curriculum development through talking, listening and thinking. In these developments she moved from the periphery of school development work to a position much closer to the centre. Through these processes of change, colleagues witnessed a growing self-confidence in her, a confidence which Vicki, herself, seems to have felt moving inside her. It was a confidence borne of increasing knowledge and a concomitant ability to work with, and communicate, that knowledge for a range of professional purposes.

Growing Through the Group

Now comes the time to blend some of my own tutorial memories with other data. To do this, I shall move across time from Vicki's rising confidence of term 2, across two successful action research projects in terms 2 and 3 discussed later in this story, to arrive in term 4, the first term of the second year.

This term became a watershed in Vicki's development as the course pedagogy changed. Now the teachers were expected to play a greater part in designing their learning programme. They were invited to identify their own learning focus, drawing upon interests and needs as they perceived them. Working collaboratively with course colleagues who shared a common interest, each small group designed a research and study programme around their chosen focus. This occupied the teachers in independent, self-directed learning for seven weeks of the ten-week term. I adopted an enabling, advisory role at the groups' behest. In the final three weeks the learning was shared with the full course group using whatever methods and resources the teachers deemed appropriate.

Along with four other course colleagues, Vicki chose to study gender issues in education. It was a broad topic and a small group. There were three women and two men. One of the men was Steven. By his own confession he was provocative and joined the group in the hope that he could examine the more entrenched views he held about women's roles. As a brave man he admitted, 'I had prejudices which were working against equality'.

He risked his reputation and his throat, it seems, by appearing, for the sake of controversy, to be more extreme than he really was. 'Some of the things I may have said were intended as humour and were intended perhaps to stir people up', he admitted. 'I think perhaps it occasionally misfired', he conceded, 'and I think people may have thought, god, that's what he really believes. Let's sort him out.'

My memory offers testimony to this, for on several occasions when I visited the small group, the sparks carried well across the table in the cross-fire. I often wondered if this group would survive the challenge of continuing to work collaboratively to the end of the task. They did, for as Steven explained, this challenge, even conflict, did not leave 'any ill feeling or any nastiness'. 'I think they were pulling my leg as much, perhaps, as I was pulling theirs', he told me.

The group was lively, provocative, contradictory. And in this challenging, if friendly, hot-house climate, I saw an energy and passion in Vicki that I had not seen before, as she and Steven parried with each other. This is not to suggest that Vicki had become a new kind of person or that a new dimension of her 'self' had been created or revealed. I may simply, as tutor, or researcher, not have been looking in the right place at the right time to have seen it before.

A serious, if challenging, humour became a feature of the group and may have served a valuable learning purpose, for it offered a direct and acceptable way of laying bare some highly sensitive issues. Nor had I realized, until talking to Steven two years after the event, that there was a part of Vicki well suited to this humorous learning climate. Indeed, she seems to have contributed significantly to it. 'We seemed to share a sense of humour and laugh at the same things', Steven explained.

Vicki's was not a trite humour. It was 'quite dry on occasions but underlying it all there is a serious purpose', Steven explained. It served a direct purpose for 'she used a laugh, I think, to make a point'. This, Steven felt, contributed to Vicki's effectiveness in the group because 'if you try to make a point you are more likely to be effective if you make people laugh'. Vicki did this successfully, Steven thought.

This was consistent with an image I retained of Vicki during the small group's presentation to the full course group. Vicki led this presentation, part of which I had videotaped for the group. For a grand finale she had read two humorous modern children's stories which epitomized the dangers of stereotyped gender role models. The stories, *The Piggy Family* and *The Tough Princess* were forthright in their humour. The gender morals were uncompromising. Various and contradictory responses were aroused in the audience. These ranged from total identification and approval to literary distaste. The laughter which the stories provoked however was universal, as was the ensuing engagement in debate about gender issues. Vicki had, through humour, managed to stir a few gender hornets nests that were lying around in the course group. She had scored. She had seduced her course colleagues down the path of entertainment and led them straight into the serious heart of the issues with which her small group had been struggling over the preceding seven weeks.

This is a very different image of Vicki, leading and engaging the whole course group, from the rather withdrawn and worried student we saw four terms ago. She looked relaxed, comfortable. She presented the groups' ideas and questions clearly and concisely. She spoke steadily and, apparently, confidently with the fluency of someone who has control over her material. She brought seriousness and lightheartedness in equal measure to the presentation. Colleagues listened, responded, engaged, argued. Vicki had been an effective presenter and catalyst.

I wondered how she had arrived there, entertaining and provoking the full course group; how she had made this apparent ascent. The small independent study group seemed to have played a part. Within its dynamic there had, according to Steven, been a consistent attempt 'to work pretty much as a team' but Vicki emerged early on 'as a natural leader'. There seems to have been some delay in starting the task because no one assumed a leadership role immediately. This delay created an uncomfortable space into which Vicki moved with a sense of frustration. She wanted to pull her colleagues together into a working group. She wanted them to get the task started. Vicki explained, 'It was an odd group, because there were no obvious leaders there. There was Steven who didn't in fact take the lead although he says a lot. And there was Malcolm and there was Pam and Carol and me. There was no dominant member, nobody that would actually lead.' She continued, 'And we hedged around for ages to see who would actually start planning and in the end I couldn't stand it any longer and so I said let's do this, this and this. So it was quite fascinating.' She added, reflectively, 'So small groups I had no problem with. It was just large groups.'

She was not the sole and dominating leader. Responsibilities were shared. There was recognition of the differing expertise and contributions each could make, for, as Steven said, 'people were leaders of different types, according to what was being discussed, how we were deciding to work, how we planned our presentation to the rest of the group'.

The group members were, in Steven's eyes, 'all fairly high powered people, all with very definite views'. Vicki, however, made the major contribution as organizer and facilitator. She had the capability to stimulate and encourage corporate thinking. She also played a vital part in drawing the group's thinking together, shaping it and moving it forward. 'I think it was a case of working at a brainstorming level almost', Steven explained. 'Vicki would be the one who would say, well, let's think about this, how many ideas can we come up with?' He went on to explain, 'once we had all bunged our ideas into the pot, Vicki was the one to do the summarizing, the guiding, where to go next'.

Managing this may not have been easy for perspectives were expressed, and challenged, forcefully. As a man and a minority Steven may have felt this more than the others. He explained that he 'felt uncomfortable once or twice because I was the minority they were complaining about'. Yet the 'prejudices and feelings' of all members received scrutiny. Any differences of views were seen as an issue for debate.

Vicki played an evaluative role in these debates, reflecting upon ideas, comparing, contrasting. Steven saw her as 'a bit like a referee, judging between the different ideas that we threw up'.

The personal style and manner in which she assumed this role was important to her effectiveness. Steven did not feel that her leadership threatened the group. Rather, she enabled the task to be developed in a challenging but reasonably safe way for others because 'she wasn't autocratic about it. She was asking our views but it was interesting that she seemed to be doing the asking and we were giving.'

Now Vicki was using personal qualities which enabled her to be a successful agent in others' learning. She was able to foster challenge in a way that changed people's perceptions without undermining their self-confidence. Steven said, 'I was challenged but that's no bad thing. It can become very cosy and you can run away from challenge but that's not what education is about.'

Being challenged by Vicki was 'constructive' because of the sense of personal caring that Steven felt she had for people. Her challenges did not contradict nor contravene her sense of respect for people. They were congruent. Nor did she offer challenge without expecting it. I asked Steven, 'What is it about Vicki that gives her the ability to challenge without offending?' He replied, 'I think it is basically because she liked and respected people and their ideas. She was prepared to be challenged. She never seemed to break things down to personalities. I think if you like people, basically you can disagree with them and if you are working on a professional level, there are several different interpretations of the same set of facts and circumstances. I think it is because of her basic like and respect for others that she could do that.'

These 'natural' interpersonal qualities, as Steven saw them, may partly explain Vicki's ascent to a new leadership role but other forces were at work. Strong motivation and personal investment were also driving her as she focussed upon gender, the topic she chose to study of her own accord, the topic for which she held a passionate commitment. This passion and this commitment manifest themselves strongly in the group. Steven felt that these were the real causes of Vicki taking the leadership role. I asked him, 'Have you any idea why Vicki emerged as the natural leader?'

To this he replied,

I think out of all of us, she probably had the most definite views on the treatment of females and the way that the system deprived them of opportunities, or certainly appeared to do.

He continued,

> She felt very very strongly that girls were disadvantaged — and by the very institutions that were supposedly trying to put that disadvantage right.

When we refer back to the biographical glimpses in the early part of this story we see the links with Vicki's experiences which, by her own testimony, helped to shape her attitudes and commitment towards gender issues in education. These experiences, attitudes, commitments contributed to the shape of this collaborative group work. They impacted on the corporate learning journey which the group travelled. Concomitantly, the corporate journey gave Vicki intellectual food for her major final action research study. In turn, the group debates helped to shape, develop, explicate ideas and passions which eventually became crystallized in Vicki's research.

It may be that this deep, biographical commitment to gender issues activated interpersonal and leadership qualities which propelled Vicki into this new 'high profile' position. Perhaps her strong feelings caused her to step forward, to shape and guide events. We may never fully know. Trying to untangle cause and effect in the complexities of the learning process is probably a misguided enterprise. Vicki herself was unable to separate the strands. Rather, her learning seemed more like an evolving ecology than a linear journey. It was, she said, attributable 'to all of it really', including 'the opportunity to spend time thinking' as well as 'mixing with people that are on the course and talking and arguing and getting your ideas sorted out'. We have to be content to speculate that term four may have been one important step in the continuous and complex learning journey which Vicki undertook during the two years of the course — and beyond.

In summary, then, we have seen here a teacher with personal qualities and style that enabled her to be readily accepted as a leader and organizer in her small research group. She had the capacity for offering intellectual challenge without personal threat. She could provoke ideas, help to organize their randomness into some coherence, think and plan ahead. Her sense of humour, which she used judiciously, contributed to a safe but challenging learning climate. It was used in a serious, not flippant manner and contributed to a conducive and productive group ethos. Her regard for people and their well-being made her an acceptable and credible course colleague without attenuating her intellectual contribution to the group work. Alongside these personal qualities, her historically rooted passion and commitment provided strong motivation.

All this may help to explain the emergence of the more confident and high-profile Vicki. Certainly, at this time, she was exuding a greater sense of belief in herself and her ideas than had been witnessed in the early stages of the course. Either Vicki had changed significantly, or my perceptions of her had changed, or both may have been the case. The evidence from school colleagues, course supervisors, course colleagues and from Vicki herself suggests that there was significant change. We began to see her differently because she was different.

Chapter 4

Developing the Humanities
Curriculum at Springfield School

Vicki's first action research study was 'An investigation into the perceptions and opinions of humanities as taught at Springfield School'. As she explained, this was a professional issue, 'being the most relevant to my situation at the moment'. She saw her role as Humanities Coordinator as a developing one in which she had much to learn, much to shape. 'I needed to work on my own knowledge within the subject', she wrote. To this end she had taken her own professional development in hand. She explained that she 'read, attended lectures and courses and drew on her own experiences as a general class teacher to put the humanities work together'.

Having, thus, extended her beliefs, concepts and practices, she felt a need to move beyond her own perspectives and 'assumptions'. She seemed concerned lest her views become egocentric or 'insular' and she felt that her thinking could benefit from inspection and challenge. Her first small-scale research study was designed with this in mind. Vicki saw this as an opportunity to add to her own learning and apply that to the further development of her work as Humanities Coordinator. To do this, she saw the need to extend her understanding of practices, beliefs, attitudes and concerns in the school generally, including those of children as well as colleagues. This was something of a tall order for a first small-scale research project, and we shall see the extent to which the study reached out towards those rather ambitious limits.

Her methodology was simple, if, as is usual, problematic. To elicit perspectives and attitudes of colleagues and to gain insights into their practices, she gained permission to distribute a questionnaire to the fifteen of her colleagues who also taught humanities in the school. In eliciting perspectives from pupils, she recruited the help of Barbara, a welfare ancillary, to interview two girls.

From the beginning, Vicki realized that the teacher researcher is in a power relationship with pupils and this may affect data validity. 'The class from which I wanted to interview the two girls was still relatively new to me', she wrote. 'Believing that this may have been a problem as far as getting the children to be honest with me, I approached the welfare ancillary who works with me. I felt she knew the two girls better than I, and in a less authoritarian and more friendly way', she explained. 'My feelings were that she could possibly achieve a more open discussion.' Vicki interviewed, too, and later compared the two approaches.

Vicki's methodological reflections were to be a key characteristic of her work from this point as she attended as seriously to her research processes as to the substantive issues raised.

These methodological reflections continued into an analysis of some of the difficulties associated with questionnaire construction. For example, in compiling the questionnaire, she became alert to the problems of personal bias. To challenge this, she sought critique from a colleague before redrafting and distributing the questionnaire. She also wanted to make it a user-friendly research instrument. 'Having devised the questionnaire I had reservations about its objectivity', she wrote. 'I felt it was too biased towards my opinions, perhaps even leading and might be condescending. I therefore asked a member of staff who had previously, successfully, completed an Advanced Diploma course to look at it critically for me.'

Here we see Vicki's readiness to learn from her own self-evaluative reflections and from the experience and expertise of someone who had trodden the small-scale research path before her. Collaboration and peer learning thus seemed to evolve naturally from a perceived research need. Vicki reported of her colleague that, 'she picked out some ambiguities and some over-involved questions which she felt were too much to ask of the staff. I acted on some of her suggestions'. Vicki was a willing learner in these ethically and technically oriented research problems, ready to listen, think, plan and problem-solve.

Vicki also used the informal course structures as a resource for her learning, deriving insight and benefit from the experience of her peers on the course. 'As one of my fellow students had experienced some apathy when handing out questionnaires', she explained, 'I made time to speak to each individual in school and to personally explain to them in detail what I was attempting to do.' This investment of time and care was rewarded. 'The response was very supportive', she added.

Much of Vicki's learning as a researcher thus evolved from her own initiative, self-direction and autonomous command of her research problems, not from the formal content and pedagogy of the course. She was steering her own development and this was important to the quality of the research.

This evaluative intelligence and willingness to learn from a range of sources may have enriched the research. Data gathering instruments were better developed than they might otherwise have been and data feedback was rewarding for, of the fifteen distributed questionnaires, thirteen 'full replies' were received.

Vicki wrote concise but detailed paragraphs in her research text in which she evaluated the effectiveness of her questionnaire. She 'felt it had been fairly successful' as a device for 'obtaining quite relevant data from a larger number of people'. Through it, she elicited a variety of data. These included 'points of view' which proved to be illuminating because they 'raised concerns of colleagues' of which she was not aware. She also discussed 'facts', as she called them, about colleagues' levels of involvement in humanities teaching as well as the nature and content of that teaching. Data also helped Vicki 'to test out her hypothesis concerning difficulties over the teaching of religious education in humanities and to test (her) doubts about split (separate subject) teaching'.

Her methodology critique seemed honest and insightful. She admitted that 'Question 12 was a total failure. It was totally ambiguous. I totally confused several of those answering the questionnaire.' As a result the questionnaire failed to elicit data that 'would have helped a great deal'. On the other hand, a final open-ended question elicited unexpected data that 'helped (her) in (her) conclusions'.

Of the experience of pupil interviewing Vicki was as critically reflective as she was of the questionnaire. Physical conditions, she hypothesized, were more than likely to affect the quality and outcomes of interviewing. As so many other teacher researchers know to their cost, the most careful of plans can be disrupted by the complexities of school organization. 'I had hoped to conduct the discussion early in the morning', Vicki explained, 'so that the children would be alert and reasonably fresh, but timetable alterations meant a change in plan'.

There were ethical considerations to encounter and report. Sensitivity to pupil motivation was one. 'As I had already consulted with the two girls on the previous day I did not want to delay longer than was necessary', she wrote. 'Hence the interviews took place that afternoon in a small secluded room which turned out to be in very noisy conditions.'

The price of ethical sensitivity was high, for in attempting to capitalize on the pupils' motivation to participate, Vicki found herself in an unconducive environment. 'I had not anticipated home economics taking place behind one of the adjoining walls', she declared. Disappointment with the data outcome was the cost. 'On hearing the result I did not feel wholly successful in obtaining from the children enough relevant information, although some interesting data did emerge', she added.

These environmental and organizational constraints often vex the teacher action researcher. They affect the nature of data and the research process, creating new problems, additional work and stress. This was so for Vicki. As a consequence of these problems, she decided to extend 'the research to include a discussion with two other children'.

Vicki had no illusions about the research limitations of the small pupil sample and was not about to fall into a quantitative trap. 'The recordings give the opinions of four children out of a possible 400 within the school', she said. 'As such it can be described only as a minute sampling and must be regarded as such.'

There was also, she recognized, a gender bias. 'I interviewed only girls', she wrote. 'Whether it would have given different results had I interviewed only boys can only be left to conjecture', she added, content to honour the role of speculation in the research process.

Vicki was, thus, aware of the danger of accepting her data at surface value. For example, in the pupil interviews, she elicited comfortable data which confirmed the effectiveness of her teaching. 'The girls appeared happy at the speed at which they were learning', she wrote. But she was prepared to doubt the data. 'Their opinion of the subject may have been genuine', she acknowledged, 'but one wonders whether it was for the benefit of the interviewer or the tape recorder'.

There were other influences in the paired interviews for which she had to account. One interviewee's responses may affect or contaminate the other's, she realized. 'Both girls expressed a desire to study more geography', she explained. 'Whether these were independent ideas or inspired by each other is difficult to ascertain.'

Barbara had been a willing and enthusiastic interviewer but there were difficulties. Vicki felt that Barbara 'tended to lead the children in their responses'; she 'reinterpreted their ideas'; she 'included some questions that were not on the original notes'; she failed to explore an issue which Vicki had identified as important to the research; she seemed unable to probe, and to help the children where they 'had some difficulty with vocabulary and with formulating their ideas'.

Yet Vicki also recognized that her own interview skill was not without its shortcomings. The first pupil interview taught her that 'it was not as easy as she anticipated' and she took the opportunity of the second interview 'to learn from previous mistakes'. Nor was the second attempt without its difficulties. Vicki's questions proved to be too open-ended. As a result the girls were not given the chance to offer the 'more in depth answers' which Vicki had anticipated. Her expectations of the pupils' responses had been unrealistic, she felt. The girls seemed to have had difficulty with the openness of the questions. Into this openness she fed more questions because the flow of talk and exploration that she anticipated did not develop. She even found herself, at one point, turning the interview into a teaching situation when she was unhappy at the direction in which the girls were taking a discussion on world studies, apartheid and racial discrimination. In the process, she felt that she 'killed what could have been an interesting insight', and wondered 'how much more could have come out of the conversation'. The questions 'should perhaps have been more thoroughly thought out before the interview', she felt.

Despite these reservations about her interview skills, Vicki found that the 'research carried out with the children was more enlightening than that with the staff'. It had raised new insights because she 'had not previously given much though to what the children's opinions of humanities were'. She set out detailed analysis of the issues which the children raised.

Much of Vicki's language of analysis of the pupil interview was the language of tentativeness. Her knowledge was provisional, uncertain, not absolute. Here are a few of her phrases.

geographical areas of the subject **appeared** to be quite important to them

The girls **appeared** happy . . .

Their opinion of the subject **may have** been . . .

They **seemed** to be of the opinion . . .

Responses 70 and 71 **could be** an indication . . .

By responses 212 to 218 they **appeared** to have . . .

The pupils raised insights into their understanding of humanities, as well as their attitudes and enjoyment. They also shared their perspectives on pedagogy. These insights acted as a stimulus to Vicki's thinking about the humanities curriculum. It prompted her into new and more complex perspectives and she claimed that it was 'a valuable piece of work'. The study 'has helped me to focus on many aspects that had not occurred to me or I had not given serious thought to', she said. As a result she felt more confident in her judgment about the action she needed to take in the interests of colleagues and pupils. Vicki explained that 'with this information' she was able to 'start on some guidelines and schemes of work that will hopefully satisfy the needs of both children and staff'. As we shall see later, these guidelines were helpful in several ways, for several people, in the short and longer term.

At this stage the research had two valuable professional purposes. First, Vicki developed some relevant understandings about research. She learnt that data are context related and subject to extraneous influences and constraints. She learnt that there is skill in constructing written and spoken research instruments. She came to understand that the researcher can learn from her own first hand experience as well as from vicarious experience and accounts of others. She recognized that forethought and planning are helpful; that forethought and planning can, even at their best, be thwarted; that a limited sample gives you limited data; that restraint must be exercised in generalizing from specifics.

Second, the study generated new knowledge about practices, attitudes and perspectives in the school. In the process, some of Vicki's own hunches and assumptions were tested, modified and extended by this knowledge.

There was some difficulty with the written text, however, in that some of Vicki's meanings were not entirely explicit to her readers even though she felt she had created meanings to her own satisfaction. For example, Vicki gave the reader little detailed insight into substantive issues which the research raised. Rather, she summarized them briefly at the end of the report with no elaboration or discussion. She did not explain her 'doubts about split teaching' nor her 'hypothesis concerning religious education'. She simply stated that the latter 'was confirmed'.

Alec's written response to the report confirmed this textual difficulty. He recognized the developmental validity of the research but was also puzzled by the 'implicit text'. 'Both in content and methodology', he wrote, 'Vicki appears to have gained and developed through this study. With some attention to structure (writing it a bit more explicitly) it could have been further improved.'

Nor does the text allow insight into the cognitive processes by which Vicki moved from relative uncertainty in data and analysis, to reasonably confident practical action. Even given the uncertainties and limitations of the research process, it seemed that Vicki was able to place enough confidence in her insights to evolve a new humanities policy as a result. Given the methodological problems encountered and the consequently indeterminancy of the data, it is unclear how the judgments upon which the policy was based were shaped. Only a little was revealed in a post-course interview more than a year after the work. Vicki said that she 'made a discussion document' from her humanities research and in the process 'was able to pick out the things that people said'. For example, she pointed out that there was no framework for skills and concept development within the school, so she 'produced a lower and upper school skills process, a spiralling curriculum'. Also, 'people wanted some sort of development through the four years, so that all came out of that particular document'. The views of colleagues formed the bedrock of policy action. Vicki was not reaching for an absolute, transcendent grand curriculum design. Rather, policy became a statement of intent that was borne of, and relevant to, the needs of her colleagues at the particular historical moment. It was context related.

The research had, indeed, caused Vicki to move beyond her earlier perspectives and assumptions. It caused her to see anew. It extended and illuminated her understanding to a point where she could incorporate the needs and views of others into a more altruistic policy framework.

So — there is research. There is new knowledge. There is teacher learning. There is policy documentation as a statement of intent. But if this is action research, what of the action?

In a mid-course questionnaire, Vicki claimed that the policy discussion document 'has led to positive changes in the teaching of humanities since September'. In addition to the concepts and skills 'directory' already mentioned, Vicki wrote of 'a rethink on strategies and methods of teaching i.e. group work, problem-solving etc., role play, cross-curricular links'. Her own practice was developing along these lines. 'My teaching too changed accordingly', she wrote, 'what I teach and how I teach'.

She also took her staff development responsibilities seriously in the process of policy implementation, realizing that she had come to 'know the areas the staff feel unsure about'; realizing that she was able to 'help out in the support teaching that I do'. She became 'more aware of teaching by example as a coordinator' as she supported colleagues in policy implementation.

Now was the impact of the policy document short-lived. More than a year later Vicki said that she was 'still using it'. Colleagues were still worried about their religious education teaching, so they kept refering back to the relevant part of the policy document. 'RE was one of the things that I discussed on it', Vicki explained, 'and that's one of the problems that people have, so I've been able to refer back to that (in the policy) to help us now'.

Richard, the Headteacher, confirmed Vicki's contribution. 'As Humanities Coordinator Vicki has introduced curriculum guidelines and practices', he explained. Her contribution had impacted across the school and he drew attention to 'the background thinking that Vicki has been able to bring to the development of the whole school humanities strategy'. In his view the school had been supported by the course, through the medium of Vicki's work and through her cognitive endeavours, for he said, 'I have no doubt that the development of that particular aspect of the school has been very much supported by the course itself'.

He commented upon the quality of Vicki's work, claiming that it reflected 'the advantages of academic rigour and the discipline of the course'. What he might have meant by 'academic rigour' and 'discipline' can only be left to speculation but perhaps he felt that the policy work for the school had been given some breath of intellectual life; some empirical muscle that it might not otherwise have had.

A year after the course had finished, I was interested to know whether practical action outcomes had been short-lived, or if they had weathered time and circumstance. By this time, Vicki had left Springfield and had taken a new professional direction as Deputy Head in a primary school but she left a legacy behind through her action research. Some of this legacy could be seen in the longer term effectiveness of the humanities policy which had 'been very powerful', according to Richard.

Speaking with the confidence of one who knew his school well, he continued to articulate the nature of that 'powerful' impact, as he saw it. He spoke of the way in which Vicki had linked her humanities coordinating role to the development of the policy and, through the two, had enabled people to start thinking and teaching more in concert than had previously been the case. 'One of the problems that the school had three years ago was that it was very separatist', he said, 'and each of the year leaders in a sense was isolated from the others, certainly in terms of curriculum'. Vicki's humanities policy helped to bind people in a common professional task and her initiative served as a model for other coordinators, as well as breaking the collaborative working ice. 'In many ways I think Vicki has made it easier for other coordinators to link the work of the four year groups because of the work she's done', Richard explained.

It was, however, a two-way affair, a symbiotic development. It was successful because others wanted collaboration, wanted the policy development in curriculum that Vicki's work fostered. Richard referred to 'the support I think that she feels she's received from the year leaders'. It was easier for Vicki to be effective because of the open and willing collegial staff group. It is hard for the Coordinator to foster development for people who do not want it. Without the willing cooperation of class teachers and their gratitude for the conceptual contribution Vicki's work made to curriculum design, the policy may have fallen on arid ground. It is doubtful, too, that she could have worked directly with class teachers without the support and cooperation of their year leaders as key figures in curriculum development. So the support, interest and readiness of class teachers and year leaders to adopt Vicki's suggestion, interacted positively with Vicki's initiative. As a consequence, the policy provided a valuable framework for planning throughout the school. 'The document is actually valued', Richard told me. 'It was actually a key part of planning for year teams. If you speak to people like Jeff, for example, about setting up the first year curriculum, you will find that the document was very useful in underpinning what they were going to cover in the thematic approach. So I think it has actually been very useful', he concluded.

Richard also felt that the document would offer a framework for curriculum evaluation as well as for curriculum planning, being 'a bedrock to come back to when we're reassessing what we've done and how successful we think we've been'.

So — there is research; there is new knowledge; there is policy documentation; there is collaborative planning. But were any changes visible in classrooms? 'I think so, yes', Richard confirmed. 'I'm sure that's been very helpful with years one and two with the change in working and style and I know it's also made quite an impact in year three with David Peterson.' And before we turned our discussion to other matters, he added, 'I wouldn't want to see Vicki's humanities study sold short in any way shape or form'. He was keen to speak its validity as a practical, useable and intellectually respectable document. It had served well the needs and development of the teachers and the curriculum. It was contributing to planning, teaching and curriculum evaluation.

So we have three partial perspectives, Vicki's, Richard's, Alec's. Together they confirm that Vicki's first action research study evolved out of, and was integrated into, a professional task facing Vicki in the historical life of the school's curriculum. The research contributed to that purpose, raising Vicki's awareness of colleagues' views and giving some empirical, if textually problematic, basis to the substance of the written policy. Further, paper policy evolved into a lived policy for teachers, informing and transforming their curriculum planning, and their pedagogy; giving direction to learning in the form of skills and concepts frameworks.

My research methodology has constrained how far we can go in the ultimate leg of this journey to discover the impact of the research on classroom practice, for we do not know much about how it changed children's lives, though the changed pedagogy to which Richard referred implied some effect. But there seems testimony enough that it brought about multiple changes of other kinds. It changed Vicki's thinking and her practice. It changed the way she worked with colleagues and it changed the way they worked with each other on an agreed curriculum.

What started out as an individualistic study took on institutional life. This was inevitable since Vicki was making a developmental link between her own needs and those of the school. Indeed, these two areas of need were inseparable as they related directly to Vicki's management responsibilities as Humanities Coordinator. Even so, Vicki's own development could not have taken root institutionally had not her colleagues been open, ready and willing to adopt the initiative. This catalysis between Vicki's development and her colleagues' openness gave impetus and purpose to implementation of the research, research which was tailor made for its particular circumstances.

The work also evidenced Vicki's capabilities as a researcher. From the start she had been critically reflective about methodology; about the effect of practical constraints on the research process and about her own developing skill as a researcher. The tentativeness with which she offered insights suggested an understanding of provisionality in the new knowledge and understanding she was creating. In addition, she readily learnt to draw upon the experience of other teacher researchers as a resource for her own learning.

The action from the study was multifaceted and long term, with an institutional existence that outlived Vicki's, since it was still influencing events after she had left. Vicki had created an autonomous action text. It continued to have a life, meaning and practical impact independently of its creator. Thus, Vicki left a professional legacy to the school that continued to create practical capital after her departure. If Alec and I had experienced some difficulty with the implicit language of parts of the original text, what little matter. I would rather know that the text had caused events that helped these teachers along their professional action paths in a constructive way, than quibble over the odd sentence or two that we had not been able to understand.

Chapter 5

Learning About Children with Special Needs

Professional uncertainty seems to have been one of the main forces behind Vicki's second research project which focussed upon the two handicapped pupils in her own mainstream class.

From the outset, her feelings about having the children in her class were mixed, vascillating from a slight ego trip 'because the powers that be decided I could cope', she wrote, to a sense of inadequacy at 'the realization that my knowledge and experience in dealing with handicapped children was very limited'. She remembered some painful experiences in early adulthood when she took a holiday job in a school for mentally handicapped children. The job was made almost totally unrewarding for 'lack of understanding and immaturity' and from an absence of help and support for the unqualified staff at the school. She left with bad memories and a hole in her arm, inflicted by 'one large boy' who 'attempted to bite chunks whilst professing his love' for her.

Neither did her formal education help. She was educated to be sympathetic to the handicapped in a distant way, a sympathy which led her to 'occasionally buying a flag for some charity'. But her grammar school education left her with a very segregationist view of the handicapped. As she explained, 'we were of the "does he take sugar" era'. Despite these autobiographical starting points, Vicki was willing to venture into yet another professional unknown.

We know little of the feelings with which she set out at the beginning of the year with Darren and Caroline, the two handicapped children, but we do know that the experience soon became a professionally reflective one, leading to much learning and much question raising. 'As the year progressed and my understanding and experience grew, as I watched, interacted and helped their growth and development in many ways, I began to ask questions about their position in a "normal" school', Vicki wrote.

There were questions about the effect of mainstream on the handicapped, the effect of the handicapped on mainstream; questions about whether the special needs of these children really were being met.

In her tentative, exploratory and doubting way, Vicki turned these questions over and over in her mind. As she watched, as she pondered, as she questioned, her experience gave way to 'nagging doubts and worries'. This new uncertainty was a way into her second action research project. The questions 'persuaded (her) to take these two children as subjects for a study' with a view to 'trying to reach some conclusions concerning their lives as handicapped children in mainstream school'.

An historical summary of provision for the handicapped in her written research report demonstrated that Vicki had consulted some relevant literature. This served to update her understanding of educational provision, taking her through the nineteenth century, the Plowden Report, the Warnock Report, the 1981 Education Act and into some current conceptualizations of special needs. Perhaps this updating contributed to the developing source of professional self-confidence which we looked at earlier. Perhaps it clarified issues and offered concepts which became useful tools for thinking and analysis. Vicki also explained that it enabled her to offer her readers an historical context against which to consider current mainstream provision.

Here we should note the teacher researcher's diligence and commitment in going down the double avenues of literature and empirical enquiry, for it has often been remarked upon by colleagues and external examiners that award-bearing teacher researchers do not appear to 'read much'. So let us commend Vicki for the relevant background reading which provided one of the building blocks for her research.

In her written report she moved from the literature into a description of her research method which was 'predominantly taping of formal interviews'. It was also multiple perspective, drawing data from the children, their parents, the welfare ancillary, the two other members of staff with whom the children had most contact. Vicki also drew upon her own insights, perceptions and observations.

There was evidence of learning transference from the methodology of the first research project. This may have helped Vicki to avoid some potential difficulties. For example, she explained that the two teacher interviews 'took place before school' and she felt it worth commenting that there was 'hence the lack of background noise'. Here was improved sensitivity to the contextual constraints of interviewing. The noisy lesson which had gone on alongside the interviews in the first research project had been borne in mind. On the other hand, Vicki also mentioned the relative brevity of these interviews in the second study. This may have been the price paid for the peace and quiet gained before lessons as colleagues gave precious, but limited, time. Here Vicki may have been continuing to discover the roundabouts and swings of small-scale, insider teacher research.

These improved conditions were not to insulate all the research, however, and the technicalities of data gathering were not, even with forethought, straightforward. Other interview data were corrupted because of the physically constraining research environment because there 'is little free space at Springfield'. And although Vicki had managed to acquire the 'practice room' for some interviews, this had given rise to 'much background noise from the music room'. Later difficulties arose as a consequence. As Vicki edited the interviews for the tape-slide material she had decided to create, she was bedevilled by the poor quality of the recorded interviews. Also, during an interview with one of the children 'the caretaker came to fit a new door'.

Such constraints are unlikely to contribute towards the ideal speech situation but they may be effective in teaching the novice researcher about the battles to be fought in the search for useable data.

Vicki's interviews with Maria, the ancillary helper, were illuminating. Maria had wider knowledge of the children because of her varied contact with them. 'Because she mixes with the children in a less authoritarian way she seems to get more insights into classroom dynamics', Vicki wrote. She picks up any home problems and is generally more aware of some of the aspects of the children's lives that members of staff often miss.'

It is worth noting here that Vicki worked confidently with the ancillary helpers in her first and second research studies and this may tell us something important of the quality of Vicki's professional interpersonal relationships.

Vicki gave thought to adjusting her data gathering approaches to match the field participants. A more open-ended, semi-structured style worked well in the adult interviews. She had 'some basic ideas of the area of subject (she) wanted to cover' but had been 'happy to let the interviewees talk about the topics, opinions and ideas they wanted to express'. Also, she drew upon her previous experience of interviewing children as she planned pupil interviews for this second study. 'Previous experience had taught me that the more conversational interviews I could enjoy with the adults would not be possible with the children', she wrote. She planned a structured approach, with predetermined areas to explore, which would be 'more of a question and answer interview'.

Additional insider problems were posed. She 'decided to conduct a small amount of classroom observation' for which she devised her own category and recording system. This presented organizational problems, as it 'proved difficult to set up because of timetable limitations'. Collegial goodwill was required to free Vicki. 'I was released from teaching another class in order to carry out this observation which necessitated someone else covering my lesson', she explained. In addition, time for data gathering in the full school day was a problem and both children had to miss one of their lessons. Also, in order to carry out her interviews with the children, Vicki sacrificed her precious and minimal non-contact time.

The limited and constraining circumstances of insider teacher research are clear. A few extra resources for teacher supply cover, for example, may have made some difference. Without the goodwill and generosity of participating colleagues, the research may have foundered.

There were other data; documentation of academic achievement; data from record cards; visual data from a mass of colour slides of the children in 'as many areas and situations' as Vicki could manage to photograph. Selections were made from these slides and an edited audio-tape made to accompany them. The edited tape was designed to offer different material from the written text. First, Vicki felt that the visual data would contextualize the study well. 'I felt that this sequence would best set the school and children in the context of the study', she wrote. Second, the tape would offer 'opinions and attitudes rather than results and conclusions'. Vicki felt that the uncontaminated views and feelings of key field participants should be presented so she edited them onto the audiotape without adding an interpretative commentary on their views.

In this range, therefore, the study offered an impressive array of data, gathered in a variety of ways. Where methods were repeated from the previous study, experience was a useful teacher. Where methods were new, commitment to experiment was a useful quality. Of the slides, for example, Vicki wrote, 'Not being a proficient photographer I set about this with more enthusiasm than expertise'. We shall later consider the demands which this combination of innocence and exuberance placed on her.

In the written text she engaged in a methodological critique equal in its seriousness to that in her first study. The open-ended adult interviews had, she felt, been successful. She had made a wise choice in adopting this approach. Even given the forethought of the pupil interviews, however, these were still hard work, yielding data that 'appear not to add a great deal towards formulating any conclusions'. New ethical problems presented themselves. For example, Vicki wanted 'to get some reactions to the children's ideas of being handicapped and what it meant to take that handicap into a normal school'. She soon recognized that this could mean wandering into some 'delicate' issues with the children which she would 'back off' if they appeared in any way to cause upset. One of the children did, indeed, show signs of discomfort, so Vicki decided not to 'probe too deeply'. The children's welfare was her prime consideration. The research here had an ethical integrity which took priority over its search for truth and perspective. If compromises had to be made they were not to be made with children's feelings. We are reminded of Steven's perception of Vicki as a caring person and this quality was evident in her research here.

A second ethical and professional concern presented itself when the 'mainstream' children exhibited some jealousy as Vicki took photographs of the handicapped children. Vicki 'overcame this by doing rather more general photographs', in order to include, in the research process, children who otherwise may have felt excluded. The cost of a few extra, if unnecessary photographs, may have felt small compared to her pupils' feelings. Vicki was alert, in her own common sense way, to the ethical implications of her work.

Her feelings for the two handicapped children became implicated and gave Vicki methodological doubts. For example, she questioned whether she had been able to remain as 'detached' as she thought she should be in the tape-slide construction; whether she had been able 'to avoid sentimentality, which is an easy trap to fall into in such an emotive area of education'. She was not sure she had succeeded in that detachment. There is little wonder in this given that she was closely involved with the two children on a daily basis. There were many daily highs and lows to share; worries, frustrations, satisfactions, achievements, hopes, fears. Professional attachment in her teaching was a necessity as she tried to understand, and respond to, the children's needs. Connectedness (Belenky, 1986) was integral to the work. It is unlikely that Vicki would be able, or want to, step out of one role relationship where engagement is essential and into another role where some would see 'detachment' as desirable. This would be to invite a spurious objectivity where none exists. On the contrary it may seem inappropriate for the teacher researcher to strive for cultivated 'dispassionate' research from which the emotive parts of self are withdrawn. To do so is to deny access to the unique insights which the emotive and committed self can offer. Separation of different parts of 'self' in this way may be unhelpful when one's own working context is being researched, and when the interests of those for whom one cares professionally are at stake.

There was valuable professional learning from failed research processes. The observations were not extensive enough to be of much value and there were problems with the category system Vicki had developed when she tried to apply it. Also, because she was dependent upon her colleagues' goodwill to release her for observation work there was a limit to what she could do, especially as she was unwilling to prey on their generosity to enable her to develop the observation instrument further. Nevertheless, the work offered other professional benefits, even though it was problematic and short lived, for Vicki claimed that she 'enjoyed the experience and found it fascinating and almost a luxury to be free to watch with such intensity what one particular child is doing'.

Similarly the photography work was problematic but it provided new professional learning. Vicki claimed that 'the process of taking photographs led me into areas of the curriculum in which I personally do not teach. This gave me insights into the education that the children received and of the interaction with their teachers.'

A research interview with Darren's mother added to the learning. Vicki felt it worth recording that this interview 'proved an added bonus', because it helped her 'to try and understand some of the problems Darren has been faced with in the last two years and how he has tried to come to terms with them'. Teacher research and teacher development were inextricably linked; the teacher learned as the researcher learned. Vicki's research journeys into data gave rise to advances in professional reflection. 'I don't feel his attitude and behaviour could be fully understood without the parent interview', she claimed. The new knowledge gave rise to new attitudes. Vicki developed greater respect for Darren as a result of what she had learned from his mother.

Vicki devoted approximately 3000 words of this approximately 6500 words research text to analysis of data. In so doing she conveyed impressions of the children which were grounded in multiple perspectives and in data from learning and assessment tasks. Vicki used the data to address the question which she had set herself at the beginning of the study, 'How does integrating these children affect the children themselves, the parents, the staff, and other children?'. She portrayed them as two quite different personalities, whose presence in the school had touched on children, teachers and organization in a range of ways. The children received more attention than others and 'are frequently spoken to in the corridors by members of staff'. 'How many of the other 308 children can boast the same treatment?' she asked. She also discovered dimensions of the children's experiences, learning and personal struggles of which she had not previously been aware, concluding that 'the children are not being encouraged to reach their full potential'. The care and concern for the children was, she concluded, leading to over protectiveness. The school was not demanding nor expecting enough because 'we don't want to upset them more than is necessary'.

Some of Vicki's conclusions were clearly borne out of data analysis. The source of others was more evasive so some epistemological weaknesses showed through the cracks of Vicki's text. Whatever the origins of the conclusions, this did not discourage Vicki from rounding them with a passionately stated professional commitment. 'We must make sure that the pressures remain on them to achieve', she declared. 'We owe it to them as we do to the other twenty-nine children in the class.' Her ideological cards were on the epistemological table.

Lapscs of intellectual clarity in an award-bearing teacher research text are not uncommon. I could have pulled many other research studies from my data box, even Vicki's previous study, and demonstrated epistemological weaknesses. Vicki's text was not too exceptional in leaving a few puzzling disjunctions between different aspects of her argument. Nor was it exceptional in leaving me wondering about the sources of particular aspects of her thinking.

These were not my idiosyncratic problems. Harry, too, had struggled with some of the disjunctions between data and argument. In his feedback to Vicki he admitted, 'My greatest difficulty is in accepting all the conclusions you reach from the data you present'.

But in the search for validity we must let our journey take us beyond analysis of the logical or argumentational, to see what practical outcomes were generated by this research.

Of Vicki's increased experience of, and skill in, research methods we have already spoken. There was also affective, attitudinal and perceptual changes which may, in their developmental importance to Vicki, have transcended the logical argument offered in the research text. The research opened a new realm of understanding that challenged initial preconceptions and attitudes towards the handicapped. In its wake, Vicki's personal regard for the children grew. This brought an interpersonal validity to the study which contrasted sharply with any epistemological shortcomings. At the end of the research text Vicki wrote, 'In carrying out this research I feel I have laid some of the ghosts of my youth. In becoming so involved in two such admirable children one cannot but feel humbled by their attitudes and achievements. The "personal tragedy theory" of disability which I had before I experienced Darren and Caroline is no longer with me. I have enjoyed the study and the learning process has involved not only different methods of study but a beginning in understanding such children.' Thus, the growth in Vicki's understanding flourished on a number of levels as ideas, understanding, feelings, attitudes interwined.

This had definitely not been detached, dispassionate research. Vicki's feelings, particularly her sense of regard, respect and empathy took on a different quality. Her heart was moved as much as her head through the research. Her professional growth had taken many varied and interrelated forms.

Nor did the ripples which the study set in motion start and end with

Vicki for Harry, as a critical and interactive reader, claimed to have had his own understanding challenged. 'I have to say that I found the work compelling from my standpoint as a teacher', he wrote. 'The study has certainly made me aware of my own imperfect understanding of the difficulties and problems, hopes and aspirations experienced by children such as Darren and Caroline.'

Such are the small changes, as one person's reflections impact on another's. One wonders how long Harry continued to ponder on these things, how long his awareness stayed with him.

All the preceding, then, is based upon the written research text which was a manifestation of some learning through which Vicki progressed. Now we can think about the tape-slide sequence that absorbed so much of Vicki's time and effort during this research; consider the purpose that it served; explore its destiny.

Along with the written report, Vicki presented some seventy colour slides of the children and the school. These were sequenced for viewing with a thirty-five minute edited audiotape. The tape consisted of commentary by Vicki, with edited selections from the research interviews with parents and teachers.

Vicki had originally intended the tape-slide sequence to be the main form for presenting her research. In the event, she decided to present it as an appendix to a traditional research report. She wrote the traditional report, she told me later, because she worried that the tape-slide alone was not 'enough' to be the equivalent of the 8000 words required for the award. 'There was very little guidance on how much or how many words it was equivalent to', Vicki told me, 'and I think you end up doing far more than you would have done if you'd done a straight number of words in a traditional report'.

So, of the required 8000 words, or its equivalent, Vicki ended up with approximately 6500 words of written text, a full appendix of transcripts and questionnaires, plus the extensive tape slide sequence which was considerable. Financial cost, too, was significant.

Vicki invested a great amount of time in producing the tape-slide material. There had necessarily been a high time investment in data gathering, script and sequence preparation, editing and final composition. There were problems to solve that were new to Vicki. She offered some insight into just a few of the technical challenges which editing and composing presented. 'It was difficult to actually decide on how I was going to do this', she explained. 'Taking sections from each of the interviews was a long process. I think it was due in for assessment on the Tuesday and on that Monday night I was up to about 3.00 still putting in the "peeps". How was I going to put the "peep" in to make it so that you knew when to move on to the next slide? That was the next thing. Then I would not be pleased with the sound level and I had to do it again', she sighed. 'It was always the sound level that was the problem, because the different tapes were all at different sound levels. But in the end I was quite pleased with the achievement.'

These challenges of composition became Vicki's audiovisual equivalent of construction in the written mode. Experimentation with the alternative forms of presentation offered by the course was on trial. There was no previous experience to help; we were finding our way. This presented problems for the teachers because the academy traditionally commodified research through word count. At least the teachers knew that a written research report was assessed, quantitavely, in blocks of 4000 words. Commodifying audiotapes, slides and videotapes was a more elusive quantitative enterprise.

In the absence of firm, clear guidance about 'how much work', during this experimental trial, Vicki decided that she had to become her own judge in the matter. The technological demands were heavy and she did not have enough time to do well all she wanted. She prioritized, balancing the time and energy available to her against the desire to communicate well her main research themes. 'I was struggling', she admitted. 'I was struggling on my own and then I had to decide what were the priorities. I couldn't do all that I wanted through the tape slide sequence and a lot of the writing as well. So I had to decide what were the most important aspects to cover in the writing.'

She had to redefine the assessment 'rules' of the academy as she saw them; she had to set her own expectations in the light of what she was hoping to achieve. 'For example, my supervisor asked me if I'd transcribed a tape', she explained, 'and I said, no, I hadn't transcribed a tape to go in, because that would have taken me however many hours. So I confidently said, no, because I've written down what I think are more important things to spend my time on and transcribing tapes is not one of them.' This she added with firm judgment.

She made autonomous decisions about what she felt were those 'important things'. 'I wrote a little bit on various reports that were out on handicapped children', she said, 'a bit of the history, which I felt was more relevant than actually doing a transcription of the tape I used. So it was things like that that made me have to decide I couldn't do it all, that I wasn't going to do it all.'

Vicki's evidence suggests that the full task of converting the research process and findings into visual and auditory text was too demanding. In the absence of clear guidelines from the academy, Vicki responded to the open-endedness with firmness, decision and good common sense. I felt both guilty and ashamed as she exclaimed, 'It was getting beyond a joke. I actually made the decision myself and that was my attitude in the end — since nobody was pointing out how many written words were equivalent to the tape slide sequence.'

Vicki's struggles and experience point to the complicated, rather bizarre nature of commodification, yet it is an assessment shackle to which the academy is chained, one which the teachers demand as a rule of thumb to measure their time and commitment. 'I don't know how you can do it', Vicki recognized. 'I don't know whether you can say a twenty minute tape is equal to so much. It's very difficult.'

However, let us not divert too much attention from Vicki at this stage, to wander into more general worries. Let us just reassert that, perhaps, the struggles associated with assessing teachers' research may be compounded where alternative, or additional forms of representation, are involved.

Yet Vicki's struggles were not pointless. They were a necessary part of making meaning, for as Vicki herself admitted, 'I suppose the floundering that I did in a lot of ways helped to clarify what I wanted to say and do'. Meaning was conveyed visually, she felt, in a way that was denied her ability with the written word. 'I knew that I couldn't actually say the things I wanted to say without actually visually showing the children', she told me. 'I mean like Caroline's smile, you actually had to see it to understand what sort of a person Caroline was and is.'

Certainly, as a reader, I found that the tape-slide sequence enriched and enhanced my understanding and interpretation of the written text. Visual information of the school and the children breathed a dimension of life and authenticity into the study that the written text alone did not elicit though the visual and auditory data did not venture into the interpretative and the argumentational.

Vicki's purposes in using tape-slide sequence were threefold. First, as we have just seen, she wanted an alternative form of visual representation in order to communicate what she could not communicate in words alone. Second, she wanted to experiment, to risk, to explore, to reach out for the new, the novel. In a mid-course interview she explained that she had done 'a risk thing — to me it was a risk anyway'. After the course, she remembered the creative challenge which she set herself. 'I was very much aware of trying to use new methods and new ways and just seeing how it worked', she explained.

'It brought a sense of achievement', she claimed. She felt good about what she had done. 'In the end I was quite pleased with the achievement. It wasn't as technically good as I would have liked it to be but it said what I wanted to say about the children, those two children.'

Thus, experiment fulfilled two of its purposes despite the labour and there was no regret about the invested time. The achievement transcended the disadvantages because Vicki felt that 'it was nice to have done something a bit different'.

In her third purpose, she intended to offer her learning to the colleagues who would subsequently teach Darren and Caroline. 'One of the reasons I did it originally', she explained, 'was to help the people who were going to have the children next to begin to understand them'.

The roots of this altruistic motive lay in a sense of accountability, a sense of debt felt in response to being awarded the privilege of day release for further study. 'We now have to be far more accountable for having this time off than we were before', she said. 'The school should be benefitting from the time out that you spend.'

Whilst her first two purposes were well served by the research, this third, more altruistic purpose was thwarted. There were two reasons for this. On the one hand, Vicki was pleased with the inherent value in the end product of her study, but on the other, as we have said, she was unsure that the quality was adequate enough for other audiences. In a mid-course interview she confessed that she felt that the tape slide sequence 'wasn't technically brilliant, I didn't think anyway'. This created diffidence and she admitted, 'To actually show that, I would have opened myself up to criticism for the way I did it'.

We cannot assume that sharing and disseminating insider teacher research in the cause of school improvement is straightforward and unproblematic. Laying one's work open and public for others' benefit is an act of personal and professional exposure for the teacher. Much of her 'self' is in that work and she may risk judgment on many levels when the research becomes public. The teacher may feel neither comfortable nor confident in that position. Attitudes and feelings will be implicated and controlling these may not be easy.

Vicki's supervisor, Harry, did not share her negative assessment of the work's technical merit. Yet his more favourable evaluation and his consequent encouragement did not help Vicki to overcome her inhibitions. 'My supervisor thought it very good', she confirmed, 'but I was very aware that it wasn't technically brillant so I didn't push it that much'.

The rhythms of the academy's examining process were also antithetical to Vicki's collegial purposes. The research was being finished and assessed at the time Vicki's colleagues might have profited from studying and discussing it. 'By the time it came back (from the assessment process) you see it was a September one — it was well into the autumn term', Vicki confirmed. This was too late for colleagues to learn from it before they received the children in September. As Vicki said, 'It would have been better if I'd been able to show it to them in the summer term, in July. So the timing was a bit wrong'.

The course handbook had outlined laudable principles for submission of research for assessment. Submission dates 'might be negotiable in special circumstances where students wish to submit work that is linked closely to developments within the school, and where fixed dates would constrain the student in achieving maximum benefit for the school from the assignment'. Laudable principles indeed, except that, somewhere along the line, either by default or lack of forethought, they had not influenced Vicki's case.

Vicki's procrastination was partly to blame, by her own admission. Given that she felt accountable to colleagues for her day release on the course, her procrastination led to guilt. 'Having decided that I was going to share the research then I felt awful that I put it off and off. I'd make a date next week, and I never actually got round to it in the end', she told me.

Perhaps this was symptomatic of her lack of confidence in the quality of the work. 'But I wasn't convinced about its technical merit as well'. She went on to admit, and confirm, 'that was something I wasn't too happy about'.

Under the surface of these explanations, there was a more deep-seated reason for not sharing her research for Vicki was not sure that her sympathetic views of the children would be shared by their next teacher. She did not want to risk making these differences explicit. 'It didn't exactly get finished until September and I had anticipated showing it when it was ready', she confirmed, 'but things moved on so quickly and the person who then had Caroline and Darren had very different ideas about Caroline. One of the reasons I didn't show the research was that I didn't want to show a different opinion.'

Vicki was not confident enough in the relationship with this colleague for their difference of perspective to be an opportunity for joint growth in understanding. 'It might have caused some sort of conflict and that was not the idea.

The whole idea of the tape was to help people to understand and be aware', she told me.

Sensitive to the possible negative effect on the relationship with her colleague, Vicki decided against sharing the research. She also decided, in retrospect, that this had been the right decision. Modesty and characteristic self-doubt were manifest in her decision, for Vicki doubted the status and wisdom of her own knowledge and understanding. She could not, as a result, make confident recommendations. 'Even on reflection, I wonder whether I was too sympathetic to these children', she thought. 'That sounds awful doesn't it — but I mean, one of the things that came out of the research was that I felt perhaps we don't push them enough. This stayed with me.' This research insight stimulated self-critique. Under its spotlight, Vicki found herself wanting. By this yardstick she also compared herself unfavourably to her colleague. 'I wondered whether she pushed them more than I did', Vicki reflected, 'and I thought, who am I to show mine as being the one that is right. So all these things played against me forcing the research on anybody in the end.'

Uncertainty prevailed over aspiration. Wisdom may also have prevailed over ambition.

What started, then, as personal, individualistic research, accumulated altruistic and collegial intentions during its development. These intentions were frustrated by a number of factors in Vicki's personal and institutional environment. The alternative forms of presentation had been introduced into the course as an aid to institutional sharing. In the event, they were of no help in the light of these other factors which worked against wider dissemination.

Here, we can see the insider teacher researcher at the centre of a set of complex forces. She is trying to make sense of various demands, constraints and circumstances in order to make a wise and appropriate judgment about purposes and audiences for her research. She has to read and understand the 'institutional text', made up of roles, relationships, attitudes and practices of colleagues, as a basis for deciding how to use her research. This is no mean task, given that she has already invested much time, energy, commitment, thought and feeling in the process of the research and in the consequent construction of her texts. If she misreads this 'institutional text', sharing may not be helpful to either side. Further, Vicki's own sense of self is necessarily implicated. Confidence in her own knowledge and certainties is being tested. If she shares the research more widely, the consequent judgments may affect her sense of professional self worth, for good or for ill. The way in which her work is received may prove to affect her feelings, attitudes and ideas about herself, her competence, her judgment.

We may wonder who teaches her to manage all this in addition to the standard demands of a research-based course; where she finds help and support in making these judgments; whether her own accumulated personal and institutional common sense prevail in the absence of formal guidance.

That Vicki felt under some pressure to make institutional use of her learning was clear from her earlier comments about accountability and favourable day release benefits. Her sense of professional obligation towards her colleagues was, certainly, a driving force. She also felt a need to reciprocate the time and commitment given to her by colleagues during the research. She wanted to pay them back for their gifts of time, interest, data. In the event, not reciprocating left guilty residues. 'I should have fed back to my colleagues, having made the effort and done the work', she said. 'Several people were involved in it as I did a lot of taping. A lot of people were involved and they never actually saw the finished result.'

Vicki had to juggle and manage a wide range of expectations, spanning the intellectual, the textual, the institutional, the interpersonal. Small wonder that, at one point, she claimed 'it was getting beyond a joke'.

The institutional impact of her second research study was, then, limited, but for Vicki herself, it had much validity. It raised her awareness of the children's needs, experiences problems and achievements. It also caused her to understand more fully the ways in which other children responded. 'It also gave me an insight into how the other children treated the handicapped', she wrote. 'This was as much value to me as the study of the handicapped themselves.' These changes in awareness, perception and understanding fed into practice. 'Being more aware helped in the way I taught and handled the children', she wrote.

Not to be underestimated, either, were the attitudinal changes which the research brought about. Vicki claimed to have developed greater empathy towards, and respect for, these children. Also, her own self-esteem benefited despite the dissatisfactions with the tape-slide text, despite her guilt at failing to share the research with school colleagues. An extract from the edited tape which accompanied the slides gave insight into the significant developmental purposes which the research achieved and some of the sense of professional mastery which it brought. Here is Vicki speaking on the audio material accompanying the written research report.

One evening, last year, when I got home, I wrote this. It's Monday the 12th, 11.40, and I had to deal with my first fit with Darren. Maria was not around, and it was an event which I knew I would eventually have to cope with. It was not a bad one and Darren did not flail. The first indication was that one of the children called out 'Please miss, Darren's having a fit'. His arm had become oddly shaped and he began to work his mouth, and his eyes stared. I knew the object was to get him into the recovery position. But he's heavy and I can feel my heart racing. I feel flushed. The children are watching to see how I am going to cope. Actually getting him down is a great physical effort. I eventually do it with the help of the children who help me with his legs. I know I must remember to keep his air passage clear and his head to one side. I talk to him all the time. I'm half kneeling on one side of him with his weight on my other leg. He is out, gurgling rhythmically to himself for about three-quarters of a minute. It seems so much longer. He begins to come round, and immediately he wants to get up. This is a struggle because he is still very unsteady. After a fit I knew that Darren generally likes to sleep. Another member of staff relieves me and takes him away. I immediately feel exhausted.

I feel a weakness in one of my legs after the weight of Darren on it. But I am a little elated. I've got through the first one and it felt like a hurdle I knew I would have to take. He had come out of it okay. I felt a bit pleased with myself and relieved. I knew that if it happened again, I could do it again.

Here is professional development in the making; alive, emotive, knowledgeable, dangerous, committed, human.

Summary

We have seen Vicki, then, through this research study, meet several new challenges, revisit a few already familiar ones and apply learning from her first study. It was a considerable piece of work in terms of the research processes, and the creation of the textual end products. There were sensitive methodological judgments as she adopted data gathering methods to suit field participants, school timetable and organization. There were many relationships to negotiate and manage from inception of the research, through the data gathering processes and at the point of decision about its institutional use. The processes benefited from existing good relationships and goodwill with pupils, colleague teachers and the ancillary helper but dissemination was impeded by Vicki's uncertainty.

Here, also, is Vicki showing a strong sense of autonomy in her judgment about the experimental mode of representation. She chose deliberately to seek risk and challenge. She was prepared to set her own norms for quantity and quality in her work.

This research involved Vicki's autobiographical and emotional being. We have seen anxiety, uncertainty, affection, worry, joy, caring as the research caused her to interact with colleagues, pupils and her own philosophy. There was a committed and emotionally attached teacher living inside the researcher role, the one driving and interacting with the other in an inseparable way.

The emotional manifestation of her philosophy showed itself in the ethical judgments she made during data gathering and in her decision about sharing the work. Where dilemmas were presented between well being of participants and development of the research, people came first. Her research depended upon this for its integrity. Its purpose was improvement. To damage people in the process would have been incongruent. Methodology was ethically consonant with the research purpose.

Even though Vicki was initially motivated to share this research, there were several reasons why she decided against this. There was not the same personal and professional self-confidence with which she fostered institutional growth through her first research study. There was more doubt, guilt, uncertainty and uneasy self-esteem because of her judgments about quality of the work and the mismatch between her own perceptions and her colleague's. In this uncertainty, the study missed its moment for institutional use. Time and circumstances moved on, so it failed to have its day for others, even though it had many days for Vicki. Vicki exercised judgment and discretion in keeping the research from more public scrutiny. Whether or not it was the most appropriate judgment, we will never know. But for Vicki it was, perhaps, the best she could manage at the time. It is a pity that she came to see this as a failure, rather than a good and wise decision.

HAROLD BRIDGES LIBRARY
S. MARTIN'S COLLEGE
LANCASTER

Chapter 6

The Gendered Curriculum at Springfield School

The diffidence in sharing the second study was matched by an equally strong confidence in the value of the third. This was Vicki's major research enterprise.

Its evolution in term 4 of the course has already been glimpsed in the early part of the story. We saw how the topic arose from a strong autobiographical agenda, one which had transformed itself into a strong educational, professional agenda. We saw the work developing in the cut and thrust of collaborative group work and being moulded into a formal group presentation. In all of this, we saw it impacting on the consciousness of the teachers on the course, as well as myself as tutor. So let us now consider where, how, and in what form, it impinged on the life of the school and on the consciousness of Vicki's colleagues.

There was a thirst in the school for insights from the research, as Vicki explained in a mid-course interview. When she was immersed in the thickets of data gathering she declared, 'The research I'm doing now, the gender issue, now I'm absolutely determined that I'm going to do a report on it.' This was imperative 'because everybody is interested', she explained. 'They keep saying, how is it going, what are the results. So they're not going to let me get away with it.'

As time showed, colleagues did not let Vicki 'get away with it'. Nor, indeed, did Vicki let them 'get away with it'. Motivation to share the study was reciprocal.

The research process itself raised new awareness and self-reflection amongst school colleagues. It was a school-wide study, so most teachers were implicated in data gathering. This may have been a factor contributing towards the keen institutional interest. Also the topic itself was intrinsically interesting. 'My own view personally is that it's an important area', Jeff commented. 'I'm hoping that it does, at some stage, feed back into the school so that we can look at the issues that Vicki's raised particularly as it's her major piece of work', he added. 'Everyone is wondering — No! I don't suppose they are that was a vast exaggeration — I'm wondering what the thrust of it is going to be. All I know is that she's researching gender issues and constantly noting down the sorts of things which indicate a prejudice one way or another. She's noting down any tendency for females to lose out here, or the macho image in children's picture books, all that kind of thing. I think we should be interested in school, despite the fact a lot of people laugh about it.'

Aspects of data gathering raised interest and humour for some time. There was the famous 'blue book' which was mentioned by almost everyone interviewed. In this, Vicki noted down a range of comments, observations, snippets of conversation that she met as she went about her daily business in the school. The blue book served as a catch-all field diary for netting data which other methods missed. It was visible within the institution rather than private and invisible as many field diaries are.

The 'blue book' aroused discussion and focussed attention for many of Vicki's colleagues. It created a sense of collegial participation as well as a sense of fun. 'And the gender issue has become very much a staff involvement thing', Vicki explained. 'It's a joke. I've got this little blue book. I'm doing it that way. Any comments or anything — and colleagues will say, that's one for your blue book Vicki.'

Had it been a deliberate device for raising institutional consciousness, the blue book could not have been better conceived. As a research instrument it may have served the institution well, for in addition to raising debate and awareness it changed behaviour. It acted unwittingly as a monitoring device for individual and institutional gender conscience. Robert, one of Vicki's colleagues, made strong claims for its value as a catalyst for change. 'Vicki's been very instrumental in that, just heightening awareness while she's been doing her research. The famous Vicki book was quite important.'

I asked Robert to elaborate. 'Well, Vicki would actually go round and take notes', he explained, 'when she did observation of classroom management and of the way children interrelated, of how staff and children interrelated, even down in the office. She had a little blue book which she wrote observations down in. Now that was enough, when the blue book appeared, to heighten awareness. It was a good tool in itself.'

Children were affected too. They were curious about the blue book and about Vicki's observational work. Their curiosity led to questions; the questions led to discussion; discussion led to new gender awareness. 'The children would say to Vicki, What are you doing this for', Robert volunteered, 'and she'd obviously tell them an outline of what she was looking at. And it was quite interesting to hear the way the children talked to her about gender issues. I remember she had a terrific conversation with some of the children on the computer once.'

'I was ear-wigging, if you like, on her', Robert confessed, not above covert data gathering himself. 'But she was talking to a group of children about their use of the computer and some of the children actually tumbled to what was behind the questions. One of the boys said, You're trying to say the boys are on here too much aren't you.'

According to Robert, Vicki promptly denied any such bias. 'I'm not saying that at all I'm just asking some questions'.

Not convinced, the boy responded, 'You are though, aren't you miss? It's about boys using the computers.'

Prone to put two and two together, the pupils made the link between Vicki's questions and the dissatisfaction which had erupted earlier from some of the girls 'because they felt they weren't getting enough access to computers', Robert explained. So the data gathering, the children's curiosity and the concern over the use of the computer merged into a valuable educative discussion between the teacher researcher and pupils.

'It was interesting how just the very fact of her being there and asking the question made the boys' awareness far greater', Robert explained. 'It started a very good conversation which I know happened later, an informal conversation, a classroom breaktime conversation', he added. 'The girls were already in quite high dudgeon about this it turned out, because they felt they weren't getting enough access to computers. The fact that the two things came together meant that they had a really very good adult exchange of views.'

It would profit us little to try to disentangle the research from the teaching, the teaching from the curriculum development, the curriculum development from the research in this brief episode. These integrated processes flowed freely, spontaneously and, perhaps, intuitively, from a drive to enquire and explore, in both teacher and pupils.

Vicki needed a tough skin in order to withstand the institutional banter which the study caused. Later evidence shows the research was regarded seriously by colleagues but it also carried much humorous flotsom along with the seriousness. 'People are aware of the work that she's doing at the moment on gender because it's the kind of thing which causes comment and amusement', Jeff told me. 'Some of the attitudes to it have been interested, but there's a level at which Vicki now acts as a butt to all the jokes, the gender jokes', he continued. 'They're not especially nasty or anything like that, but there's a feeling of, "Oh dear, we'd better not say that because Vicki's about".'

This humour may have been an institutional defence mechanism, a way of making overt that which was otherwise difficult to speak. The humour may have served to cover embarrassment when a gender-slip was made in the presence of one who was so gender-conscious. It may have been a way of laughing-away any transgression of the new norms which Vicki's research was beginning to establish.

According to Richard, the headteacher, humour made an important contribution to the school climate; to the way relationships were conducted; the way thinking was developed; the way the school developed. Disagreement was also a regular and important feature of staff discourse, he believed. But it was healthy disagreement because of the constructive way in which people handled it. Disagreement did not close people off from each other. Rather, it opened up possibilities for growth. 'What I think is also very powerful', he explained, 'and again it reflects, I think, the people we have here, is that although people will disagree about things and have doubts — and I think doubts are very important to have — I've got stacks and stacks', he added 'but people can say they disagree and it doesn't actually by and large change the working relationship. I think that is very healthy.'

Other teachers in the school had told me about the humour phenomenon in staff discourse and in the management of ideas. Antony, a main professional grade teacher, saw humour as a device for facing challenge; for dealing with change in an open way which was institutionally acceptable and healthy. 'I think it's part of taking things on board', he said. 'It happens to everything in the school, especially to formal proposals. We're having a school uniform next year. It all went through the same humorous phase.'

This controversial school uniform issue generated open ragging and bantering. These served both sides of the managerial process of challenge. On the one hand, open humour offered an acceptable institutional format within which dissenters could express their perspective. On the other hand, it brought dissension to the surface and to the attention of senior management. Whilst the teachers had to deal with the challenge of the change, senior management had to deal with the staff response to that challenge. 'A cut-out child was produced', Antony told me. 'And we dressed it in the staffroom and suggested a school uniform, with binliners and the rest', he said. 'And I thought it was very healthy because the Head accepted it and took part. The Deputy and all the hierarchy took an equal part in it too, so it seemed to be part of the acceptance phase.'

The communal humour also mediated and attenuated the differences of opinion between teachers and management. When all were laughing at the same joke the differences behind peoples' smiles dissipated. Senior management went along with the humour. There was no attempt to quell it, intervene, or contradict it. There was managerial wisdom. This helped to conserve an open climate. Challenge and difference became instruments of change whilst maintaining a healthy and accepting collegial spirit. 'Well, senior management don't start it', Antony explained. 'Again it's bottom up pressure but once they realize it they don't struggle against it. They join in.'

As I probed Richard's perspective on humour, I met a swift affirmative, 'That is terribly important here'. He told me of the white NOBBO board in the staff room. This was a device for drawing out, capturing and sharing any *ad hoc*, brainstormed ideas from anyone who felt the need to express themselves; a legitimation of professional graffiti. The NOBBO board encouraged staff participation in a creative way. So the professional graffiti was managed and used purposefully and, often, humorously. 'You would have seen the NOBBO board in the staff room', he said to me, 'and that's terrific. It really is ever so powerful for relieving tensions and keeping the humour bubbling'. He went on, 'I mean, I have to sort of check it carefully before PTA meetings, because some of it is really terrific stuff. But it is very powerful and useful to us all!'.

Here was an institutional device for encouraging and legitimizing openness. It gives us insights into leadership style, staff climate and ethos. Openness, free expression, forthrightness were all encouraged through the strokes of the felt pens on the white melamine NOBBO surface.

This, too, may help us to see why Vicki's major gender research eventually played such a positive role in staff development. There is no doubt that the research opened institutional sensitivities, for it challenged people's beliefs, attitudes, professional and personal practices. It leaned hard against people's feelings and ideas. And it did this in a way which became progressively more and more public. In a less open, less challenging, less humorous climate, it may have had a very different welcome.

So let us continue to look at the life of this research as it moved further into the influential data gathering stage, into its written form and its subsequent second-stage of institutional existence. And Vicki's research text itself tells us, in plenty of detail, what emerged from the months of observation, discussions and blue-bookery. Let us also glimpse at the way in which Vicki structured the enquiry, for that will indicate the issues which were raised and developed within the institution. It will also tell us more about Vicki's learning about gender and research.

Vicki originally had three questions, all institutionally related, all broad. First, she was interested to explore 'the attitudes and opinions that the children are subject to by the staff, the curriculum and the ethos of the school'. Second, she asked, 'Is there a difference in expectation and attitude of the male and female child at school and in their perception of the male and female role they will fill in later life?' And, as if these $64,000 questions were not enough to be going on with, Vicki asked, 'How do children formulate their image of what male or female is? Where do the influences come from and what are their attitudes to it and to each other?'

Broad though these questions were, they represented a considerable narrowing down. By now Vicki realized that in empirical enquiry and intellectual pursuit 'one question immediately leads to a dozen more'. Maybe she had come to accept that compromise and pragmatism are often the order of the day in carving out enquiry starting points.

Methodology was a challenge and a vexation at one and the same time. On the one hand she needed a methodology that was appropriate for 'what (she) was . . . attempting to do and discover'. On the other, she wanted the research to be a continuing methodological learning experience. So she asked herself, 'what methods not so far attempted in previous research could I adopt to continue the learning process in action research?' Appropriateness was in competition with her desire to experiment.

She decided, initially, to develop her skill at questionnaire design, over which she had gained some mastery in her first research. But she soon realized the problems of reliability and validity which would be raised. She did not wish to question her colleagues' integrity nor doubt their honesty in giving questionnaire data, but she questioned whether colleagues' accounts of their professional practices would actually give an accurate indication of such practice. In other words, she trod that vexing path which many researchers before and after have trodden in questioning the gap between our rhetoric and our reality, between what we think we do, what we say we do, and what we actually do. She recognized that colleagues' may have professional perceptual blind spots, as well as acknowledging the possible existence of her own. Of the questionnaire proposal she wrote, 'In the process of trying to devise suitable questions, it soon became apparent that however I phrased the questions and however honest my colleagues believed themselves to be, there was a strong possibility that the answers would not necessarily reflect practice and I included myself in that category'.

The doubts were sufficient to send Vicki in search of other methods. 'Philosophy and practice in teaching can be poles apart', she wrote. 'A questionnaire then was the wrong medium as was interviewing, because the same problem would arise.' She concluded that 'the only feasible method was observation'. And so, the blue book was born.

The next methodological vexation to be confronted with the blue book was the problem of personal bias. Her own preconceptions and prejudices would, she realized, determine the data that she would collect. 'As I was making the decisions about what I felt was relevant and not', she wrote, 'this method immediately became subjective. I believe myself to have been scrupulously fair, using comments that both upheld and threw out any assumptions or theories I already held, but this cannot be guaranteed'.

Harry confirmed that this issue of personal bias troubled Vicki for some time as she expressed concern about the 'subjective' nature of her research. The method placed ethical and epistemological demands on her which she recognized. She knew she needed to locate herself more clearly in the data than she had with previous approaches. 'It perhaps puts more onus on the part of the researcher who takes on the responsibility of making sure that the data collected is well balanced and fair', she wrote. 'It is a research skill that needs a more confident approach as the researcher is relying on her own opinion; everything she brings, especially to this emotive type of topic, is going to affect her decisions. It becomes, therefore, less safe and more speculative', she concluded.

Harry discouraged her from seeing her personal position in the research as a disadvantage. Instead, he encouraged her to celebrate the personal quality and insights which 'subjective' and 'insider' perspective could offer. But despite Harry's persuasions, Vicki never fully resolved the doubts, though she did continue with her blue book. 'Having been encouraged to attempt this form of data collection, I still have misgivings about it', she admitted.

Her own written account of the substantive nature of the blue book corroborated what others had said. She wrote of the kinds of data she recorded, and how the method developed. 'I found myself at one stage becoming more concerned with staff-to-staff relationships than with staff-to-children. But even this was interesting data . . . As I progressed with my research, I felt I was less inclined to jot down comments and single events, and more inclined to analyze subjectively whole events, impromptu, unplanned occasions. There was a Sunday morning football match; a maths course that involved children; an observation from a Masters' degree colleague which helped my research as well as his; the drama lesson that suddenly threw up data.'

She wrote of the raised awareness of colleagues, as well as her own growing self-awareness. This led some into volunteering data for the blue book. 'It became apparent as my research continued that staff were very much more aware of what I was doing', she wrote. 'As I myself became more critical of how I treated boys and girls, to a lesser extent so were the staff becoming more aware of their own practice. I would be told anecdotes and given quotes concerning a wide range of issues', she explained.

This voluntary, collaborative development may have counter-balanced to an extent the 'subjectivity' that caused Vicki anxiety. As such, blue book data became determined by colleagues' own views, so data selection became communal.

In no time at all, data gathering became something of an obsession for Vicki and as a fellow researcher, I identified with her when she wrote of this. She recognized that the blue book could seep into parts of life that other methods fail to reach. At the same time she saw how it began to take on a life and power of its own, controlling and possessing her. 'Once the decision had been made, everything was data', she wrote. 'It had its advantages and disadvantages. The main advantage is that I have been able to form a far wider perception of the gender issues in general, both inside and outside school. The main disadvantage is that it becomes a way of life. I found I couldn't stop collecting data. Every event or happening has been viewed as data collection, even the recent Funday!'

Vicki told me that once she started looking more keenly for gender inequalities, she began to see them 'everywhere', in situations to which she had, in some sense, previously been blind. The research fostered more 'looking' and, in the process, it fostered more, and different, 'seeing'. Vicki's mind was wide open and into it flowed a mass of new information.

Lest it be thought that this was a private problem with which Vicki had to deal, it should be remembered that the blue bookery, and, thus, Vicki's research obsession, maintained its high visibility in the school. It therefore continued to touch colleagues' lives, and nerves, in different ways. Vicki told of a colleague's frustration on feeling that life was regularly being given a double meaning as Vicki treated all existence as research data. 'Oh Vicki, give it a rest! was the exasperated comment of one of my colleagues', Vicki explained, 'when at 9.00 p.m. one evening on a school holiday I was making observations and taking photographs'.

Such are the feelings insider researchers may invoke in those around as they pursue, relentlessly, their keenest research enthusiasms, driven by interest, curiosity and the excitement of the chase. Dispassionate research may have little to do with this level of personal immersion in the game of enquiry.

The blue book was not all, functional though it was on many methodological levels. There was an analysis of some children's curriculum books. Vicki 'tried to determine how they were presenting the world to these children'. There was also a taped discussion between some children based upon their responses to 'Piggybook'. This was one of the gender stories which Vicki used in her presentation to course colleagues and which caused hilarity and fierce debate between the teachers. The pupil discussion was a creative alternative to pupil interviewing because Vicki's earlier experiences had left her dissatisfied. 'I have learned in previous research that (the children) very often haven't formulated any thoughts or opinions on those issues which you are trying to research. I did not want to be in a position where I was leading discussions by my questions.' The Piggybook had led to lively discussions previously with some children so Vicki set the tape recorder and left the children alone. They had the book and a sheet of simple instructions and questions to structure their discussion. She also did a gender analysis of 'literature, comics and to a lesser extent advertising' which all 'helped to formulate . . . conclusions'.

There was also a questionnaire for gathering data on her second question about children's views of gender roles. This was piloted with a small number of children and alterations were made in the light of the trial. Vicki did an ethical analysis on the piloted questionnaire and 'withdrew some questions that had led one or two children to take the opportunity to attack certain members of staff', which she 'felt was inappropriate'.

The final questionnaire was used with children from each age group in the school. Vicki decided to be pragmatic and not include all the children in the school because 'the analyzing of the data would restrict the time (she) could spend on other research'. Time constraints meant that she had to tailor her methodological suit to fit her situational cloth.

She had to devise a common questionnaire that all children could read well and to which they could give full written answers. As a result, she decided to 'help out in writing the answers for (the youngest) children as (she) did with some of the less able older children'. Here, again, we see her methodological intelligence at work. Her craft knowledge as a teacher supported her new developing role as a researcher.

A critical stance towards the development of the questionnaire pointed to a basic dilemma posed in its construction. 'I was fairly pleased with the final copy, although I will be the first to admit it was too long', Vicki wrote. 'It would probably have been possible to amalgamate questions to make the whole thing less complicated. For example, (some) questions were both long-winded and confusing . . . but finding that balance between not leading the children and leaving the questions too wide open is a fine one.'

She had created problems. 'The fact that I created one questionnaire for the (whole) age range was, perhaps, the biggest mistake I made', she believed.

This mistake would have cost her dear had she not fortuitously administered the questionnaire to the youngest children first and, therefore, recognized the difficulty. Thus, she had been able to retrieve the situation to some extent. 'With approximately half the first year class I had a one-to-one interview to complete the final parts of the questionnaire as by this time they were struggling. In this way I was able to salvage what at one stage looked like failure.'

Vicki was well aware, as in the previous study, of the limitations of small scale, and small samples, though she was now more confident in her purposes. 'Although I have analyzed the results in some cases in percentages and priority list', she wrote, 'I am aware that little store can be put on the actual figures themselves. Using such a small sample . . . invalidates any major conclusions.' She agreed that 'what I have been looking for are tendencies rather than concrete results'.

Validity and reliability were also, she recognized, affected by the many and differential factors influencing field participants' responses. 'With so many variables affecting the children's answers, results must be viewed speculatively'. Children may have been influenced by Vicki's teacher role; they may have been seeking to give socially acceptable, rather than authentic, responses. 'Very often children will write what they think they should rather than their own opinions', Vicki thought.

Here, then, we see the broadening of methodological horizons which Vicki anticipated. This was a lengthy research process. 'I had spent almost a year observing, reading and discussing, as well as collecting articles, quotes and various other tangible data.' In this time she was continuously reflective about practicalities, ethics, reliability and validity in data gathering.

From her experience, she moulded and shaped data gathering techniques in response to previous experience and in response to piloting. She was sensitive to possible ethical by-products of the research. She set limits on the scale of data gathering, offsetting advantages of quantity, perhaps, with advantages of variety of data. She also delved into some complex and difficult gender questions for which she chose to involve approximately half the children in the school and many of her colleagues. With the visible nature of the blue book, and the institutional scope of the study, Vicki assumed a public profile. Along with that went challenge and ragging.

The 'findings' which her colleagues awaited were many and varied. From a numerical analysis of the children's questionnaire returns, Vicki concluded that 'reading was the favourite pastime of the girls' with a greater percentage of girls than boys claiming that 'they read on a regular basis'. Also, the stories which the children claimed they read 'separated almost completely into accepted gender divides'.

Analysis also reinforced Vicki's own perception that the boys were dominating the winter play area at break times. The girls did not register this as an issue of much importance, as Vicki had done, but 'several groups of girls saw it as unfair, not only because of lack of space, but also because the boys, they felt, were deliberately rough or would not let them join in'.

Favourite toy choices demonstrated a gender divide in which 'Dolls and cuddly toys rated highly with the girls compared with lego, transformers and cars for the boys'. Likewise, there were gender differences in the jobs which children claimed they had to do to earn extra pocket money, and gender differences in the way children spent their pocket money, once earned.

Analysis of children's curriculum preferences suggested that maths became less popular from the first to the fourth year for the girls but remained consistently popular for boys. Science was not a high preference for most of the children. It was seen as a 'low choice throughout the school with all the children, apart from third year boys'. Popularity of computer studies was inconsistent for the girls, rising from the first to the second year but then dropping markedly in the third and fourth years. For boys, computer studies remained consistently popular across all four years. The reverse was the case for drama. It had an erratic reception from boys and a consistently good reception from girls. As for future job preferences and expectations, gender stereotypes prevailed, with girls aspiring to become hairdressers, shop assistants, teachers, housewives, and boys dreaming of becoming pilots, footballers, detectives, doctors.

Vicki tried to understand how school practices, including 'the curriculum and general ethos of the school', might be conspiring to perpetuate stereotyped gender 'images and attitudes'. She questioned the method for calling the daily attendance register, pointing out that boys were always called before girls. This, she thought could be seen as a form of discrimination against girls. 'When the boys are always in the register first and therefore always at the top of the class list, the discrimination against the girls is constant', she assumed. She wrote, 'We reinforce it every day when we call the register and on the hundreds of other occasions when the class list is used'. She was unable to give evidence of the gendered effects on children's self-images though she highlighted the habitual 'historic' nature of this practice in the school. Such practices continue, institutionally, 'because we have always done it that way', she advised.

Her data did, however, suggest differential gendered treatment by staff of pupils. From her observations of 'the way staff treat boys and girls', she constructed three teacher categories. First, she identified teachers who, despite believing that they treated all children equally and fairly, nevertheless reinforced gender stereotypes in their practices. This included instructing girls to clear away the paints and instructing boys to 'move the tables'. In the second group were teachers who were aware of gender discrimination. Yet they found it difficult to change because of their own deep-seated, autobiographical views on differential roles in our culture. In the third group were teachers who were highly gender conscious and committed to changing practices to deal with discrimination. Even so, Vicki claimed to have witnessed unconscious gender bias in at least one of these colleagues. She claimed to belong to this third group herself but also cited evidence of her gender blindspots. For example, she wrote of an occasion when she was proud of putting her practice where her principles were when needing to move furniture from one classroom to another. 'Earlier this year I had to move classrooms and being aware of the stereotyped characteristic we encourage, I asked one boy and one girl if they would please help me to move my desk'.

She could have been well pleased with her conscious practical affirmation of her ideological stance had not a linguistic gender slip contradicted her, and let her down. 'With a feeling of great righteousness at having displayed such a liberal attitude, I asked them to "manhandle" the desk to my new classroom!.' And she may have continued to be unaware of this contradiction had not one of the children mirrored it back to her. 'It was, in fact, one of the girls who drew my attention to what I had said. I had not even been aware of the language I had used', she admitted.

Continuing her exploration of the gendered nature of institutional language, Vicki moved on to share her findings from published texts in the school. Her 'simple survey' of the books which had been bought for the literature course in years 1, 2 and 3 suggested a heavy predominance of male over female main characters. This was in the ratio of 3:1 (year 1), 6:1 (year 2), 6:1 (year 3).

Vicki could not, did not, hide her emotive response. 'This (the predominance of male main characters) is perhaps more alarming when considering that reading was the main pastime on which girls spent their time.'

The 'alarm' was generalized to other areas of the curriculum, particularly to history. In the next stage of her research text Vicki asserted that 'the dominance of the male and male attitude is prominent in other areas of the curriculum, for example in history'. Vicki substantiated this through reference to gender analysis of some of the schools' history texts and concluded that 'it is extremely difficult to teach history giving a balanced view. The material is just not available'. She had scoured the schools' text books and publishers' catalogues for gender conscious history material, to little avail.

From the interviews, questionnaires and observations, Vicki developed a well grounded exposition of the children's stereotyped views of gender roles, gender work, gender aspirations, gender attitudes to adventure, risk and challenge. She concluded that 'stereotyped roles are firmly established with these children'.

In addition, she tried to understand how 'children get their ideas of maleness and femaleness'. Her sources were eclectic, including the data from her observations, interviews and questionnaires. She drew upon other sources such as the Lego catalogue; a gift advertisement suggesting that girls have 'choices' and boys have 'challenges'; current school experiences, the Saturday school soccer match, the recent class trip. These data were drawn upon remorselessly to build a picture of the gender scales tipped firmly in favour of boys' active self-images and girls' passivity.

The questionnaire data again stirred Vicki's emotions; her concern, her alarm. Her written research text gave clues to the feelings within her analysis. She wrote of the worry roused by some of her observations. She expressed a sense of sadness at what she saw as girls' limited self-aspirations. 'It does seem to me very sad that instead of seeing their future as a development of themselves, they see their own role purely in connection with a husband or a child.' Perhaps, the children's view of womanhood and its possibilities fell far short of Vicki's own strong views.

There was also a sense of shock felt when analyzing gender images in the comics which were most commonly read by the children in her survey. 'I was even more shocked than I thought I would be', she admitted.

Alarm, worry, sadness, shock. One could argue that this is not the usual language of research. Yet if Vicki wanted to account for herself in the enquiry, it is difficult to see how much more honest and authentic she could have been in constructing her research text. Her feelings were made visible for all to see.

Nor did Vicki try to hide her gender ideology from her reader any more than she had hidden her commitment towards the handicapped. In discussing the gendered nature of language, for example, she referred to 'the furore that has met suggestions that "chairman" be changed to "chairperson" '. For Vicki, this was no trivial semantic matter. 'If our aim is to equate the standing of men and women in society', she declared firmly, 'then surely we must try' to change the attendant language.

Vicki's language here is the language of persuasion, of personal conviction and her gender principles were explicit. There were, thus, many linguistic ingredients making the pot pourri of Vicki's written research text. Thought, feeling, ideology and autobiography were its multiple qualities. Its subjectivity enriched its authenticity. And whilst Vicki brought rigour and system to data analysis in the best way she knew, she had no illusions about her own role in the biases of the research. Hence, there was no pretence to dispassionate and spurious objectivity. This was neither appropriate nor desirable. Indeed, the personal, and more emotionally risky, nature of this third research enterprise was a major driving force which led the ensuing practical outcomes. This subjective validity prevented the research study from lying around gathering practical and institutional dust. Rather it turned it into research which gave life to institutional thought and practice.

Let us move on then, to consider where the work impacted beyond the field work events which we have just encountered, for impact it did. There was little gathering of metaphorical dust in the early life of this research. Changes emerged.

Vicki was well aware of the difficulties to be encountered in influencing deep seated elements of the culture. She believed that change had to be approached gradually and carefully if it were to be effective. Without gradual care, people would become defensive in order to protect themselves. 'I feel it has to be a gradual process', she wrote. 'It is better to take more people with you at a slower rate than try to move too quickly and be blocked by hostility.'

She had a realistic understanding of the deep-rooted nature of gendered perception and, therefore, of the need to be patient when eager for developments. 'Change in such a fundamentally traditional area of our culture cannot be dealt with overnight', she believed. But were the subsequent developments as slow and difficult as Vicki supposed they might be?

Some of her suggested practical action steps had already been implemented at the time she wrote the research report. They included revision of name order in attendance registers for year 1, from gender to alphabetical; more story books offering alternative female images or what Vicki called 'the liberated princess books' which 'all reverse the traditional fairy tale image of the princess'. Changes in gendered use of language were slow, for Vicki told us that the 'change of the traditional he to she when referring to a child is still an unusual event', though progress was being made. Nevertheless, these examples showed that the gendered culture of the school, and the gendered behaviour of its members, was beginning to shift in new directions even before the research report was finished and shared.

In order for the research to affect change more widely in the school, Vicki needed to transform her written text. This is not to suggest that it was presented in an unpalatable style. Far from it. Within the formal examining process of the academy, all who had contact with the text — Harry, myself, the external examiner — found it an engaging, intriguing, provocative if, in parts, challengeable, read. Rather, it is to suggest that transformation of the written research text for the school audience was necessary in the face of the heavy pace, energy and time demands of school life. Vicki said of an earlier study that it was offered to colleagues in an open way but had not actually been read, despite interest. So it was with this third study. The fifty-two pages of research script plus the appendices would not fit comfortably inside the precious days, hours and minutes of school colleagues' lives.

Antony confirmed that colleagues had been invited to read the report. 'She's invited us to read her study, but she hasn't stuffed it down our throats.' A certain reticence and modesty was evident. 'But I think that's partly to do with Vicki's personality. She is a very modest person and lacks a lot of self-confidence, if you like, at times'. Vicki may also have been nervous about the high risk and high exposure involved in sharing her writing and so, for these possible reasons, the text which she prepared for assessment in the academy did not serve her school colleagues well.

The opportunity to transform the research text into a different mode came shortly after its completion in September. By now Vicki had finished and left the Advanced Diploma course. She had been asked by Christine the Deputy Head, to give a report on the gender research at a staff meeting.

The meeting began, rolled on through discussion of this and that. Time and the agenda ticked away leaving Vicki's report stranded in the last five minutes. Richard turned to draw Vicki in to the remaining time. With an emphatic no, she resisted the invitation to share, with such brevity, the insights of a year's research work and the influence of a lifetime's socialization. Pam, one of Vicki's colleagues told me, about the occasion. 'It was arranged for the report to come within a staff meeting', she explained. 'Because the staff meetings are now an hour long, everything's always rushed.' And Vicki, at the end of the meeting when there was five minutes left . . . said, No, I refuse to talk about it in five minutes.' As Vicki herself told me, during a discussion long after the event, 'I felt it was too important to be put into five minutes.'

When the report to the staff meeting was aborted, Vicki took the initiative. She spoke to Christine, the Deputy Head. Christine had sympathies with Vicki's research topic. She also had a role in supporting and encouraging colleagues in their professional growth. To this end she encouraged communal sharing of individual learning. She had helped the Headteacher to create a system within which this could happen. Vicki offered to share her research on a formal staff development day which was part of the system. 'All I was going to do originally was to give out the recommendations', Vicki explained, 'and I thought that people needed a background to it really. Then also, very soon after the (aborted) staff meeting another colleague had put down to feedback from his Master degree course and I thought, "Oh yes, feedback!" So when the staff development days were actually put out, in-service was one of the things that was discussed. If you actually wanted to feed any in-service in, that was your opportunity to do it. So I went to Christine and said, "Perhaps I could feed back my research on one of those days. It would give me more time." We needed to have more discussion of it. So that's what happened. The staff meeting was thrown out, so discussion of my research went on a lot longer than I anticipated.'

There was a powerful interplay, then, between organization of school-based in-service, encouragement and support from the Deputy Head and Vicki's personal commitment and initiative. This interplay turned a potentially short research report on equal opportunities at the staff meeting into a much lengthier and more significant staff development experience.

Christine acted as Vicki's critical friend in the planning stage when the structure, content and pedagogy of the staff development session were being shaped. 'I said to Christine that I would do it', Vicki explained, 'but for her own peace of mind she wanted to be there just in case. And I also wanted someone to shut me up if I talked too long as well, which I was very conscious I might do. We had an hour-and-a-half and I divided it into three sections. I went to Christine and said, "This is what I plan to do, what do you think?" She said that it was fine.'

Vicki was reassured by Christine's judgment. And when the day came she was reassured by Christine's encouraging presence. Christine was there in the background and the foreground. She cushioned the nerves and fluster which overcame Vicki when her presentation began. 'It was useful because Christine was there at my elbow', Vicki told me 'It was just somebody there to help me along, so she was very valuable.' Vicki's character reference for Christine was unequivocal. She possessed qualities which supported others' growth and for Vicki these had been beneficial. 'She's very interested in this as well', Vicki explained. 'Well, she's interested in everything. She's nice to have there because she encourages. If I'd wanted to do it all, that would have been fine, but she's always there as a backup just in case you flounder.'

And flounder a little, at first, Vicki did. For despite the confidence coming from having made good preparation before the event, ('I wasn't nervous because I'd prepared it', Vicki at first said) her certainty and composure tottered when she began. 'Well I *was* nervous' she admitted, 'but it was just that when I started to talk, it didn't flow to begin with and I was tripping over my words and all the rest of it. You know, my colour rose.'

Not only was Christine an encouragement as Vicki took this hurdle with her new professional skills, but so too were Vicki's colleagues. She felt their implicit encouragement. 'I know the staff and I knew whatever I did they would be kind', she explained. 'And I could feel them saying "It's alright. It's OK. It's fine".' Here is evidence of the collegial, interpersonal climate in the staff group; the sense of mutual support; collaborative encouragement; emotional and personal sensitivities.

Vicki's anxiety settled as she brought life into her material. Her presentational skills rallied and she was away on her new professional venture. Now she had the learning of her colleagues more firmly and formally in her hands than she had ever had before. 'And after about ten minutes or a quarter-of-an-hour', she recalled, 'when I started to talk, when I got into talking about the questionnaire and then started to get some feedback, and once the conversation started to flow, then it was easy'.

There was human moral responsibility associated with this developmental venture for Vicki, for lest it be thought that she was the only one to suffer nerves on that day, we should note the apprehensions in the staff group. These were there even before the day began and Vicki's colleagues were certainly not coming complacently to the issue. The research process — and especially the blue book, as we have seen — had raised awarenesses, discussions, self-reflections. It had even changed some practices. Debates had been borne, sensitivities exposed, thinking challenged and advanced for several members of staff. Some colleagues were still uncertain about the issue. 'Quite a few of us were dubious as to what equal opportunities meant', Pam told me. Vicki was holding all this in trust as she led the day.

Given that this was Vicki's first substantial responsibility for in-service delivery, her achievement seemed remarkable. A fainter heart might have avoided the challenge of leading an in-service experience for a large group of colleagues on such a personally and emotionally charged topic. To be effective, she had to seek a challenging, appropriate, but safe pedagogy. The research text in which she had invested so much time and effort for the academy and the course examiners was not appropriate for this school audience. Nor were the purposes the same. The academy sought to assess, to validate. School colleagues sought to learn, to use, to develop. New text and new methods of communication were needed. So the written assessed text was superseded by an interactive professional learning text, mediated principally through the spoken word during the morning and through a variety of challenging activities. The written text was sifted, reorganized and reshaped for this new purpose as it was transformed from writing to speech.

Some preparation seemed important to set a climate of relevant ideas before the event. With some last minute forethought, Vicki had succeeded in arousing interest and debate the day before by creating a thinking environment in the staff room as the most obviously used communal area. For this she mounted some stimulus material drawn from her research data and written text.

Thus, the new transformed in-service 'text' offered a flexibility which the written autonomous text did not. Through the in-service talk which Vicki stimulated, ideas and meaning could be shaped, developed, modified, elaborated in a way that the finite written text alone could not allow. Vicki was there, active, connected to her words and ideas. She was there to explain, translate, rephrase and reshape ideas at others' behest. Transformation of her ideas from writing to speech, and from the isolated, disconnected text to the communal in-service text, held new and distinct possibilities for sharing and development. 'On the wall the day before she'd put a few articles from *The Times Educational Supplement*', Pam told me, 'and various quotations from a number of people throughout the ages. That got quite a bit of discussion going the previous day.'

This last minute forethought, Vicki claimed, paid dividends in terms of setting a reflective atmosphere and of engaging participants' ideas, ready for the formal input the following day. It was a useful pedagogical strategy, given that it had been borne out of minimal deliberation.

'I did the quotes before which was a very good thing', Vicki said. 'I didn't actually give it a lot of thought. But I did it the day before. I thought I might as well stick it up during break, it will cause some sort of interest. And that got people thinking, because one or two discussions started the day before. That was good, because people began to formulate thoughts and ideas ready to bring to the next day. So that was nothing I'd planned but it worked very well.'

The characteristic institutional humour which we have already seen was brought into play by this preliminary material. Antony suggested that the banter may have been a manifestation of the challenge, acceptance and change process. It may have been a necessary institutional strategy for confronting new and sensitive ideas. 'The display produced the usual batch of person-quippery', he said. 'You always get this. The staffroom itself has a great deal of banter, probably more than any other I've ever worked in. That's part of accepting something I think in a school. It has to go through the banter phase, I think.'

So, with her nerves fluttering and colleagues assembled, Vicki begun by presenting some key issues from the study. 'I started off by talking about what equal opportunities was', Vicki recalled, 'then I thought I owed it to my colleagues to give some idea of recent research. So I looked at some of the recent research on reading schemes and science and computers and all that sort of thing.'

Her own research came next. Now Vicki was presenting to the institution an image of itself. Pam told me about it. 'Vicki put forward various findings which she's concluded from her research. She'd looked at how, perhaps unknowingly, the females' equal opportunity isn't quite so equal within our school, even though I think we're quite a progressive school. She brought forward ideas about language and the books that males and females like. She brought forward ideas within humanities, science, French, every part of the curriculum really. She raised issues about artists within design; how there are very few of us who know the lady artists. She made us think about the ideas that we specifically put forward to the child.'

The atmosphere became interactive as Vicki moved in an out of the delivery mode and as colleagues responded with questions and comments. Presentation of the questionnaire findings was particularly effective in drawing colleagues further into the issues. It was the questionnaire results 'which of course, generated a lot of discussion', Vicki claimed, because they reflected the practices, attitudes, habits, perceptions of the school back to itself. A mirror was being held up.

Vicki's introductory input lasted longer than the twenty minutes which she had planned because colleagues became readily engaged. 'I talked for a bit longer than I'd intended but that's because we had a bit of to-ing and fro-ing.'

Even so, Antony welcomed its relative brevity and the way in which Vicki had selected her material. 'Vicki gave a presentation first which I think was sensibly short. It didn't try and explore the whole scene but it dipped into some of the issues which we might consider.'

Then it was into groups and out with the felt-tipped pens. Here Vicki drew upon the pedagogy of the Advanced Diploma course and upon her own experience as an adult learner in that context. Her methods had 'echoes of the Institute', Vicki admitted.

First, colleagues were invited to articulate a concept of equal opportunities from a gender perspective. Second, implications for practice had to be considered. Third, this thinking was shared in the plenary group. There was, however, a greater task ahead. The day's processes were to lead towards ideas for a first draft school policy. 'Really she set the target of us trying to evolve a school policy about equal opportunities — about gender issues in general', Antony explained.

Of this target we shall hear more later but let us take a quick look, here, at the staff group moving into their small groups, attempting to utilize a balance of what may have been considered the male and female perspective. Small groups of three were the desired norm, though this created difficulties. Men were at a premium; a scare commodity. 'From there we moved into small discussion groups which were obviously mixed gender groups', Antony told me. 'We evolved those ourselves. We tried to go for groups of three and so there would be seven groups of three.'

'And people chose their own groups did they?' I asked.

'More or less, by looking around to see if there was anyone basically without a man. We were quite short so we tried to balance it out', he replied.

'Spread the men out?' I asked.

'Yes, spread the men out', he confirmed.

And, of course, the ratio of men to women on the staff ('. . . it's about three to one', Antony said) was not reflected in the gender structure of senior management. 'But of course, of those men, there's the Headmaster and two of the four year leaders are men', he elaborated. 'We've just had a new year leader appointed last week who is also a man', he confirmed. This became an issue for discussion later in the day, as a debate was raised about the gendered nature of the institutional management structure.

The groups stayed on task. They tried to be explicit about the gender principles upon which they shaped the curriculum as they tried to organize and translate their views into commonly agreed ideas for policy.

Antony was certain that gender awarenesses had been shaping professional behaviour and that Vicki's work had influenced this. But this all lacked coordination, purpose and direction at the policy level. 'In these groups, we set ourselves the task of coming up with recommendations for an internal school policy', he recalled, 'because we haven't had a formalized policy before'.

Vicki felt that this small group pedagogical strategy had been particularly successful, generating lots of ideas and lots of individual involvement. 'In fact the small group discussions were the ones that they liked. They went on with those for a long time and a lot of discussion came out of it.'

Her own preference for small groups had influenced the methods she used with colleagues. 'Whereas people won't say anything in a group of twenty', she believed, 'as soon as you put them into threes and fours the actual discussion goes on'.

(The written text did, in the event, find a niche in the morning's discussion, for Jeff, the only colleague to read it, used it to resource the small group debate. 'He could remember the things I had written', Vicki recalled. 'And every so often it was, Can I borrow it to show them this bit?').

Antony recounted the important issues and sensitivities raised in the small groups. He pointed out first that Vicki had challenged colleagues to relate their discussions firmly to analysis of practical possibilities. She had been firm and decisive in steering them away from a theoretical discourse that led nowhere in practice. 'When she set us a target of evolving a school policy', Antony recalled, 'Vicki said, I don't want sort of grand phrases, I want identifiable nitty-gritty things that you think could be changed in school'.

This they did. The range of possibilities generated was wide, covering children's needs, strategies for staff self-evaluation, development and support, gender analysis of staffing and critique of staffing policy.

'I was terrifically heartened by the way that the staff took that on', Antony told me, 'because some groups responded in a very personal way. There were great things like realizing that fourth year boys have particular needs as an equal opportunity issue'. Also, colleagues decided to help each other with their personal change processes. 'There was a recommendation from one group that the staff should be critical friends to each other, and of each other, and in a friendly tone try to be critical and make constructive recommendations.'

People, thus, recognized the need for intercollegial support and help in their continuing process of professional questioning. They also had a feel for the particular style of interaction that would be most effective in that process. They needed to be challenged but this had to be tempered by sensitivity. It had also to be positive and constructive.

The gendered structure of staffing in the school was confronted and one group chose to talk about a staffing policy for the school. This was a sensitive and immediate issue because, as Antony pointed out, 'the Head was reading applications for the fourth year leader's job' at the time. The staff as a whole 'had made it very clear that there ought to be more women in positions of authority'.

Richard sympathized with the problem of gender imbalance in senior management but he also pointed out the contrary gender imbalance across the staff as a whole. 'It was a very interesting dialogue', Antony remembered. 'The Head said, "Yes I take all of that on board, but I have more women in the school than I have men and that balance has got to be redressed"'.

These were large and unresolvable dilemmas but colleagues had been able to sustain open and acceptable confrontation. 'That was a very interesting up-front dialogue that took place there', Antony concluded.

At one point, Antony felt that the Head may have been threatened by the discussion of the year leader appointment which was already underway at the time. Discussion of the appointment became a whole staff affair during the in-service day. Antony thought that Richard may have had gendered preconceptions about the appointment and may, thus, have been discomforted by the communal debate. 'I think maybe the analysis of the school appointment policy threatened him', Antony speculated. 'I think if he hadn't been in the middle of that appointment it would have been far less threatening. But he'd sent out the advert before Easter and had a pile of applications on his desk.' Still in speculative mode Antony continued, 'we all suspected that there would be a male, but no-one broached him on the subject. Well we did, but he pulled his horns in like a snail at that point and seemed a little challenged by that'. Admitting to the speculative and subjective nature of his explanation, he added, 'I can't really give you any concrete evidence apart from the feeling, and I know I wasn't the only one to feel that'.

When Richard volunteered his reflections, this suggested threat was not evident. He spoke positively and supportively of the opportunity which the day had presented to discuss this appointment. 'There's obviously an ongoing conversation about the quality of opportunity for men and women for promotion', he said, 'and we were able to talk about the number of applicants for the two posts we have to fill in September. They are both men who are coming for interview.' The gender imbalance had been questioned by some of the teachers yet Richard intimated that open discussion of it had been healthy. 'The short list was nearly all men and we discussed why that was, so that was a helpful space to talk about that.'

There was wider discussion of the structure of promotion, both inside Springfield and in the education system in general. He felt that there were difficult issues to face but he had welcomed the chance for substantial discussion with the teachers. 'So that was a helpful space to talk about that and to talk a bit about difficulties women feel they face in terms of promotion', he continued. 'So on that front it was very useful, and as I was saying, those things don't go away. They're ongoing concerns. People apply and get turned down. People get tired and fraught and those things seem to hurt more at particular times in the term than at others. But that was a good space on the in-service day to have a lengthy discussion about that particular aspect of equal opportunities.'

The debate about the two appointments had raised differences, speculations and uncertainties. There was no simple and singular agreement or solution. Although 'the applications were seventy to thirty male to female', no females were, initially, short-listed. This, according to the Head was 'because they weren't of the right calibre'.

Even Antony was unsure about adopting a policy of positive discrimination in a bid to alter the gender structure of senior management for if a woman had been appointed that would, as he pointed out have made 'the gender imbalance even greater within the school'. Contradictions, dilemmas and differences such as these demonstrated some of the complexities facing the school in evolving their equal opportunities policy.

Yet the small groups were able to sustain, contain and promote these difficult and complex debates. Antony was impressed by their effectiveness. He spoke of the range of personal and institutional outcomes that were generated and the real sense of relevance and ownership over the agenda which colleagues felt. 'The range of conversations that took place within these groups I thought was very impressive', he said. 'It was going from the formalized structuring of the policy of the school, right down to everyday issues of how we approach each other and children in the staff and classroom. I was heartened by this. It felt very constructive. It felt as if we were doing things that mattered. So many times you're in a working party and you come out with these wonderful statements that sound great and you're very pleased with them. Then a month later their effect is almost nil. You do it as an exercise because they're self-satisfying if you like.'

Vicki's in-service provision was qualitatively different for Antony from others he had experienced. There were tangible, immediate, small-scale practical outcomes and Antony valued this. In particular, he mentioned how his small group had discussed the reordering of the class registers. 'I think the true value was the low-key recommendations made. For instance, we have class lists. Boys are first then girls and many of us have been complaining about it for a long time. We were able to bring that up in a formal way and develop a whole school format. From September those are going to be just in alphabetical order.'

In his small group, colleagues had agreed that this was no trivial issue, even though the practical action steps seemed small scale, even low-key, to use Antony's phrase. He went on to explain how a gender ordered class list affects other practical professional decisions in a way that perpetuates inequality of treatment.

'Why did people not like those old lists?' I asked.

'It begs a whole load of questions', he replied, 'like you tend to ask the boys to do things first because they're first on the list. If you're going down a class to give children attention and you run out of time, it quite often means that the boys get the attention'.

Such practices do not exist in isolation, he pointed out. As Vicki had suggested in her research, each of these small inequalities may add to a larger, more worrying set of practices. 'I think some classroom studies have shown that boys are far more adept at gaining attention anyway and at advertising their presence and it simply compounds that effect', Antony said. 'Anything based on a rota with a class list at its roots, with time against that rota, is going to be weighted in favour of the boys, so we felt that an alphabetical order would be a better solution.'

An alternative solution had been offered. 'Some people had suggested positive discrimination by putting the girls first.' This had been rejected. Colleagues in general felt that it would reproduce inequality in a different form. There was consensus. 'We felt as a staff that wasn't the right thing to do', Antony said.

During the small group discussions, many had started to place their own circumstances and behaviour under their analytical microscopes, as Pam reminded me. For example, far from feeling overly-threatened by many of Vicki's ideas, some of the men had responded positively and assertively. In the discussion on boys and gender stereotyping, for example, Richard had spoken of aspects of his personal and domestic life. 'The men were coming forward with even more definite statements on what should be done to stop discrimination against girls', Pam recalled. 'The Headmaster put forward the fact that at home he comes off the Lego technique and his wife goes on it. And he also stated that when they get in the car, he's the one who automatically goes to drive and he believed you have to try to stop yourself sometimes and hand over.'

Pam had contested and challenged this perspective with an alternative interpretation of power. As a woman, she could, and would, choose not to drive. In making this choice and in refusing to drive, she would exert power and control over her man. 'I said to the Head, yes, that's fine, but its no good pretending. I mean, I don't enjoy driving, therefore I automatically say, to my husband, "well, you do it". So if people heard that, they'd realize I was giving the order there, wouldn't they, rather than letting him have his own way for driving. You can play it either way, can't you?'

Many ideas for the draft policy document were raised in the small group work and there was a felt need for these to be shared across the full staff group. So the next pedagogical strategy, as any in-service goers will have predicted, involved a large piece of paper on which the group ideas were posted, and a wall upon which the large piece of paper was posted. Vicki was reproducing her in-service experience from the course. 'The definite points which came out from the groups were then put on a piece of paper which was put onto the wall', Pam explained.

Colleagues attached much importance to this part of the process. They wanted to ensure that the ideas raised in the small groups were well represented and that there was a sense of their goal having been achieved. 'That was where we had asked for extra time to be given to this', Pam told me, 'because we all felt as a staff that it was important to bring this to a conclusion and to see if there were any ideas which came up on that morning that we could introduce into the school in the present curriculum. This we did.'

Pam specified the practical action steps to which colleagues committed themselves. She spoke of the attention to be paid to gender language and to gender images in the learning texts used by pupils. This would be a responsibility and management task for the school language coordinator. But changing the language culture was also seen as a responsibility of each member of staff. There had to be daily awareness and monitoring of gendered talk. The teachers were concerned to evolve measures that would affect the language culture on a significant scale. 'The language coordinator said he would look for books which were written with wording on an equal opportunity level', Pam explained. 'He would look for book resources with a balance between boys' and girls' stories. Each individual member of staff would try to be aware of what they were saying and the language they were using towards the children.'

Teachers would also offer new role models and images to children in school. Traditional stereotypes would be challenged and changed. Such measures would try to influence the gendered nature of the curriculum and the gendered perceptions of pupils. 'And also we decided to help the aspirations of girls', Pam continued, 'to perhaps pull them out of the jelly-mould and put them into the ideas of computers and science, and perhaps the subjects where there is a tendency for them to accept they weren't competing'.

This suggestion was rooted in insights from Vicki's research, particularly in her analysis of the curriculum preferences of older pupils. 'We were very aware of the figures which Vicki had read out from the pupils in the upper school. When the girls make options, the options aren't for the computers and science, the CDT areas. It tends to be for the other areas. Perhaps we should put input into this issue.'

There were many other suggestions 'nailed' to the paper 'nailed' to the wall, all of which Christine, the Deputy Head, coordinated into a comprehensive list. This was later typed on one side of A4 paper and circulated to all staff. This gave a set of initial guidelines for the staff to use in practice. The format was simple, accessible and brief. The language of the document reflected some of the substance of Vicki's research and the reflections of the staff upon it during the day. The catalysis between an individual teacher's research and the school response was beginning to show. The document was headed

'*Equal Opportunities — Gender*' with a sub-heading

'*Suggestions* made as outcomes of Vicki's research and subsequent staff discussion'

The first and lengthiest section asked simply 'What can we do?'. It was a call for realistic, practical action. Here is the full list.

What can we do?
- consider role models in the curriculum
- push female aspirations
- encourage boys to value females' worth in society
- in the long term try to offer a more balanced adult role model with the community and outside
- in school aim to increase awareness in everyone — professional staff, non-professional staff, children and, through them, their families
- provide opportunity but don't take away the choice
- make choice situations explicit
- help boys to feel it's OK to be sensitive and show it
- consider particular areas of need for example, first year girls and fourth year boys relating to age and development
- list children in alphabetical order (class lists, registers, records)
- look at materials used
- seek female representation from business and industry
- be critical friends to one another to encourage new perception in ourselves
- form a pressure group to encourage publishers to produce more material showing girls and women as successful in all areas not solely in domestic roles and showing boys and men as successful in domestic roles and other areas

Such aspirations to change the gender culture of the school were wide ranging and the list implied a need for a multiple structural approach. Change was sought at the level of individual consciousness of pupils; 'encourage boys to value females' worth in society', 'help boys to feel it's OK to be sensitive and show it'. There were aspirations to change the consciousness of groups in school other than pupils, expressed through the phrase 'in school aim to increase awareness in everyone — professional staff, non-professional staff'. There were wider aspirations to influence institutions outside the school; the family, 'children and through them their families', the education media, 'form a pressure group to encourage publishers to produce more material showing girls and women as successful in all areas'. The policy implied that gender consciousness of pupils is multifaceted and that it is constructed in response to several socializing agencies and experiences inside and outside school. Changing only one aspect of the learning environment of the child may not, thus, be adequate.

The staff recognized that they, too, needed to change if the curriculum was going to move forward for children. Norms, perceptions, practices, attitudes and expectations were all implicated. The gendered culture of the school had to be examined, changed, monitored. Staff invited themselves to 'be critical friends to each other to encourage new perception in ourselves'. At the level of cultural expectations, they are asked to 'push female aspirations', 'provide opportunity but don't take away choice'. To promote new attitudes, staff should be encouraged to 'help boys to feel it's OK to be sensitive and to show it'. To change behaviour, they were asked to 'provide opportunity', 'list children', 'seek female representation', 'consider particular areas of need', 'look at materials'.

This approach to change through agencies in school, in the family, in the outside community and at the multiple levels of norms, attitudes, perceptions, expectations and behaviour, constituted what could be seen as a major shift towards new socializing processes. In its directness, its range and its practical thrust the list could be seen as something of an activists' charter. The staff were ready and willing to keep moving forward.

Yet the document also reflected, quite simply, the general staff attitude towards the type and pace of change sought. Whilst these aspirations could be construed as radical in many ways, the staff were not impatient people. They were neither impatient to achieve their goals nor impatient of themselves as active change agents. The consensus attitude to change was modest and pragmatically realistic. The second part of the activists' charter asked a simple question, 'How can we best manage change?' and posed two simple, but powerful, suggestions.

First, a positive and firm staff attitude was proposed; 'serious staff commitment', the document said. Second, targets for change and progress needed to be small, manageable and by implication, realistically achievable. Also, progress needed to be steady, 'gradually, by selecting small objectives!' This echoed the recommendations which Vicki had made in the written research report: 'So the recommendations I would suggest are: 1. Make lots of small moves rather than radical change. Isolate small objectives that can be achievable.'

Commitment to slow and small change seemed to be Springfields' way of taking threat out of the change process. It was also, as Vicki suggested in her written report, borne out of a belief that modest and measured change would be more effective in this particular school. Alan articulated the substance of the staff's thinking on this. 'I was very heartened by the number of people who recognized in their groups that any changes that were to take place would have to be slow and maintained, rather than revolutionary', he told me. 'We felt changes wouldn't be maintained and sustained if they weren't evolved and slowly worked out.'

Pam mentioned more specifically the possible retrogressive effect of a more militant aggressive attitude to change. 'We felt it had to be done slowly over a long period of time', she said, 'quietly, without the militant attitude coming in because we agreed as a staff that you then just tend to lose the motivation that you desperately wanted to put in'.

Not that staff felt they had been confronted with, or challenged by, a militant or aggressive attitude from Vicki or anyone else. 'Does that suggest that Vicki is seen as a militant?' I asked. Pam confirmed that this was not so. Vicki had not attempted to impose her views and will over others by aggression, threat or intimidation. Vicki's style had been strong, socially sensitive, committed and sure. 'Vicki has very definite views, very strong views, but will certainly accept reasoned argument from anyone else', Pam confirmed. 'I think you'd have to feel quite strong if you went into an argument against Vicki, where she was so adamant on the issue', Pam added, 'but I certainly wouldn't say she was militant, but she is very adamant'.

This analysis of Vicki's style was echoed by Antony and it was a style which, we saw earlier, was important to her success in offering group leadership in term 4 of the course. For Antony, it was this combination of commitment, her non-threatening way of expressing that commitment and her engagement with reason, that made her effective as a change agent. Her sensitivity of, and awareness towards, others' feelings and views was effective, he felt. 'I think what is good about the way Vicki does it', he claimed 'is that she does it with sympathy'.

Vicki's modesty, to which Antony referred earlier, was one of the keys to the success of the school's professional development day. The catalysis between her modesty and her clarity of commitment brought about serious staff engagement with the issues. 'Vicki appreciates her value a lot more than she did', Antony continued 'But she's still not one readily to push herself forward. I think that's why the INSET, the staff development day went so well, because her person was exactly right for it. If anyone had come at it at 100 miles an hour, it would have met with resistance, but because she came at it with her personality — strong views gently put — I think that was exactly right'.

So, the activists' charter expressed a commitment to a gentle but significant change. This had, perhaps, been influenced by Vicki's own views, as well as by her own personal style. These views, however, were not naive. The third part of the policy ideas document articulated a few reminders that values are not necessarily shared by all, even given commitment, reason and modesty. Nor was it inevitable that goals would be achieved. The third heading thus read,

> '*But we must remember that:–*
> * there will be individual differences despite any policy
> * an interest in Equal Opportunity is an ideological stance
> * it may run counter to current movements in society
> * this puts us in the role of reformer
> * it might prove increasingly difficult to achieve'

People realized that even within Springfield school, structural changes would not be easy. In particular, staffing structures, both professional and non-professional, mirrored the very inequalities that the staff were hoping to influence. These inequalities were being perpetuated, despite people seeing the need for change and despite their clear-sighted aspirations. 'The gender awareness is there, and I think the boss is very aware of it too, but changes are slow', Antony explained. 'We've got several levels here. There's the thing you can change very quickly, which is the way you talk to children, and though you slip back you can change that pretty quickly. You can change formalized groupings of children that might constrain certain groups. What you can't change are structures of staffing. The children go in there and see the cooks, and they're all women and they see the caretaker who's a man organizing the cleaners who are all women. That sort of hierarchical structure is going to take a long time to change.'

Paradoxically, the school was reproducing the institutionalized gender structures and images that ran counter to its educational intentions. Perhaps the paradox was inevitable at this stage in Springfield's development and Alan felt that despondency over the status quo would not be productive. 'You've got to be realistic about it. It's no use taking things on and getting depressed about it.'

Yet it was recognized that the school had a difficult job ahead in the face of other influences bearing on children's perceptions. 'Even if we do get our act together', Antony added, 'we're a very peripheral influence'. These difficulties did not discourage the staff from progressing with hope and optimism.

In addressing itself to three dimensions of change, the 'what', the 'how' and the contextual or structural field, the policy ideas document reflected aspects of Vicki's research report. Thus, the individual teacher research enterprise influenced the staff development enterprise. Vicki's individualistic research led organically into institutional policy and institutional action.

So, the morning drew to a satisfactory, if vibrant, close back in the staff room. The small group work had generated debate, difference, consensus, ideas, plans and the professional debates had wandered inevitably into personal territories. Christine had coordinated and scribed the first draft consensus list which was later to emerge on the A4 typed sheet. Now, with a gap in our knowledge and data, of who said what to whom and what people did when the large sheet on the wall was full of ideas, the scene moved to lunchtime in the local pub.

It was inevitable that discussion, reflection, introspection and theorizing would not stop when the staff development session finished. The learning and change process is rarely, if ever, contained within the formal time and boundaries of the planned and delivered curriculum. We saw this to be the case with the Advanced Diploma group as the teachers developed themselves over coffee outside the library. And we see it here with the staff down at Springfield's local.

Some of the personal debates which had grown from the professional focus during the morning continued over a pint and sandwiches. For Antony, this was as important to him as the formal discussions of the morning. 'It made quite a difference to me', he claimed.

Exploring personal biographies had helped people to understand some of the professional issues. With their own educational experiences as the starting points for learning both men and women gained greater insight. 'Some of the girls, particularly, reflected on their own education, the women, sorry, reflected on their own education when they were girls which was quite interesting', Antony told me. 'So did the men and some perceptions that people got became far clearer when they were aired like that.' Starting with reflection on the 'self', thus, was a powerful sense-making, meaning-making, learning strategy.

Collegial empathy continued in the pub, too. 'A lot of the pressures on people at home were aired as well', Antony explained, 'and that was very good. It was good to support each other.' The woman teaching full-time as well as running a home was given special thought. 'Quite often especially female members of staff are under terrific pressure because they run two careers, and that pressure, you know, we were able to analyze it a little.'

Also comparisons were made between what were seen as the more satisfying domestic tasks of men, compared to the never ending tasks of women. Women's tasks lacked a sense of resolution, fulfilment and completeness. 'We were talking about the nature of the tasks that men take on. Men tend to take on fulfilment tasks, if you like, things that have fixed results, a fixed end', Antony recounted. 'Put a shelf up and you can stand back and you've done it. Whereas the female role tends to be the Forth Bridge task, you know what I mean, the ones that are repeated and cyclical and once you've done it, you do it again, you clean the bathroom and next week you clean the bathroom and so on. And men, although they will take on that role far more often today, they can still step out of that and do something with a fixed result. See what I mean?'

Yes, I did see what Antony meant, though I may, had I been in the pub, contested the analysis in some degree. As one who was recently terrified out of her bed in the middle of the night when books, files, data and shelves came crashing off the wall, detaching themselves from inadequate rawlplugs, I think I would prefer the regular, if persistent, completeness and satisfaction of putting away my whiter-than-white pile of ironing in the airing cupboard. However, these lunchtime deliberations were sufficient to cause Antony, at least, to think about domestic roles in his own home and to continue to encourage his wife and himself to 'take on the other tasks'. But he recognized that 'It is not easy'. He recognized that the pace of change was slow because of the need to analyze and come to terms with one's own history, position and circumstances. 'It's not easy', he admitted. 'It's a slow development in recognizing my own situation.' And the process of gender self-analysis was not comfortable. 'I think everyone feels threatened by an analysis of roles.'

Here, then, are some of the thoughts, feelings, experiences, attitudes, beliefs which were touched by the research discourses of the formal and informal encounters of the day. They were discourses about the professional, the personal, the autobiographical, the domestic, the interpersonal, the societal and the institutional. They were discourses that people approached with some trepidation but also with a voluntary and fairly open spirit. They were discourses that were helped along by Vicki's strong but gentle style as professional development agent; discourses that prompted self and institutional reflection and evaluation. As Pam had done previously, Antony applauded Vicki's capacity to stimulate challenging self analysis. It was this quality that was one of the more effective forces generating the discourses which led to change. 'I felt that, through my union contacts, I know sometimes militant feminism can be quite a destructive force because it makes people take sides', Antony believed. 'It makes people align one way or the other and feel very challenged. And that's certainly not the case here because if anyone does feel challenged, it's through self-analysis and the kind of guilt that brings out, rather than through being confronted directly by uncomfortable truths. So I think that's one thing that Vicki's managed to bring. That's a great asset.'

Complementing this, however, was a perceived liberal attitude towards feminism from the male members of staff. Richard felt that constructive, open, and change-inducing discourse had taken place because the men were not resistant to the gender challenges. On the contrary, he felt they were sympathetic to much that had been raised. 'The men on the staff you might describe as atypical for a school', he believed. 'I think they are pretty much aware of the topic and are sensitive to the issue. It would be difficult to pin a chauvinistic label on any of them', he claimed. 'I hope I can include myself in that, though others may not perceive me like that. It can raise tensions sometimes because some people tend to be over vociferous in things they say about how put down women are, and are very critical about others', he believed. 'That can become a tension in a staff room but that really hasn't happened here. I think that's as much to do with the sensitivity of the men on the staff as it is to do with any sensitivity that female members of staff have brought to bear on the conversation', he concluded. This gentle catalysis of male and female which was brought about by Vicki's agency changed the gendered culture of Springfield.

The activists' charter saw immediate and practical light of day. Some curriculum outcomes were generated almost immediately. One of these related to the nature of female images in history. 'I've decided to do a humanities topic for the next six weeks on women in the twentieth century', Pam acclaimed.

In gathering book resources for this, Pam met the problems of limitation and bias that Vicki had articulated in her research report. Pam acknowledged that the staff development event alerted her to these problems. It would be necessary to do an analysis on the few books she had been able to obtain and she was not sure whether resources would be adequate for what she wanted to do with her pupils. 'I sent to the library for books on women in all fields in the twentieth century', she explained. 'I think I've got about fourteen from the County Library but I think it's going to be quite hard work. To find the information will be quite hard work for the kids.'

'Is that because the books are not appropriate?' I asked.

'I don't think they're available', she replied. 'I've got to look through our own books, humanities and the twentieth century, to see what's available there.' She was beginning to see the validity of what Vicki had tried to convey.

'I think I'm becoming more aware of what Vicki was saying at the time on the staff development day, and how little is done.'

She planned to challenge stereotypical gender roles through drama. This would raise the issue with her own class and also with the whole school through the more public curriculum of the school assembly. 'I was going to introduce it in fourth year assembly', she said. 'We did a little play within our class where we changed role-play, with women for all the men and this kind of thing. We were going to put it forward to the rest of the school in assembly to see whether they could differentiate the sheer fact that it was women playing men's roles.'

Other immediate outcomes included the gender aware topic on Australia which Vicki had mentioned. 'Last week we had an Australian Day and rather than Ned Kelly we did Nellie Kelly', Pam confirmed.

Gender awareness had definitely been enhanced in the school, according to Pam. This was particularly so for some resistant teachers, whose gender consciousness was not as liberal as that of some male colleagues. 'The awareness of the staff had changed', she believed. 'As I say, it was very good from the men but I think they're quite aware and didn't perhaps need an awakening as much as some of the women did.'

The staff development event had made an impact on these women colleagues, who, by Pam's testimony, had previously met gender issues with apathy or disinterest.

'Has there been any resistance to it amongst some members of staff?' I asked.

'I don't know about resistance so much as perhaps apathy towards it', Pam replied.

'And you're saying that's coming from the women? How does Vicki handle that?'

'I don't think it's specifically directed towards Vicki', Pam replied, 'I think it's just a case of, you know, "Well, I think you're making a mountain out of a molehill" attitude and, you know, "If I remember to do it, I'll do it and if I don't I won't".'

Pam thought there were still great areas of insecurity in some of the women teachers that caused them to feel threatened by the analysis going on around them. There may have been new surface responses developing but deeply engrained views were still operational. 'A lot of women are insecure with it', she said. 'I think they feel quite threatened by the idea of really having to come to terms with it. They might mouth about it, but when you get down to the nitty gritty there's still a lot of in-bred ideas within them'. Socialized into dependency, some still held stereotyped, and unrealistic, beliefs about fulfilment through the male-female relationship. 'They look at the man in their life as going to change their lives, and anything will be done for him. Perhaps when they get over the initial love, romance, it will all come back to normality', she sighed.

There were, thus, different starting points, different gender perspectives. The staff development event had affected the perspectives of the more resistant women and there had been progress but these differences would make whole school change a complex, challenging, even fragmented, business. The activists' charter would be unlikely to receive an even hearing, let alone smooth implementation.

The staff development event had, nevertheless, stimulated everyone and drawn most people into critical analysis. The personal discourses had touched most people's perceptions and experience. 'The impressive thing was, though', Antony said, 'it got everybody involved and it gave a lot of people the chance not just to look at it in terms of school either. I know loads and loads of people talked about gender issues in the home and family as a result of that'.

Given this level of engagement, how did Vicki feel about the event and about her role in it? We must not forget that this was her first attempt at offering a structured professional development experience for colleagues. Her professional skill and her sense of self were implicated. We already know that she experienced the equivalent of first night nerves, despite good planning and preparation and despite a clear emotional and intellectual commitment to her material. But we have also seen the design and pedagogy of the event working well, capturing the commitment and enthusiasm of colleagues, generating constructive challenge, discussion and decision-making. As Pam said, 'I think she handled the day well.'

Even after her initial nerves subsided there were difficulties. For instance, Vicki had misgivings about the way she had handled presentation of her questionnaire data which suggested science to be an unpopular subject in the school. She wondered whether Annette, the Science Coordinator would interpret the research results personally, seeing them as a judgment on her teaching. As Annette was new to the school her teaching could not possibly be implicated. Even so, Vicki wondered whether a personal briefing before the event would have been politic. 'I know that the Science Coordinator was devastated by the results', she told me. 'But I knew she would be. I'd thought about that and it was all researched before she came to Springfield. Nevertheless, I had to alleviate her problems', Vicki continued. 'I did panic at one stage and wondered if I should have actually shown the results beforehand but I think we were able to get over the difficulty. I thought I could persuade her not to take it personally and I don't think she did in the end.'

Annette had been positive, despite being 'devastated'. The two reactions seemed to go together and the devastating questionnaire results had propelled her into immediate action. Straightaway she started looking for female role models within science. She planned to bring women scientists into the curriculum whenever possible and appropriate. 'She found a list of twenty women scientists within the twentieth century. So I know she looked at role models within science and she's bringing their names forward within the lessons where appropriate', Pam explained. This may well have brought its sense of relief and reward for Vicki in the light of her earlier apprehensions.

There was explicit feedback, too, which caused Vicki justified pleasure and satisfaction. 'I had an official "thank you" from the Head, of course'. Other responses were generous and spontaneous. 'Lots of people have said how much they enjoyed it.' Some were more detailed and particular. 'But the people who have actually come up to me personally have been the men.' The atmosphere that had been created was particularly appreciated. 'A lot of colleagues said what a relaxed atmosphere it all happened in. Some heated discussions were going on but they enjoyed it.'

Even the personally threatening nature of the work had not detracted from the pleasure or benefit of the learning experience. 'But one male member of staff, who later came along and said how much he'd enjoyed it and how valuable it was, had admitted at coffee break on the staff development morning that he was feeling somewhat threatened.' Some people were in a heightened state afterwards. 'A lot of people were very elated, not a lot, several of them were quite elated', Vicki said.

Despite the heavy demands that the work had placed on people, Vicki felt it had been worth the trouble. The investment in her research had clearly benefited the staff development event. This, in turn, had benefited her colleagues' learning. Vicki experienced satisfaction on seeing that her research and her learning could be employed on this scale and for this purpose. Her efforts paid multiple dividends. 'I think we were worn out after the morning', she said, 'but I feel it was very much worthwhile; the whole process of actually doing the research and the learning that I've gone through; the fact that it has actually been used and been some good. That was great. It really is good.'

It was characteristic of Vicki, however, that she was unable to rest on any laurels she had thus earned. Pride and satisfaction were matched by a concomitant guilt. 'I still feel guilty about that second research study, though; that I didn't ever feed back.' Satisfaction with her institutional contribution was dampened. That contribution had not in her eyes, been adequate. Thus, we see guilt and modesty taking the edge off pride and satisfaction.

Now, it was 'on with the future'. It was agreed that the staff development event was neither the beginning nor the end of the development process. Pam speculated that there would be further prompts and input from some of the keener members of staff. 'We've certainly got ideas for a policy written from the day. They will be used for future reference and will remind us about what we could do', she said. 'I would think that we are going to be talking about it again. When, I don't know but I should think either Christine or Vicki will bring it up. Or another member of staff will put some input in, not necessarily drawing from outside research but perhaps looking at something which has occurred within the school.'

There was indeed formal follow-up in the form of a staff meeting with the purpose of establishing a working party. The meeting was designed to consolidate the outcomes of the day and to advance policy. 'The second phase was a consultative staff meeting', Antony explained, 'at which some more formalised results were drawn out of the staff development day. From that the next stage is that a small working party is going to produce the final results, so I think it has achieved some kind of concretion from that start, which I thought was very useful.'

Policy was not to be constructed in a structural vacuum. Local education authority guidelines on equal opportunities were on the way into schools and so Springfield's activists' charter would be developed against these guide-lines. 'We're now waiting', Vicki explained. 'There is a policy coming from the local education authority. We didn't think there was much point in creating our own policy without this, so I've got all the bits and pieces of what every-body has said and when the other comes we'll amalgamate them and make some policy from them.'

There were the inevitable doubts about the long-term, permanent nature of changes even given the immediate success of the staff development event and the practical effects of the research process. 'The proof of the pudding's going to be time', Antony declared.

Whilst not wanting to appear sceptical, Antony recognized that a written or spoken commitment does not automatically ensure practical change. 'Even when you get as far as the formalized written school policy on equal oppor-tunities, quite often those are lip-service policies, aren't they, which don't actu-ally alter the day-to-day running.'

He had intuitions that the changes had been more than a transitory eph-emeral affair, however, because of the attitudes of the staff group to change. 'If you asked me if I felt the signs were there, I think because of the mixture of staff we've got (they're very open and amenable to change) I don't think it is a short term awareness, consciousness-raising exercise.' Optimism was in his soul.

Even so, Antony and his colleagues recognized that their commitment to change could be thwarted by the power of other forces outside the school. They had pondered on this when drawing up the structure of the activists' charter. 'There is a conspiracy of interests. If you look at adverts showing the family roles, any batch of adverts is horrifying from that point of view. When you look at that, you realize how little our influence at school is. So although we might perhaps get a fairly concerted front at school and align ourselves, and perhaps more successfully avoid some of the mistakes we've been making in the past, I think we're up against a huge amount from society. Vicki's all too well aware of this.'

To what extent therefore was Antony's mixture of optimism and de-spondency realized in the proof of the pudding of time? As we move on from this particular historical moment in the school's development and take a glimpse some eighteen months on from the staff development day we can see the extent to which the candle, lit on that occasion, continued to burn.

Thumbing through and through my data from Springfield in the draft writing process, I became curious to know more about the life of the gender research policy. Vicki had dropped her pebble of learning into these institu-tional waters some year-and-a-half ago. The splash and the waves had been strong and immediate. But were the ripples still in evidence after all this time, as Antony had foretold, or had the impact been transitory and ephemeral?

I phoned Christine, the Deputy. Could I come and talk to her about these matters? Were there any long-term dividends? What had happened to the pro-posed equal opportunities policy?

Christine's response was as open, inviting and interested as ever and her description of the destiny of the written policy was direct, if gaily delivered. That was easy to answer, she implied. It had simply been buried. It was lying, metaphorically, under the full weight of papers, documents, brochures, demands and expectations of the Education Reform Act and the National Curriculum. We exchanged expletives and made a date for a formal interview.

Being, by now, an experienced teacher researcher herself, Christine had constructed a richer and more interesting methodology for me than the monolithic interview I had planned.

She had placed my long-term research questions on the agenda for a full staff meeting. As she said, 'it's not just my views, my talk, that counts. Let's have some staff. So in readiness for talking to you. I put it on the agenda for the last staff meeting.'

As we settled to the formal interview, now better resourced, Christine produced the minutes from the staff meeting as a prompt. As data on their own these were, she realized, problematic. 'I've got the difficulty that not everything we said in the meeting has been minuted.' So we were content, indeed grateful, to draw on the wealth of remembered insights from the meeting that spilled from Christine's memory into the tape recorder.

Two significant events had occurred since we last met after the staff development day, a year-and-a-half before. The Education Reform Act had hit schools. Also, Vicki had left Springfield to take a Deputy Headship in a small rural primary school.

Christine confirmed the impact of this first event. It had halted the formal writing of the gender policy as other policies had taken precedence. 'It wasn't done', she started. 'We have been — I mean the policies we have written', she added, 'the technology one and the sex education one'.

There seemed to be more policies around than hot breakfasts. 'We have had policies coming out of our ears, one way and another', Christine added.

To have simply produced a written equal opportunities document for accountability or political purposes would have gone against the grain of the consultative process. Consultation lay at the heart of the development ethos and procedures of the school. 'And if you're going to do it as a whole staff, it's a case of when you can get it all together', Christine explained. 'It's easy for someone just to sit down and write one thing, but it's definitely time that's needed to do a policy together.'

Time was not a commodity in excess of needs at Springfield, nor at any other school which was responding in a serious professional way to the new external political demands. Like most other such schools, Springfield had been trying to stretch time to match work demands and barely making them meet.

Much time had also been given over to discussion and consultation for a multicultural education policy. This had come, not from within the school, but from the external demand of the local education authority policy guidelines. Here was another relevant and important part of the school's work on equal opportunities but it had taken time away from development of the gender work.

Christine and Vicki were to work together on the written multicultural education policy document but Vicki's departure from the school put unnatural time pressures on this task.

'Vicki left at Christmas', Christine explained, 'and we were supposed to be addressing the multicultural policy. So it came in late summer or early September of that year just before Vicki left. The idea was that she and I would work on it. Then she left. The local education authority put a deadline for getting the policy in to them which was awful because you needed a lot of time.'

The principle of developing a consultative and collaborative policy was in danger of being displaced by the external demands of the local education authority. Christine, however, held on to her principles and would not capitulate under these pressures. Policy would still be generated from the thoughts and practices of Springfield participants. It would be grounded in the lived practical and intellectual realities of the teachers. Vicki's impending departure did not panic Christine into premature and inadequate policy-making processes. So when Vicki left and the written policy text had not been produced, Christine took over the baton. 'In that spring term', Christine said, 'I took the multicultural policy. I went to year meetings and together we discussed policy issues and put together something which was then developed and altered.'

She did not develop the multicultural policy in isolation from other initiatives. The work became linked to the humanities policy. Another colleague, Heather, had developed this from the sound beginnings which Vicki made through her first action research study. 'Heather has taken over humanities', Christine said. 'We went back to the humanities policy afterwards and put that together, with the multicultural work.'

She leant over to me and passed a sheet of A4 paper headed

Springfield Middle School: Towards a multicultural education policy — for discussion.

It had two opening paragraphs on philosophical concerns and then a direct link into humanities. 'Further to this, through the humanities working file, we draw attention to the following', the document read.

Having come to discuss the destiny of Vicki's gender research work and staff development work it was startling and curious to meet again, unsolicited, Vicki's first research study. She had completed this almost three years ago and now Christine was making natural reference to it in the current curriculum. Christine was talking about the impact of the Australia week on the curriculum. It had led to a similar French Day on 14 July, conceptualized and planned against the framework of the humanities policy document. 'Ah, so the humanities policy is still around is it?' I asked rhetorically.

Not only was it around it was still proving very useful in curriculum thinking. 'The humanities document is still in use', Christine explained. 'Heather is looking at it, but we still use it as a document', she confirmed. 'Most of the actual unit planning, the topic planning, is based in the humanities policy document.'

Vicki's document was now being reviewed by Heather. She had the task of making it responsive to current government initiatives and legislation. 'It has to be altered in the light of the National Curriculum', Christine explained. But until this new version emerged, Vicki's original was still proving useful in curricular planning and teaching.

Christine also explained how Vicki's document supported her thinking for the multicultural policy statement. 'I used it as a part basis for the multicultural education policy document', she said, 'because I went through some of Vicki's writing there highlighting what appertained to a multicultural approach'.

She had tried to link two strands of curriculum thinking together, the humanities and the multicultural. She was also grappling with a more unitary curriculum conceptualization that would draw several related areas and issues together. 'So I tried to collate it all, as a starter for people to address', she explained.

Thinking in metaphor was helpful. 'I like the idea of this umbrella', she said, with some intrigue. 'I couldn't fix in my mind whether it would be a multicultural education umbrella', she continued, 'with all your things like child protection, abuse and little categories under these, or whether it would be an equal opportunity umbrella with multicultural education as part of it.' Not to miss a staff developmental opportunity, she had, she said, 'used that as a basis for discussion' with the staff. A conceptual shift had taken place over time at Springfield, since Vicki's work. 'We didn't come to a final agreement on it', Christine admitted. 'But it was quite an interesting start to our thinking about where aspects of the curriculum fit into our minds. Because I think you have got to have pockets, you see, and you can cluster a lot of these things that are about the child together.'

Indeed you can, I pondered. And I mentally noted the significance of this interesting turn of events, for the two apparently discrete parts of Vicki's research, the humanities and the gender policy, which were created at different historical moments, had been fused. They had been synthesized in this particular way, for this particular purpose, at this particular time some several months after the author of the research had left the school. And who could ever predict, through scientific or any other research method, that particular educational event. It had an historical birth all of its own. Indeed these two research events of Vicki's had taken on an institutional existence and a life of their own independent of Vicki, their originator. They had an autonomous life that continued to have an influence and impact on others' thinking irrespective of what Vicki was now doing or thinking. Vicki had left parts of her self behind through her research in the minds and actions of institutional others. And these parts of her self continued, autonomously, to shape Springfield policy and practice.

And so, without seeking it, nor even having passed a thought about it because my eyes were firmly fixed on the gender research, I had been handed this little nugget about the continuing history of Vicki's first research initiative.

So, Vicki had moved on, leaving behind an incomplete task in the willing and interested hands of the Deputy Head. The Education Reform Act had started biting and demanding from the outside, changing, it appeared, the formal institutional task and development agenda. Also, directional pressure from the local education authority was shifting the institutional tiller this way and that. Had the gender initiative, therefore, truly been blotted out in all this? Did it only live on in the intellectual deliberations about whether to conceptualize multiculturalism as a sub-category of a broader equal oppor-tunities policy?

It is well to remember, and remember again, that policy and curriculum exist on many levels, and that the most significant of these is the lived policy that exists in school between human beings going about the daily business of teaching and learning through interaction. It is in this sense, through human interaction, that the gender policy survived at Springfield. The good inten-tions to develop formal policy documentation had been aborted by the ex-ternal demands and pressures. But newly-established gendered behaviours, attitudes and customs had continued to survive and bed themselves down into the habits of the institution. With the help of time, vigilance and repetition, they were taking on the qualities of familar, if pubescent, culture.

By the teachers' testimonies, Vicki's work had struck home and stayed home. 'The general feeling was that it had quite a great deal of impact on us long term', Christine claimed.

The immediate changes, such as reordering of registers, had been main-tained. There had been other initiatives; for example 'positive discrimina-tion towards girls on the computer', Christine said, 'because boys were taking over'.

This had led to girls' only sessions during lunchtime. Also, the staff had continued to monitor language for its gendered assumptions. 'We're very very aware of what we are saying', Christine said. 'We are picking each other up all the time on anything that is sexist. We know we are doing that.'

Nor were the children's uses of language left unmonitored. Teachers were intervening where pupil talk signified gender attitudes and conceptions that were not consonant with the newly establishing values. 'We do intervene on child comments', Christine said, 'if there is a sexist comment. We do intervene more'.

There were other slow, but consciously created advances, as some mem-bers of staff attended to role modelling. With a predominantly female staff it had been difficult to offer female role models in stereotyped male domains. Even so, there had been a deliberate and concerted effort to do so, especially in more technical activities such as computing, video work, media activities. Staff development had been a priority. Overcoming the women teachers' own in-built gendered responses to these areas had been one of the stumbling blocks but Christine had deliberately given this a keen importance. Progress was being made. 'We are a little worried about role models', she explained, 'because there aren't so many men in this school as women and women tend to be a bit frightened of some activities. I've made it my quest this year to get computer friendly because I've set up so much in-service for everybody else in this school and there is never space for me on it because of their need. So

I'm trying to tell myself that this is priority for the year. I'm going to get this show on the road — things like using equipment, video cameras.'

In the earlier stages of this quest, Vicki had also played her part in visible and practical ways. 'Vicki and I really tried to push it by standing there fiddling around with a video', Christine reflected 'And we worked together to try to get other women to see the importance of this because men are taking their own development quite easily, and the woman weren't.'

In the face of this female reticence, some of which Pam had earlier predicted, Christine was soldiering on, taking new and changed role modelling into the curriculum. 'I've done a media studies package for the second year with the idea that the children and teachers can see me using the video', she explained.

Given that this work was for use by a year group of teachers, it had the potential for influencing, aiding and supporting some of the less secure female teachers. 'It's really aimed at the women in that group because both men are quite with it', Christine added.

Tackling the 'quiet girl syndrome' through regular monitoring of practice had been another continuing institutional development.

'How do the teachers do that?' I asked.

'Well, I think there is a lot more thinking about who we actually address in the classroom', she answered. 'I mean, you do notice that it's very easy to address boys a lot in the classroom. It's a sort of control thing as well, because they can be lively and one tends to think they are going to be the naughtiest.' The endemic gender stereotyping of boys had thus also been examined. 'I think we've even changed in that now', Christine added.

More positive attention and reinforcement for the girls paralleled this change of attitude towards the boys. 'It means going for the girls' ideas, and praising girls as well as boys', Christine concluded.

She had challenged gendered behaviour in games lessons, too. Team games were mixed yet boys had their own style of playing and so had the girls. Thus, there was a division of styles within the mixed teams. Christine analyzed this with the children. 'The boys were not throwing to the girls', she explained, 'and the girls complained to me. So I faced that issue with them. We split into two groups, a girls group and a boys group and we noticed how the girls played. It was true, the boys argued the whole time and the girls just got on and followed rules and stuck by what people said.'

The analysis had led to action; the action had led to change. Single sex groups were tried. Mixed groups were again tried. In time the discussions and analysis with the children changed their games behaviour.

'This week, I told them how pleased I was, that after half a term the games lesson was coming to terms with gender. We'd tried all sorts of combinations and so I put them back into the original groups. Lo and behold we had boys throwing to girls. That's the best game you've played, I said, and it was lovely.'

Curious to get a sense of the children's perspective on this, I intervened. 'How did they feel about it?' I asked.

'They were pleased, I think, that I wasn't nagging any more', she laughed.

It is impossible to know the grace with which the children took this new gendered behaviour. Perhaps some accepted the models presented by the authority of their teacher for less than gender-sensitive reasons. They may have been conforming to new gendered behaviour to please or obey the teacher or they may, indeed, have undergone genuine changes of attitudes. Who can say. Methodologically, I was not in a position to probe further into this, time and resources for further field work having run out, so the rest is speculative.

Continuing efforts were also being made to select appropriate gendered literature for the curriculum. This was still the problem and struggle it had been for Vicki. Others had now joined the task force since Vicki had raised awarenesses. Richard, too, had joined in. 'Still there are a lot of male heroes rather than heroines in the books we have got at the moment', Christine said, 'but the Head has tried to purchase more'.

In these practical ways, the changing gendered culture of the school was being made manifest. Also, gender awareness was sufficiently developed by now for the members of this newly emergent culture to spot tokenism when they saw it. Intolerance of a minimalist approach to equal opportunities was emerging. 'There are a lot of books that are just putting females in as a token gesture', Christine claimed, 'and that is what we have got to be careful of. It is quite hard to find the equal number of books that have got this strong female image.'

The changes that had emerged since the staff development event were thus several and various. There were personal changes of attitudes, values, awareness, language and behaviour. These were manifest in interaction with each other, with the children and through curriculum provision of activities and materials.

There was no simple sense, from Christine's account, of the changes being uniform across the staff group, nor sensational in their effect on institutional life. Developments were moderate and differentiated. Yet they were progressively secure, gradually adding to the steadily changing gender face of the institution. Even so, the teachers felt that these changes were, for the most part, limited to the professional group. The changes had not reached in any significant way, they felt, the external school community. Nor, they felt had the children changed very much, though Christine's work with the children in mixed games may have been an exception. 'The staff think that we have changed but we don't think the children or parents have changed', she said.

The teachers had suggested that old established attitudes to maleness and authority were still endemic in the parent community. Christine had discovered in some of her own research for her Masters' degree course, for example, an almost Victorian conceptualization of the male teacher. He it was who reigned uppermost in the disciplinarian hierarchy. 'There was an interesting thing come through in my research', she explained, 'that parents wanted the children to have a male teacher here. They would rather have a male teacher here — and the Head has noticed this as well — than a female teacher. They wanted a strong disciplinarian in a male.'

Women who matched men teachers in this gave parents cause for concern.

The combination of femaleness and a certain type of discipline did not fit their gendered preconceptions or expectations, Christine had discovered. 'But when strong discipline crops up in a female here', she continued, 'parents don't like it. A disciplinarian female, perhaps, doesn't fit their image. We have more complaints about any female disciplinarian than we do about men.'

This reinforced Antony's earlier concerns about the weight of culture and tradition outside the school bearing adversely upon the change and development task. Christine also believed that further changes beyond the staff group would be slow. One the other hand some of the teachers' own attitudes were so deeply engrained that stereotypes were still being unconsciously reproduced in certain professional practices, despite the steady progress made since Vicki's research. Christine recalled a recent incident as the staff were organizing a parent-teacher social event. 'I will tell you something else that I noticed in our PTA minutes', she proffered. 'I read the minutes from our last PTA when they came through and I said to the Head, oh gosh, we actually decided this in the arrangements for the coming Barn Dance. Listen. And the minutes said, the bar will be run by Mr So and So, raffle Mrs So and So. And it said, all the ladies will help with the serving of the food.'

Such an incident showed a contradiction between expressed institutional philosophy and endemic personal behaviour, between the conscious striving to establish new cultural norms and the deep contradictory pull of personal history. It showed the interface between old, unacceptable custom, and new preferred possibilities.

At this interface, the challenge of critical self-reflection was embraced such that institutional learning and change were able to take place. First, the occasion was used to feed developing staff awareness. 'I said to the Head that we must have decided this, look at it', Christine said. 'He could see. And I spoke to the staff about it.'

Out of this, the new gendered possibility was decided. Roles would be exchanged. 'So we decided that Richard and the other chap who is on the PTA committee would do the food and I would be on the bar.'

Second, it was used as an opportunity to raise the gender gauntlet with the parents, pushing the boundaries of challenge, learning and change a little further into the tough outside community. 'I spoke to some of the PTA people', she went on, 'to our chairman of the PTA when he came in, because the staff think it's a very good way of going through the PTA and getting parents to think about equal opportunities'.

The chairman had been positively responsive despite his own personal gendered contradictions. 'At home my wife and I are equal', he had told Christine. Whilst thus claiming enlightenment, he turned to the hoover 'because he had brought straw in for the Barn Dance', adding, at the same, time that 'he never knows how to work a hoover'.

Christine had been quick to challenge his personal contradiction, in line with the growing institutional determination to raise new awareness whenever possible. 'But I said to him, you've just claimed you're equal', she recounted. 'Oh we do equal work at home', he had replied to her, 'but I never touch the hoover'.

Christine continued her mission on the night of the Barn Dance with some of the women. They responded positively and one joined her in new role modelling. 'So I spoke to some of our women', Christine explained, 'as they came into the barn dance and they said, yes, right, and one of them said I will come on the bar with you'.

Not all responses were affirmative and supportive. Some gender sensitivities and prejudices were touched. 'I spoke to the father who had set up the bar and he told me I was talking a load of rubbish', she said, 'and that it was a stupid thing to make a fuss about'. Christine had to shoulder the ensuing hostility as a price to be exacted for straight talk.

Here, then, old cultural norms and behaviours were being examined and challenged at the interface where parents and teachers meet. Also a similar personal challenge was taking place where the teachers, awarenesses raised, met their own latent and estranged attitudes in contradictory professional practices. What was said, and what was done were not always coincidental. Congruence between gender philosophy and gender practice was not always evident. Yet some of the battles between the old and the new were surfacing and being fought in public institutional arenas. The challenges that Vicki had set in motion with the staff group were still evolving in various shapes and forms, in and beyond, that group.

Despite this contradiction between emerging gender beliefs and aspects of gendered practice, some gender maturing had, almost unconsciously, taken place in the institution. This maturing was made apparent at an institutional interface between the internal culture and an external agent. Christine told me of a recent visit from the Home Economics Adviser to the school. The Adviser overtly expressed her delight at seeing the headteacher, a mere male, taking a mixed cookery lesson. 'Richard was just about to do a cookery session as part of his design work', Christine explained 'And she went absolutely over the top with admiration about it.'

'Because he was a man?' I asked, for clarification and explanation.

'Because he was a man and was a headteacher, doing cookery', Christine obliged.

This had brought a shocked response from teachers because Richard's behaviour was, to them, not exceptional, not particularly progressive nor praiseworthy by their own cultural norms. To them it was normal professional behaviour, to be expected within a professional culture sensitive to gender equality. It was, in effect, no big deal for either a male, nor a senior manager, to be engaged in the domestically oriented curriculum. The teachers felt that the Adviser's behaviour was somewhat immature and patronizing (or, perhaps, matronizing). The clash of attitudes highlighted the state of the developing gendered culture.

This was not, of its kind, a singular incident. There had been other occasions when less developed gender attitudes of people outside the school culture had made the taken-for-granted, internal attitudes evident. New members of staff crossing the cultural boundary from the outside, for example, had similar effects to the Home Economics Adviser. New male teachers surprised at their obligation to teach cookery had raised a 'so what' attitude from established staff. Also, there had been 'other people outside the school' who had expressed 'surprise that some women are doing craft, design and technology', Christine explained. She smiled, widely. It was not a smile of complacency. It seemed, rather, a smile of amusement and bemusement.

'So you are saying that you've come to take these things for granted?' I asked.

'We now take a lot for granted', she replied. 'It may be a measure of our advancement that we are surprised at these attitudes of other people.' Yesterday's conscious gendered culture may have been settling into today's unconscious behaviours, attitudes and practices.

There were other indicators of institutional maturing. For example, none of the staff felt that equal opportunities was in a state of institutional weakness any more. Christine had conducted a staff review of perceived development priorities and needs. There were varied responses but none signifying strong concern about the state of gender development. Indeed, many were aware of a new state of maturity. This is not to suggest that complacency had set in though Christine was cautious about becoming overly optimistic. Rather it is to acknowledge that staff were aware of the progress that had been made and that, set against alternative and competing demands on their time and energy, they deemed it unnecessary, and impractical, to give gender issues further formal developmental attention. 'On equal opportunities only three said it wouldn't, couldn't, benefit from a specific review', Christine explained. 'Seven said it didn't need any specific review . . . and then we had five saying it was satisfactory. One said that it was strengthened and nobody said that they regarded equal opportunity in school as a weakness from what we were doing.'

Christine was guarded about these responses and may have had strong feelings herself about what still needed to be done. 'It seems to me that when you address something and have talked about it, people think that's enough for now, because it is in their minds, it's been brought to the surface and that is enough to be going on with.'

The staff, however, recognized that their practice and behaviour had developed even though formal written policy had not. The Education Reform Act may have blocked the way of formal policy endorsements but the forces which had been set in motion by Vicki's work had been powerful. They had propelled practical change and development through the potential barrier of the Education Reform Act. 'In a whole staff meeting everybody had a coffee', Christine said, 'and people were talking about how we were dealing with gender issues, what sort of attitude we were taking on as a staff, rather than that we need to write a policy. But in fact if government changes hadn't been in the way we'd have probably done the written equal opportunity policy, with time, before now. It's overload that's stopped us.'

The practical maturing would, she thought, enhance the maturity of a written policy, had they time to formalize it. The passing of time with its consequent nourishing of change could enrich written, as well as lived and enacted policy. 'We could have written it straight after Vicki's talk', Christine said, 'but it would almost have more strength, wouldn't it, now, because we actually have practised it'.

This, then, was the continuing story of the waves set in motion by Vicki's research on gender. The initiative achieved a state of autonomy, no longer dependent for its existence upon either Vicki's drive, nor Vicki's presence. Others continued the struggle for change in various ways, enabled by an open staff attitude and climate and by the coercive policy requirements from the local education authority. Central Government legislation could have dammed up the motion and, to some extent it did, but the waves found a way through the barrier, continuing into people's daily lives and behaviours.

But what about Vicki's own continuing story? In what way, and in what sense, did the initiative and the struggle of her major action research study, now living in the institutional culture at Springfield, continue to exist with, and within, Vicki herself?

These questions were not followed in depth in my research field work. There are a few brief notes on file from a short visit I made to Vicki in her new school, ten months after she took up post. The main purpose of the visit was to collect Vicki's research texts which she agreed to let me analyze again more closely for my own research. In the event, we managed to have a general chat about her new job and circumstances. In the course of this, we moved onto talking about equal opportunities, gender issues in particular.

Vicki was adamant that she would not try to initiate any curriculum development or change on equal opportunities in her new post at present. Her new colleagues on the staff were, she felt, not ready to engage seriously in this kind of discourse. In addition, there had been some difficulty in her relationship with the Headteacher, a man of middle years who had been Head of the school for several years. He had, apparently, embraced the opportunity at selection interview to appoint an energetic deputy who was willing to take initiative and bring changes to what seemed a stable but relatively static school. This corroborated what had already been told to me informally by the local adviser who had been involved in Vicki's appointment. Things had not quite turned out like that once Vicki was in post. Maybe Vicki had wanted to move more quickly than the Head felt was desirable. Maybe, when his wish for change was tested, it was found to have less substance that at first appeared. Maybe Vicki's style and strategy, well matched to the interpersonal climate at Springfield, was not as well suited to this new context. Whatever the explanations, Vicki met frustration and conflict as she tried to stimulate change in her new post. In this climate, addressing equal opportunities was, she judged, not a wise thing to do.

There was a second reason why the lid had to be put on the well. Like the staff back at Springfield she and her new colleagues were facing the National Curriculum juggernaut. There was, she told me, simply too much else to do. Curriculum and staff development priorities had been determined by central Government. Equal opportunities was not on that agenda.

Thus, the support, interest, opportunity which Vicki had built at Springfield were not present in her new post. She had read her new situation as best

she could and decided to suppress any immediate hope of institutional gender development. The particular institutional chemistry and ecology of Springfield was not replicated in this new context. What had been possible and apposite there, and then, was not so in the new here and the new now. The action-oriented self of Vicki that had been allowed to grow and influence at Springfield had now to be packed away. Neither the time nor context were fertile for gender challenge and change, as Springfield had been.

Vicki tried to keep alive, however, her gender beliefs and practices in her own classroom with her own pupils, though she was clear that she would not try to generalize practices beyond her class. All in all, it seemed, according to Vicki's testimony, the time was not right, nor the professional environment ready. She would have to draw back. And, like some other teachers on her Advanced Diploma course who had initially been loath to give me research access to their school, Vicki would have to live with her ideological isolation in quiet, until better times and circumstances prevailed, if they ever did.

She handed me her written research texts and the box containing the tape slide sequence from her second research study. We wandered around the school, made our way through a bustling dining hall, exchanged courteous and warm greetings with the headteacher in the school entrance. And then I was on my way, picking up, as I left, a government leaflet written for parents to inform them of the National Curriculum, and of what they could be justified in expecting from their child's school. Needless to say, I could find no reference in this leaflet to equal opportunities, the humanities, nor the special needs of special children as I read through it back in my room at the Institute.

That was the last contact I had with Vicki until almost a year later when I presented the draft case study for her comment, appraisal, critique and validation. More than two-and-a-half years had then passed since Vicki's gender staff development contribution at Springfield. The start of her Advanced Diploma course had receded some five years into both our histories.

Summary: Drawing Together the Threads; Seeking Explanations

Close scrutiny of Vicki's gender research has allowed three broad areas of insight. We have learnt more about Vicki. We have thought about the nature, purpose and destiny of the research text. We have puzzled over the many factors which contributed to the successful use of the research. First, then, in learning more about Vicki herself, we have seen a little more of the gendered past that we met in the opening of the case story. This gendered and personal past informed Vicki's developing professional career with its fits, starts, rejections and frustrations. It was a past that clearly motivated her time at Springfield, a time that coincided with involvement on the Advanced Diploma course. The strong feelings generated in her past brought motivation, commitment and application to her major research study. In that, she linked her commitment to the Advanced Diploma to a commitment to her school. This dual commitment, and the course it ran, placed new and risky

demands on Vicki. We saw her taking the opportunity to continue learning about methodology, about methods of data gathering and some of the ethical, interpersonal and organizational challenges posed. Her data sources were more varied and experimental than in the previous two research studies. The blue book was particularly innovative but it was also more institutionally visible than anything she had previously used.

Because of the reception of the blue book in the school, Vicki needed her interpersonal wits, judgment and a good emotional shield about her. The humour that had helped in raising challenging issues in her Institute course group also served her well in the face of the institutional banter raised by her blue book methodology.

She also needed her common sense and sensitivity to handle a number of methodological dilemmas involving colleagues' and pupils' feelings. She chose on each occasion to err on the side of human need rather than the needs of the research. In return, she benefited from the regard of colleagues who gave voluntarily of their precious and pressured time for the purposes of her research. As before, time and environmental constraints continued, in places, to be a problem, causing Vicki to make methodological compromises, as she had done in her previous research.

As never before, we saw Vicki's consciousness being possessed by the research enterprise. And we saw her utilizing her own subjective perspectives in the research process. This was no comfortable matter for her. On the one hand her own perspective was clearly a valuable source of data alongside the other multiple data sources. On the other hand, it caused her to be anxious about overly-contaminating the outcomes of the research with personal perspectives. There was no evidence that this tension was ever resolved. Yet we can see that her subjectivity, at the level of personal motivation and ideological commitment, gave birth and growth to the study. Somehow, she needed to celebrate her commitment and her historical identity in the research. At the same time, she needed to lay them open for scrutiny, challenge, critique and possible change. We have little evidence in the data that this multiple subjective balancing act was either consciously attempted or consciously achieved. We know that Vicki continued to worry about the way in which her control over the blue book might bias the research but we have no evidence that the research changed her belief that women and girls were the disadvantaged sex. In contrast, there was evidence in abundance that the research caused her to analyze the gendered nature of life at Springfield in a more detailed and complex way than she had ever done before. This evolving perceptual complexity served, rather, to reinforce her existing beliefs and suspicions; to give sharper, more detailed articulation to the problem of unequal opportunities as she saw them.

There was further evidence of her use of professional resources in the research process. We saw her drawing upon existing teacher craft knowledge and skill to design her data gathering instruments, matching her understanding of children's literacy capabilities to the structure and content of the questionnaires and interviews. This craft knowledge was also evident in some of the research interactions with children, as teaching and learning moments near

the computer were created from research moments. The two were insepar-able as research detachment was superceded by professional engagement with children's questions, observations and curiosities. These incidental practical action outcomes were, on such occasions, deeply embedded, camouflaged almost, in the research process. In this, they defied the linear orderliness of conventional action research cycles; they showed that professional action outcomes cannot always await the deliberations of longer term analysis and theorizing. When the practitioner researcher wears the dual hat of teacher and enquirer, theory often validates itself, as Elliott (1981) reminded us in the full and immediate flight of practical teaching moments. And so it should be for researchers who are more concerned with improving the world through studying it, than with studying the world with no obligation to improve it.

The shift in Vicki from reticence to overt institutional confidence was tangible in this third research study. This may have been borne out of mastery of her subject — knowing her stuff — as well as being grounded in the new mastery of the skills required to undertake important staff development. She had made significant advances as a student, a teacher researcher and a profes-sional development agent in the school. Concomitantly, the school climate offered support and self-confirmation for Vicki which may have contributed significantly to her self-confidence. In general, her colleagues regarded her well as a person, a professional and a colleague. Their positive, if challenging, responses to the research processes and to the staff development event made this evident. They also accorded the same seriousness to the gender issue as Vicki herself had done. This may have contributed well to Vicki's certainty and confidence in the appropriateness of what she was doing. The staff pre-sented themselves to Vicki as an interested, if challenging, reference group. In such supportive and affirming circumstances, the growth of self-confidence was highly likely. Vicki's tangible confidence, thus, may have flourished as well as it did because of the rich, enabling institutional soil in which her growing personal certainty was seeded.

Alongside this growing confidence, Vicki had been given more respons-ibility within the school. It is difficult to say whether Vicki's new confid-ence caused senior management to offer this institutional responsibility, or vice versa. Her new confidence and new achievement through responsibility may have been so inextricably related that it would profit us little to try to isolate the one from the other. Yet the catalysis of the two was quietly powerful in terms of moving Vicki, and her institution, forward. If we add to this chem-istry the central drive of her deeply held beliefs we have a picture of a power-ful and influential person emerging from the wings of relative anonymity and diffidence as time and circumstance ripened. Christine gave voice to these changes in Vicki when I followed up the case story. 'I remember her as a fighter, fighting for an ideal', she said. 'She had a definite quest in life and a quest in her educational philosophy. Her attitude suggested that the status quo wouldn't do, that we need to do something about it.'

'Was she always like that as a member of staff?' I asked.

'No, I mean it was quite different when I came here', Christine recalled. 'She was going through the experience of being taken on permanently and I found her quite retiring to start with; keeping a lot of thinking to herself and not saying much. That was my first image of her', she confirmed. 'I think the fact of her being given responsibility opened her up completely. It was like a fire', she added emphatically.

I felt that 'fire' was not too strong a metaphor to suggest the changes that I had also seen in Vicki as her major research study took shape and as her influence grew on the Advanced Diploma course. Her growing confidence was transported back and forth from the course context to the school context, each, perhaps, feeding the other.

The second broad area of insight from this analysis of Vicki's gender research relates to the nature of the written research text. The analysis has allowed us to reflect upon the relationship of text, as product, to the less tangible, less visible processes of the research. No one should ever expect that the fullness of the research process, even in relatively small-scale research, could ever be captured in the written research text. Selections for text always have to be made and the selection determines the story which is finally told. This, we know, is an inevitable fact of text creation. On the other hand, the text can offer understanding and insight that would otherwise be lost in the million fleeting moments of an unrecorded research process. The written text thus records and describes lost moments for permanency.

It also becomes a vehicle for the researcher to create his or her research meanings. Many thoughts are not thought, nor developed, nor modified, nor changed, until they become subjected to the will of the pen or word-processor. Text creation becomes meaning creation and meaning creation becomes mind creation. So analysis of Vicki's text also becomes partly an analysis of her mind. Yet it was difficult, in parts of her text, to separate Vicki's mind and ideas from deeply affective and ideological aspects of her being. Her research text was not devoid of passion. It did not give rise to clinical, purely propositional, passionless analysis and theories. On the contrary, the language of autobiography, the language of emotion and the language of ideological persuasion were prominent features of the text alongside the more propositional qualities. This is not to deny that data analysis and her argumentation were, in most places, clear, reliable, well grounded. But argument slipped on occasions, as Vicki chose to leave her data and grounded theorizing behind in favour of grander, if less logical, discourse. So, at one and the same time, we saw Vicki extending her gender understanding of Springfield through a well conducted research process, while also using the research to substantiate and confirm previously established views on equal opportunities. Thus, the research and the research text were ideologically self-confirming for Vicki whilst adding detail, rigour and depth to her empirical understanding.

The third research text also offered greater insight than had the previous two into the parallel institutional changes generated by the research process, though the text did not stimulate many of these processes. Colleagues' awareness of the research, and their responses to the blue book, brought about changes in people and practices, long before the finished text. As we saw, action does not always await the formal outcomes of the research before finding its moment. Indeed, it is worth speculating on whether the earlier changes, before the staff development day, would have been any less significant had Vicki failed to write up the research.

On the other hand, the substantial nature of the finished text gave Vicki much to draw upon for the staff development day. She had relevant materials, well endowed arguments and well grounded institutional insights in the text as resources for other people's learning. These she drew upon in a process of textual transformation, matching the selection and employment of the research text to her new audiences and new purposes. For the new purposes of school-based professional development, the written text was mediated through different kinds of talk, through individual, oral presentation, incidental colleague discussion and more formal structured group discussion.

By the time I collected Vicki's gender text for my research, it had already served several purposes and several masters — mistresses even. In its creation and construction it had served Vicki's own developmental purposes as a vehicle for extending her thinking as well as expression of self; it had served the purposes of the course examination process, speaking to the audiences and requirements of examiners and the awarding academy; it had served Vicki's colleagues in their quest for further learning, understanding, self-explanation. By the time it became research data for me, it had lived three of its lives and earned its keep.

The third area of insight offered by our analysis of this gender study takes us deeper into the institution itself and allows us to speculate upon the combination of circumstances which explains the success of Vicki's research.

Something was learnt of the school by looking at the links between research and practice in Vicki's first and second studies. Much more was revealed through study three as we saw the research impacting deeper into school development processes. This gave us a chance to look at the kind of professional environment that allows individual teacher research to impact on the school. There were features of the school culture which promoted sharing, dissemination and consequent change. The Head of Springfield subsequently suggested that there were three key factors at work, and the data in the case study bore out his analysis. First, the people who made the culture were important; not just their ability but their openness to professional learning. Participation in various kinds of professional development was a cultural norm and a cultural expectation. Richard felt that this level of professional involvement improved capability in the school. I asked him, 'Have you any views about what makes the gender research that Vicki did helpful in the long term to the school?'

'I think first and foremost', he replied, 'because of the calibre of staff that we have'. He paused, and then added, 'I'm under no illusions. We are very lucky in that we have a lot of very talented, committed, thoughtful people. And a lot of that is linked to the in-service training that they have received, not just on long courses but also in things that have been going on in school, in house. That makes a big difference.'

It was, as I came to see it, a positive professional development climate.

I remembered being told of a list that Christine had compiled for in-service analysis. The list analyzed the recent INSET experience of the staff. It was impressive. Everyone had pursued some further professional development. Many people had done a lot. A few had been substantially involved. The school also had a history of involvement in Advanced Diploma courses. Two members of staff were currently studying for their Masters' degree. Regular in-service work was nothing unusual for these people.

Richard also spoke of the staff group as, almost, a professional in-service brotherhood (or, as Christine later pointed out, a sisterhood). This made Vicki's dissemination task much easier. She was not the marginalized teacher in her school as were some of her course colleagues, looked at askance as a professional pecularity with strange addictions to learning. 'I think that some-one like Vicki is lucky in the sense that there are lots of converted people around her', Richard explained. 'I was in a primary school this morning', he went on, 'where one teacher there was feeling very much burdened down by the lack of development of interest by colleagues around. Trying to make an input in such a school when you have been off on a course is just very very difficult.' And on another occasion he explained, 'So the sort of environment we have at Springfield makes a big difference to how you can input when you come back from that sort of course.'

In addition, there were helpful team structures and processes in the school within which ideas, participation and change were encouraged. 'One of the ways in which we work here', Richard explained, 'and it's a fairly recent development since I came, is to work in teams. It's a much more open society if you like. We have a whole range of different groups who meet and discuss issues and these range from whole staff consultative meetings to year team meetings to curriculum management meetings.'

He felt that these team discussions helped to foster a more open climate in which ideas such as Vicki's could implant themselves. 'So there's a great deal of open debate within the school', Richard concluded. 'I am sure — I know — that's very healthy. There is that sort of structure within which to bring back the skills and make a contribution to the development of the school and the direction of the school.'

This learning needed to be well managed institutionally for it to have any general benefit beyond the individual. People gave much time and effort to their individual professional development but this had not, in the past, been matched by time to share their work institutionally. Both Christine and Richard were trying to bring more coordination into this so that individual in-service could also become a richer resource for the school. There was now more school-based INSET which drew upon internal institutional expertise as well as drawing upon learning generated by external INSET. Christine and Richard had also devised strategies for improving information flow. Informa-tion and publicity about external INSET was now better targetted to inter-ested individuals in order to ensure that it did not get lost in the mass of staffroom paper. At the outset, they ensured that interested people received potentially relevant material before a course. 'There's an awful lot of discussion between the Head and I about who goes on a course and what good it will do the school, whether it is a viable position', Christine explained. 'All the course information comes to me, then the Head and I look at it and think of people who would benefit and who would enjoy it because they are travelling down that road themselves.'

Thus, the Head and the Deputy held as compatible the needs of the school with the needs, interests and preferences of the individual. Their management of INSET information was linked to their view of school development as well as to the professional encouragement of individual teachers. 'So it might be for the school, like if something on computers comes up and we are trying to build a certain teacher up because he or she seems interested in computers and the computer teachers keep leaving, we then see if they are interested. So we do a lot of offering.'

They were moving the culture of individualism into one of individualism within the collective. It was an emerging culture in which individualism became more consciously targetted for the benefit of the group. It was a better targetted, more responsible individualism than had previously been the case.

Subsequently, information about course attendance became open and communal, rather than private and individualistic. This had the advantage of encouraging greater collegial interest in others' learning; greater cross-fertilization of ideas. 'I put out a bulletin every week of everything that's happening', Christine explained, 'They all know who's been on what courses'.

Christine paused with a certain mischievious look in her eyes — a not uncharacteristic look of hers. 'You can hear them in the staffroom', she continued, 'saying, how did you get on, and, what was it like'.

She offered a fleeting insight into one of those impromptu processes by which external INSET drips into the fabric of the school. 'You see, Vicki just came in the staff room and the Head popped in and said straight away, how was the course, and Vicki started talking all about it.'

The Head felt strongly that improved management of INSET was another of the keys to successful dissemination and application of individual teachers' learning. Time, space, support and coordination were institutional enablers. 'I think the other key factor', he explained, 'is the way in which those individual sorts of interests are kept alive and managed by Christine in particular. Because the space is given to these things. There is planning. Things are written up and they are valued and hopefully there is some implementation from them.'

INSET, then, was seen as investment for the school, and teachers' learning was seen as a source of institutional capital. The business of capital investment, profit-making and profit-sharing needed his leadership. 'We're talking about management', he explained. 'My key responsibility is to make things happen, to manage the situation, to manage the staff and the direction of the school. Yes, I see that as very much a key role to make sure we make the most of the investment, which is considerable for people like Vicki who have been away on courses.'

The school, thus, had a developing style of leadership which offered direction and structure. Within this, individual growth could be encouraged and promoted. Within this, too, teacher development became linked to institutional growth and development.

Structures, processes and enabling management do not function independently of the people working within them. Richard understood this. More was needed than good management and he realized that a combination of circumstances and drives explained the success of Vicki's research. Added to the staff drive and the management drive was, he knew, Vicki's own personal style; 'strong ideas put gently' as Antony had said. There was also her sense of purpose; her aspiration to change her professional world in some small way. 'Along with management, obviously', he believed, 'is Vicki's commitment and involvement and willingness to try and make something happen as a result of the time she's spent'.

The open research agenda of the course had been helpful. We know this from other research (Ovens, 1991). It had been important both to Vicki and to the cause of school development that the teachers on the course were allowed, required even, to choose their own research focus. Course members often ask that research topics be prescribed for them. There is a singular reason for resisting this pressure. Those working in classrooms and schools are much better placed than members of the academy to match research focus to practical and professional needs or interests of the school.

There is a Stenhousian (1975) teacher-centred ideology lurking there; a commitment to promoting teachers' voices and teachers' perceived needs in educational research. Not all course members share the academy's views on this. Some find self-direction difficult in the early stages. Vicki was not one of those. Her autonomy was crucial for matching research to perceived need. This added depth and quality to her school-based research. After her first research study, she explained her thinking to me. 'I liked the fact that you can choose the research areas. But even within my own supervision group we disagreed about that. When we first started, three of the teachers in my group decided they would much have prefered you to give a title but I've liked to be able to do what I've wanted to do. That's been very valuable for me.'

What was particularly interesting about Vicki's gender research was the way in which her personal, idiosyncratic, self-chosen research became, ultimately, the driving force for school development. The research gave rise to 'bottom-up' motivation and change which was fuelled by 'top-down' facilitation, encouragement and support. Indeed, when clearing the case story, Christine reminded me that the 'bottom-upness' had been important to the reception which the research had received. It had been important to the staff, she felt, that Vicki was not a member of senior management; that the staff saw her as 'one of us, not one of them'. Vicki was not another figure of authority 'pushing them around' but a valued and trusted colleague of their hierarchical peer group.

In time, this chemistry between individualistic bottom-up motivation and top-down facilitation worked for Vicki's individual development and for school development. Gone was my early hypothesis that negotiation of the research agenda was required to optimize school development. Gone was my supposition that idiosyncratic, individualistic research had little chance of contributing to school development. Gone was my hypothesis that the research agenda needed to match the whole school development agenda if it were to bring about change. Vicki had worked from a starting point which was deeply rooted in her own history, not that of the institution. The personal flame that had grown from that personal spark had, for more than a brief time, lit up the institution. The glow was still apparent in several shapes, forms and persons long after the event. Here was personal development made institutional through the means of passion, commitment, reason and collegiality. Here was personal development made institutional through the means of modest, if challenging, self-management and enabling, well-structured, institutional management. The idiosyncratic agenda had become a communal agenda, bypassing a formal process of negotiation.

And I had learnt a lesson that generated a new, if more obvious, hypothesis. I had learnt that, perhaps, there is an unpredictable chemistry between each unique teacher researcher in her school and her unique small-scale research project. Each is different from the next. As such any prediction about the impact of award-bearing teacher research on the practical world can only, at best, be a naive and simplistic enterprise. Vicki's three research studies impacted differentially on the school for different reasons, not least because Vicki and her colleagues chose that it should be so. None of us could have foreseen this.

But not even the passage of time gave any firmer prediction about the life span or usage of the gender research. When I rang Vicki, now in her new post almost two years, to arrange delivery of the draft case story, she asked if I would return her gender research text too. The Head had, she explained, been involved in drawing up school development plans. Equal opportunities was a compulsory category. Her new moment had arrived, she felt. Her old passion was to be revisited. She had told the Head about her Advanced Diploma research and offered to lead some staff development. Almost three-and-a-half years had elapsed since the end of Vicki's course. The Springfield staff development event was two years and nine months behind us. A chink had appeared in the previous institutional wall which Vicki felt she had seen in her new post. And she seemed fit to sieze the day once more.

Time Passes

Fortune was not going to smile so readily this time, however, even though equal opportunities appeared on the school development plan for the next two years. The Head chose the three priority items which the plan required. Equal opportunities appeared because of the local education authority's requirements, not, in Vicki's view, because the Head saw it as important. On the contrary, she believed him to be antipathetic. They had differences of views. He could not, for example, understand the fuss being made about segregated and gender related competitive games. Boys played football and cricket. Girls played netball. That's the way the world was meant to be. Why should it be changed?

Vicki aired her beliefs and feelings. Their relationship became more formal, more frosty. It was clear, Vicki felt, that the Head required loyalty and agreement from her on curriculum matters, not challenge and difference. What she had learnt at Springfield about disagreement, difference, challenge and change was as nothing now. What she had been there was a hindrance to stability here. She grieved for her cultural loss.

Nor did the school development plan cut any ice. The two other priority items always seemed to consume the development time along with 'all the other things' from Government education reform. The equal opportunities policy failed to gestate.

The following year the Head retired. A young man took his place. This was his first headship. He was eager to please; eager to negotiate; eager to foster full staff involvement in many decisions. In his second year he devised a collaborative approach to the design of the school development plan. Individually, each teacher decided what they thought the development priorities should be. The ideas were pooled. Seven priorities were identified. These were rank ordered. Equal opportunities was in the top three. Vicki tried not to show her joy too publicly.

During the new Head's first year Vicki had made it her business to acquaint him with her action research interests. With this in mind, he now asked if she would like to take on the task of developing the equal opportunities policy. 'You're interested in this Vicki. Would you like to do it?' Would she! She tried not to show her enthusiasm too publicly.

For starters, she suggested that they might look at the use of playground space. The top area was dominated daily by the top year boys playing football. What did the majority of the children feel about provision? The question uncovered a hornet's nest.

To follow, Vicki told her colleagues about classroom research which showed how even the most aware teachers distribute their attention with great inequity. Why didn't people visit each others' classrooms to find out for themselves? the Head suggested. Everyone said that this was an interesting idea. Vicki would make the necessary arrangements. She tried not to show her enthusiasm too publicly.

When I last saw Vicki she was looking forward to a much needed summer holiday after a gruelling year at school, a year into which she had also fitted a great deal of further professional development through INSET. Learning to be a Deputy with the new Head over the last two years had been fascinating but taxing. Change, difference and turbulence had been inevitable even though the new climate, ethos and curriculum ideas had been almost universally welcomed by the staff. Now the honeymoon period was coming to an end. The new Head was proving to be human like the rest of them and Vicki was already calculating the interpersonal challenges ahead in the staff group. She could see the stresses and strains to come. If there were grumbles, people came to her. If there were dissatisfactions and tears they were shed on Vicki. ('It needs a woman's touch', she said. 'I think I have to be the part of him he can't be himself.') Yet Vicki had no shoulder for shedding her tears, frustrations and exhaustions. She was learning endurance and she needed her holiday.

But his heart was with Vicki's on many issues and there was a shared desire and drive to test and develop beliefs through practice. So although Vicki was desperately looking forward to a rest, she was also joyfully relishing the prospect of working, at last, on the equal opportunities policy in the coming school year. After all, she had been waiting a long time. It was over five-and-a-half years since she left Springfield and she was certainly determined to seize this day with heart, head and both hands.

Meanwhile, Back at Springfield . . .

Shortly afterwards, I bumped into Jeff. It was a delight to see him. Five-and-a-half years on from my last formal fieldwork contact with Springfield, Jeff was now Deputy Head and had been for some three-and-a-half years. Christine had moved to take her own Headship shortly after Vicki left Springfield. Jeff replaced Christine as Deputy. Vicki had updated me on these developments but I had seen neither Jeff or Christine during that period, even though we had spoken from time to time by telephone.

We met unexpectedly at a seminar on gender policies in schools. Jeff explained that gender had slipped off Springfield's dominant agenda since Vicki's and Christine's departure and he felt that this was no longer an acceptable state of affairs. The school needed a new 'gender leader' (Rudduck, 1994) for since Vicki and Christine had left, no-one had quite filled their passionate places.

The school had maintained many of the changes wrought by Vicki's and Christine's influence those five years and more ago. Indeed, colleagues still made reference to Vicki's gender beliefs and attitudes, reflecting upon what Vicki might have said or done in particular gendered situations. She was still in people's heads and hearts. ('Vicki would have said that' or 'Vicki would approve of this', Jeff had overheard colleagues say.) Also, curriculum practices and consciousness were still gendered in the way they had previously been. 'And we have three key science teachers who are all women', he said with some pride and pleasure. But gender issues were not, he felt, receiving the overt attention and priority they needed and deserved. 'Other things have dominated', he said, with some sadness and frustration.

We both knew what 'the others things' were. We exchanged observations about the manifest affects of Government education reform on school development and the 'child-centred way of working' as Jeff unashamedly called it.

Gender equality needed a new impetus at Springfield, Jeff felt. He had come along to the seminar in order to think about these matters, in order to seek that new impetus.

We chatted for some time about the challenges teachers face as they meet contrary gender attitudes and beliefs in the home and community, rehearsing discourses of Vicki's staff development day some some six years ago. The seminar had also explored this. There was still much work to be done, Jeff felt. For example, he had recently overheard a boy at Springfield wishing for a return of the days when men were able to 'knock women about' without fear of retribution. The teachers were shocked and worried.

Springfield colleagues were noticing a widening of the values gulf between themselves and the children. There was more violence, less care and concern for people, property and truth, less reciprocity. The seminar had spoken of the depressing effects of economic recession on many communities where secondary school gender leaders were working (Rudduck, 1994). This had made many teachers cautious about challenging home values. It did not seem appropriate for the school, as an institution of authority, to be adding to the negating problems of unemployment and increasing poverty which many families were suffering. Perhaps Springfield was caught, too, in these negating social and political waves of depression. The economic recession had caused a values recession. Gender equality may be one of the casualties.

But Jeff was not fatalistic. He was prepared to consider shaking the equal opportunities baton again and stimulating a new wave of agency. He and his colleagues had to believe that schools could make a difference. The struggle would go on.

We parted, vowing to keep in contact.

Chapter 7

Valuing Teacher Action Research

So — thank you to Vicki and her colleagues for all they have shown us. And I am compelled to remark on the intricacy and complexity of the case inside the originally muddled contents of this black box.

In pursuit of understanding the nature and effect of teacher action research, the story has had much to say. It caused me to look well beyond the surface understanding one has of the teachers as they come in and out of the lecture room at the beginning and end of the award-seeking days. It caused me to peel away the outer, and relatively thin, layer of my initial 'knowing' of teachers such as Vicki. In this process I gained a richer and more respectful sense of the multiple challenges to be overcome by the teacher researcher as she seeks to extend her learning for her own benefit through empirical enquiry; as she seeks to please the academy's tutors and examiners in construction of her written texts; as she seeks to reflect upon and develop her practical professional work for her pupils' sakes; and as she seeks to contribute some of her professional learning to her colleagues' development and the healthy growth of her workplace. She has these several audiences and these several purposes, with the concomitant task of trying to reconcile them all in the same teacher research process. The consequent achievements constitute significant success.

The case has also taught me to decentre as a teacher educator and recognize, yet once more, that all that is learnt is not necessarily taught. Vicki was not dependent solely upon my tutoring for the complex tasks she undertook as researcher and agent of change in her school. Much was learnt from experience and the reflection she brought to bear on it. Much was done and achieved through the agency of her maturing wisdom and judgment. The course provided a stimulus, a support, some knowledge, some guidance. The learning was enriched by Vicki's initiative, commitment, power to act and reflect. The case taught me humility and challenged me to re-evaluate my own role and importance in the teachers' learning and development.

My journey into understanding from Vicki's story led me into thoughts on research validity. I was constantly haunted, from my first field work days, by the difficulties the academy faces in judging this teacher action research for an award. In what sense can we or should we speak of the validity of teacher action research in an award-bearing context which places these several and varied demands on the teacher and from which these several and varied achievements arise? This was not amongst my initial research questions but it became a prominent and pre-occupying one when the triangulated school questionnaires and interviews were underway. The data made it evident that many of the teachers' research studies for academic assessment were generating practical processes and outcomes in school of which I had little previous understanding and which our validation criteria failed to capture. Vicki's story gives but one illustration. Other studies, untold here, revealed similar good and engaging news though some were less fruitful.

In addition, it was plain that the nature, benefit and outcomes of some of the teachers' research processes were not always adequately represented and manifest in their written texts. The finer detail of some of the school based processes that emerged when I was writing Vicki's case story only added to my sense of chagrin. Many of the teachers' written studies had the semblance of the literary tips of practical icebergs. Yet the work was being formally judged only in terms of what I called at that time, product validity, in contrast to the emerging knowledge of process validity. This was problematic if the texts did not adequately represent these complexities in and from the research. It is doubtful that many research texts do, or could.

Also, there was evidence from the teacher questionnaires and interviews of other learning beyond that formally expressed in the research reports. There was evidence of perceptual and attitudinal changes generated by the research that caused teachers to think, perceive and feel anew (Nias, 1987), as well as to act in new kinds of ways in their classrooms and schools. Vicki's story reflected some of this but certain descriptions and accounts which were expressed in the research questionnaire and interviews did not always surface in the written texts, though some, as we saw, did.

Whilst, thus, pondering on the diligence of the teachers I found myself pursuing a conceptual struggle over the notion of validity in teacher action research. We know that the concept of validity in research has, in the past, been concerned primarily with truth criteria (Altrichter, 1986; House, 1980) which post-positivist views of knowledge have problematized (Ford, 1975). Further, beyond these contemporary vexations about the nature of knowledge lie new forms of research which are driven by purposes other than primarily the production of knowledge; that are committed to the application of knowledge to action, to change, to improvement. In addition, there is a commitment to teacher development and school improvement through the action research which many institutions of higher education now foster. Teacher and school development are the prime organizational purposes; action research is one of the dominant development methodologies. In this context, therefore, research is oriented towards different qualities and purposes from other, more traditional forms. It cannot, thus, be regarded in entirely the same light so 'nervous borrowing' (Winter, 1993, p. 315) of criteria from other paradigms may be only partially helpful.

A concern over whether the research was 'true' in an epistemological sense became gradually replaced, therefore, by a concern over articulating ways in which the research was deemed to be worthwhile. I borrowed the concept of 'worthwhileness' from House (1980). In articulating alternative approaches to validity in evaluation he abandoned a narrow view of validity as 'prediction' (p. 249) which he saw as 'the traditional notion of validity' (*ibid.*) choosing, instead, to talk of the qualities of worthwhileness of evaluations, of which he felt there were many. 'In a broad sense I take validity to mean something like worthiness of being recognized,' (*ibid.*) he wrote.

Simons (1987) was helpful, too, speaking of validity within the context of naturalistic generalization. The 'problem of validity bedevils most researchers' (*ibid.*, p. 25), she wrote, a comforting thought to one who had already spent many long hours worrying over it. Simons pointed out that evaluators and researchers have conceptualized validity in many ways. Nature, purposes and audiences are all relevant determinants of validity moving beyond the monolithic criterion of 'truth'. In exploring validity, we need to consider relevance, appropriateness and useability of the evaluation, she suggested.

All of this certainly complicates the issue of validity but also allows us to consider how, why, and to what effect evaluation and research impact on people's lives and circumstances.

This search for a congruent way of perceiving validity in action research is of concern to many (for example, Carr and Kemmis, 1986; Altriches, 1986; Altrichter and Posch, 1989; Cochran-Smith and Lytle, 1990; McNiff, 1993; Elliott, 1994). Pam Lomax (1993), for example, has struggled with this difficult challenge as a teacher educator within her own award-bearing work with teachers and argues a case for five possible criteria, 'to do with ethics, rigour, logic, the practical and aesthetics' (*ibid.*, p. 113). Richard Winter, Stephen Rowland and a group of colleagues (Clarke *et al.*, 1993) also offer a set of principles and expectations which, they suggest, should govern the construction and validation of action research reports. At the time of writing this book, their exploratory ideas had been subjected to open debate with interested participants at the 1994 Collaborative Action Research Network conference at the University of Birmingham and at the 1994 Third World Action Research Congress at the University of Bath. At the Classroom Action Research Network seminar, Orton Zuber-Skerritt spoke of a tortuous struggle which colleagues endured in Australia as they, too, pursued this validity challenge, framed as a debate about defining the characteristics of action research (Altrichter *et al.*, 1990). Their debate was, she admitted, complicated and difficult, even though it appeared conclusive — a list of agreed criteria emerged.

Consensus is not easy. Struggling to find a common set of criteria for the entire action research community may be misguided in this obsessive age of standardization within Western economies. Localized approaches which develop from our unique contexts may be equally appropriate providing they are not corruptingly insular. Further, the action research community is a broad and varied church, crossing continents and political contexts. A blueprint approach to criteria may deny this.

The researcher's development is also a consideration. We would, for example, probably expect greater rigour in its many forms to be evident in the work of a teacher who had successfully completed a Masters' degree course in action research than from a novice about to step into the first stages of a research-based Diploma — though I have to admit that Vicki's novice research intelligences challenged some of my assumptions, as well as forcing me into further reflection. The journey from novice to expert may be long, complicated and differentiated and we may well expect more from full-time academics who hold research and publications responsibilities than from the Masters' degree and Diploma teacher.

Yet there is a tension between a developmental and a standards approach. A developmental approach allows greater tolerance of the unique journeys which teacher action researchers make as they develop their action research craft but this may make it difficult to agree and impose common standards. On the other hand, a rigid standards model can only offer absolute targets for the action researcher to achieve; the personal, professional journey is subordinate.

In trying to define standards and criteria in action research we also need, thus, to recognize and honour developmental and situational differences; to support 'validity pluralism' (Altrichter, 1986) as well as searching for any essence which characterises and unites all good action research. This does not imply letting go of a search for basic standards. Nor does it mean that 'anything goes' providing the action researcher has experienced development. Far from it. A developmental perspective need not be incompatible with a search for standards if standards-seeking becomes a qualitative, rather than quantitative enterprise; if it entails a search for acceptable qualities, or principles, embodied within action research rather than an exercise in ranking and rating one piece of research against another. Also, development is not a neutral concept. In exploring the worthwhileness of an action research project, people's values and beliefs about what the work should do, what it should be for and how it should be conducted will inform discussions. Development implies growth towards worthwhile ends. Those worthwhile ends are our personal and collective qualitative standards.

There are, however, paradoxical gains and dangers involved in defining detailed lists of standards within an essentially developmental paradigm. Qualitative standards can, on the one hand, offer clarity and guidance to action researchers but they can also be interpreted mechanistically and prescriptively to the point where individuality, divergence, creativity and risk are crushed. It would profit the action research community little to prescribe standards which were so tightly defined and applied that they became a validation straitjacket, squeezing the breath from development and innovation. Yet it would be dishonest to pretend that we do not have beliefs about the essential qualities which good action research should try to honour.

Power is an issue, too, for there is a shared concern about 'outsiders' enforcing unnegotiated and inappropriate criteria on teacher action research (Lomax, 1993; Clarke *et al.*, 1993). In an essentially democratic research methodology such as action research, it is incongruous to rely upon one, sole arbiter of worthwhileness, so the monolithic validating voice of the academy does not sit comfortably, even though it is an important voice, and one which may thoughtfully enhance the debate. Lomax (1993) poses the problem in terms of 'who is competent to judge' (p. 124). Clarke and her colleagues (1993) recognize that we 'must avoid making yet another set of "technical" prescriptions as a means of controlling others' research' (p. 491). There is, thus, a case for multiple perspective validation in this multiple perspective paradigm; a case for democratic validation; a case for validation 'through the intersubjective agreements of individuals who are sympathetic to the efforts of the enquiring practitioner' (McNiff, 1993, p. 104). There is a genuine opportunity for 'caring for the varieties of others' perspectives' (Winter, 1994).

We have already seen the range of purposes and audiences which Vicki's work, for example, served. And we have seen that members of those multiple audiences had valuable contributions to make in speaking the worthwhile-ness of the research projects. School colleagues knew their school, knew their children, knew their needs. Their knowledge and expertise gave them good grounds for contributing their validating perspectives. Vicki, too, had her considered views. She knew herself from the inside. She named her own developmental journey. She articulated needs of children and curricular in the historical life of the school. She reflected upon her colleagues' positions within her research processes. She was well equipped to validate the worthwhileness of her own research from her informed and committed professional perspect-ive. As agents of the academy, teacher educators, too, have understand-ing and interest to contribute. They will have their particular experiences as teachers and researchers to offer. They may be better acquainted with research perspectives, issues, possibilities than school audiences. They will know of, and be sympathethic towards, the hardships and heartaches involved in con-structing research texts that aspire to speak everything to multiple, anonymous and highly critical audiences. They will, ideally, be both theorists and prac-titioners of action research themselves who contribute their validation per-spective from a knowing and experienced position. They will be reflective practitioners who understand, and probably agonise over, the contradictions and ambiguities inherent in their difficult roles as guardians of academic 'standards' within an essentially developmental enterprise.

From multiple perspectives, the democratic validation enterprise takes on a different hue. It becomes less a competition for power and the ultimate dominant judgment; more a reflective exploration of worthwhileness as viewed from several exchanged positions of interest. It is less of an hierarchical enter-prise involving the giving of grace from one powerful and privileged party to an aspiring underclass; more of a mature, respectful and symmetrical pool-ing of different experience and expertise. The academy ceases to behave 'like doormen at exclusive clubs' (Belenky, 1986, p. 104). They shed the mono-lithic, adversarial, 'separate knowing' (*ibid.*) mode and enter into 'connected knowing' (*ibid.*) in which there is less pretence towards an ossified objectification of absolute criteria; more of a belief in evolving inter-subjectivities. Democratic approaches do not disconnect the action researcher and her community from the research at the point of validation. Instead, they continue to utilize, connect and integrate the many informed voices in pursuit of further understanding about worthwhileness. Each voice may sound different. Each voice may make a helpful contribution. Each voice may learn something from the others. The validation enterprise may be a developmental experience for all interested parties. The many voices that engaged constructively in the pursuit of understanding and action during the research are not silenced at the point of validation but continue to play their unique and different parts.

Democracy demands time, effort, energy and often founders on the hard rocks of human overload. Matching validation processes to multiple perspectives is not easy. It places greater onus on the already over-burdened teacher researcher and her colleagues to engage in validation reflections. It requires them to prepare and present their voices alongside the academy's; to gain access to children's perspectives where possible; to find ways of expressing their informed judgments about the research. It requires of the academy new ways of encouraging, and accounting for, these voices in the validation process. It problematizes the role of external examiner as ultimate judge and jury. The parties need to talk, share, exchange, listen. These ways are likely to be more costly and time consuming than the solitary disconnected 'marking' of research essays and dissertations.

As the overload on schools and higher education increases through government reforms, democratic validation may appear little other than a theoretical luxury we can ill afford. Yet we cannot ignore it if we are to strive for congruence and push the boundaries of our own developments. Many higher education institutions which support teacher action research are making huge strides with teachers and schools in a hostile political and economic context.

As a contribution to this involved debate I offer, in the following chapters, a set of developing ideas within which discourses about the validity of teacher action research could be conducted within a democratic framework. These are not offered as a definitive list, nor a bundle of hard edged academic criteria. Rather, they are offered as possible perspectives which teacher action researchers, their research communities and their awarders might bring to collaborative validating discourses. They are also offered as a potential resource alongside others' ideas in the hope that they may contribute to this developing but complicated field. The five areas — knowledge, text, action, development, collaboration — emerged from three sources; from reflections on the nature, purposes and outcomes of Vicki's research; from the main themes which consistently arise in the action research literature; from reflections upon the difficulties and struggles faced by my own academy in validating developmental research in a standards oriented academic culture. The discussion bears in mind the 'developmental and situational' as well as the 'standards' concern; it recognizes that each teacher action researcher and each of his or her projects will be unique but it also looks towards offering a view of the qualities, or qualitative standards, which might reasonably be expected.

I have chosen to frame these ideas about validity within the wider concept of 'valuing', for this allows us to move beyond discussions about worthwhileness into a spirit of celebration; into public acknowledgment of, and regard for, teachers' action research. I also use this concept as a reminder to myself that it has deeper, richer human meanings than its current monetarist connotations.

Small scale teacher action research is not valued at a structural level in Britain. Major research funding bodies, for example, recognize its methodological uniqueness but continue to award resources to alternative forms of research (Elliott, 1993). In so doing, the funders, as Elliott says, appear 'blind to the fact that methodologies being developed in the context of action research are providing new solutions to the vexed question about how research can be utilized to inform policy and practice' (p. 17). Action researchers in schools are still bedevilled by lack of funding to attend courses, projects and associated groups that foster and support small scale enquiry. They scratch and scrape to raise finance to attend the Collaborative Action Research Network conference so that they can disseminate their research more widely as well as meeting, and learning from, other action researchers. Few manage to find the necessary release time from school, nor the associated necessary funding.

In a broader context in Britain, wisdom and insight of the educational practitioner has been savagely scorned, abused and ignored in the processes of government educational reform (Dadds, 1992). The practitioner's voice has been negated in all but the technicist reform discourses. Only when centrally controlled educational change ran aground on its own internal inconsistencies and inefficiencies were teachers and headteachers allowed into the debate. Even then, the parameters were centrally defined. Teachers were not invited to express views about the worthwhileness of the centrally designed curriculum and assessment arrangements; only about their technical manageability.

The consistent devaluing of teachers' judgments at a macro-political level has become a national scandal. Negating teachers' informed and thoughtful professional voices constitutes a waste for children. Further, it damages teachers' self-esteem and endangers their willingness to see themselves as responsible, experienced and competent knowers. A nation cannot care for its children by abusing their teachers.

This is not to romanticize the whole of the teaching profession. Nor is it to indulge in 'uncritical glorification of action research' (Zeichner, 1993, p. 200). Rather, it is to argue that the valuable and valid work of teachers like Vicki is going unrecognized outside the award-bearing context and the relatively small circles of the action research community. When we study these small scale action research projects we witness the benevolent resources for change — and for good — which they offer children. It is lamentable that they are not yet recognized and valued more highly by those who hold political power and purse strings. For these reasons I invite the reader to step further beyond an exploration of validity into the realm of valuing, in the hope that we will, as a potentially caring nation, one day learn to regard and respect the quality of professional contribution we have seen here, in the pursuit of improved educational opportunities for children.

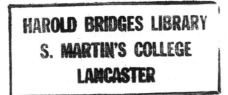

HAROLD BRIDGES LIBRARY
S. MARTIN'S COLLEGE
LANCASTER

Chapter 8

Valuing Knowledge and Understanding

Epistemological considerations are high priority, for who would deny that the purpose of any research enterprise is to create knowledge and, in the process, improve our understanding of the worlds in which we live and operate. 'In carrying out research the purpose is to try to make some claim to knowledge; to try to show something that was not known before' (Bassey, 1990a, p. 35).

This pursuit for new understanding does not have to be on a grand scale for it to be recognized; we do not have to discover the origins of the universe to qualify. Bassey acknowledged the worthwhileness of the small scale and the particular. To gain respect as research it is important that enquiry be a conscious, ordered process, one in which the enquirer is critically reflective about the work. 'However small, however modest the hoped for claim to knowledge is', Bassey wrote, 'provided it is carried out systematically, critically and self-critically, the search for the knowledge is research' (*ibid.*).

There are many interesting ways of viewing the epistemic qualities of Vicki's research for it is clear that all three studies created new knowledge and understanding. First, we could consider its quality of newness, for Vicki created many original insights into the humanities curriculum, the learning of two special needs children and gender practices at Springfield. She revealed knowledge which had not previously been made explicit or public. It is impossible to say that all the knowledge and understanding Vicki offered was new to the world, for who can ever be sure what lies dormant in the heads of those around us, even though we may think our thoughts are highly original. The claim that all research knowledge should be new and original is, thus, problematic. What may seem the most creative and original of thought for one researcher may appear to be self-evident, long-established truths to others. One person's novel insight may be another person's old wheel. In this, familiarity with the relevant field of knowledge through 'the literature' is helpful but limited. What was more important for Vicki's situated research was a need to understand dimensions of her own professional context. Others' disseminated knowledge and research could not adequately fulfil that purpose. She needed to create her own understanding of her own situation. This she did. Herein lay her claim to originality. Her questions and subsequent understandings were unique.

We should note, however, that the new knowledge became useful to others in the development of their understanding as well as Vicki's. The reactions of school colleagues to the humanities and the gender research work in particular suggest that the research and related in-service processes generated new knowledge and understanding at the wider public and institutional level. Vicki reflected the institution back to itself in these two studies, thus allowing it to see itself in many new ways.

In its turn, Vicki's research also generated a chain of new reflections for other people outside the school. External validity became enhanced. Others who interacted with Vicki's work were able to relate to its internal epistemic qualities and also transferred their reflections to new contexts. We saw, for example, how some school colleagues self-reflected on domestic gender practices as a result of addressing some professional gender concerns which Vicki raised. And Harry, Vicki's second research supervisor, concluded his written feedback by asking, 'and please may I borrow it for use in my own school'. Harry admitted in his written feedback to Vicki that he had found the work 'compelling and thought provoking'. And I cannot deny that I also reflected anew upon my professional gender practices as a result of engaging with the Springfield gender story.

Thus, the claims to new knowledge can be seen as multifaceted. The research generated new knowledge and understanding for Vicki, her colleagues, other readers. A chain reaction of new thinking evolved from the knowledge base which Vicki built.

We should also reflect upon the nature of the knowledge and 'truths' which Vicki created. But let us not get too worn out with the age-old epistemological goose chase about whether knowledge is 'out there', in a positivist sense, for the researcher to discover, or whether it is 'in here', in a phenomenological sense, by courtesy of the knowers perceptual making. I will admit to having been seduced towards this familiar trap at several points in the case study research, to little effect. Finding an epistemology to one's liking is no easy matter, but during one such period of distraction, I felt I had found a friend in Richard Rorty (1989), who suggested that truth may be 'that which it is better for us to believe' (p. 10). This was a tempting perspective which would have certainly terminated the epistemological struggle. Yet it is an inadequate perspective, especially in trying to gain insight into the experience of personal change generated by Vicki's action research. We know that challenge, conflict and discomfort may often be necessary for the creation of new understandings. Ideas which challenge our existing knowledge may not feel to be 'that which it is better for us to believe' at the time. One wonders, for example, at the discomfort Vicki and her colleagues may have felt when the research reflected back ideas and insights they did not particularly wish to confront. Yet it also seemed evident over time that people were making gradual and successful adjustments to the uncomfortable ideas in the research. Practices and attitudes changed such that those ideas which were, at one time, not better for them to believe, became accepted and operationalized. So Rorty's playful proposition offered an epistemology which was only partially helpful. And if Vicki had only utilized that which it was better for her to believe, then we would have much to say about her research epistemology that was critical.

On the contrary, all three research studies adopted a multiple perspective approach in the construction of research knowledge. In this, Vicki extended the boundaries of her own understanding by drawing upon, understanding and assimilating views of the world as others saw it. She adopted a 'collaborative resource' methodology (Winter, 1989, p. 56), working predominantly with phenomenological rather than objectivist epistemologies (Lather, 1986). Her personal knowledge became connected knowledge (Belenky, 1986) as she sought to understand, and empathize with, ideas, feelings, perspectives of colleagues, children and parents.

Vicki arrived at her methodological decisions and insights mainly through her good common sense views of how best to conduct her enquiries and through the reflections on experience gained by the doing. She realized that she could only usefully extend her understandings of the research issues by talking to relevant others; by trying to determine how they saw the world; by utilizing 'organized common sense' (Fullan, 1991, p. xii). She spent little time grappling with complex epistemological and methodological literature and language. Rather, she arrived at multiple perspective enquiry through a personal, experiential and common sense route, not an abstract and academic route. Along this route, growing personal knowledge and confidence were allowed to thrive.

Winter (1989, p. 56) suggests that collaboration between the researcher and the field participants allows access to complexity and to alternative perspectives. It enables the researcher, in analysis, 'to move outwards from (the) inevitably personal starting points towards ideas which have been interpersonally negotiated'. Collaboration is, thus, concerned to challenge, rather than confirm initial assumptions through serious exploration of different views of the world. In Vicki's case, the insights generated from the collaborative research prompted her away from many perceptual starting points, into newer, more communal perspectives. It also challenged and changed many assumptions.

Lather (1986) claims too that this multiple perspective methodology is necessary for enhancing the 'construct validity' (p. 270) of the research, as it draws upon the perceived truths of the research participants. In the process, the 'counter patterns' (*ibid.*) which multiple perspective methodology raises help to extend the constructs of the researcher. It is also a safeguard against the perpetuation of an egocentric researcher perspective. Vicki's collaborative resource offered methodological checks and balances against the research perspective becoming overly personalized, even though the final assembling — the shape and form — of the report, lay in her hands.

Lather further suggests that the theories from the research must be shaped and stretched 'by the logic of the data' (*ibid.*, p. 272) and we saw this happening in Vicki's work. She made good use of her data. There were many insights in all three research studies that were shaped and stretched by its logic; her changed perceptions of the two special needs children; her developed understanding of colleagues' attitudes to their humanities teaching; her new knowledge of gender issues. These well grounded, 'logical' insights enhanced the internal epistemological validity within this multiple perspective approach. Vicki, thus, created new understandings and knowledge from a wide range of data and from a wide range of field participant perspectives. She used her data faithfully and with integrity.

Even so, she struggled to the end with the epistemic basis of the gender study in particular, as she tried to come to terms with the influence of 'self' on the data. There was a research dilemma here for her. On the one hand, to explicate 'self' in the data was epistemologically appropriate, as Harry had tried to persuade her. 'Any attempt rigorously to eliminate our human perspective from our picture of the world must lead to absurdity', Polanyi wrote (1958, p. 3). And absurd it would have been for Vicki to deny the value of her existing professional knowledge in the research, or to deny the power of her passionate commitment to the research project. Both these enhanced the motivation behind the research. They also probably enhanced the quality of understanding within the research and the consequent practical developments. On the other hand, to make herself visible and known in the research process, she felt, was no guarantee that her preconceptions would be overcome — if, indeed, they needed to be. Vicki maintained a nagging doubt that her biases, beliefs and historical passion would stand in the way of clear thinking. There was textual evidence that this happened in a few places though these moments of self-intrusion were outweighed by the myriad multiple perspective insights arrived at through 'the logic of the data'. The clear thinking and the passion ran side by side, and whatever Vicki's doubts, whatever the influence of Vicki's self on the research insights, there was no evidence of the 'rampant subjectivity' that Lather (1986, p. 271) warns us to be guarded against in phenomenologically oriented research.

Whatever approach to 'truth' informs the creation of research knowledge, it is clear that passionate and committed teacher research such as Vicki's is driven by affective as well as cognitive epistemologies. Knowing and theorizing were not simply activities of Vicki's intellect. Her feelings as well as her ideas were much in evidence through the accounts of 'self' which she explicated in the text; they were both sources of her research insights. The affective, in its turn, also assumed the autobiographical. What Vicki brought from her past informed the questions of the research, the ways of conducting the research and the sense she made from the research.

Far from undermining the epistemological validity of the research, the affective and autobiographical contributed to the driving forces which shaped research knowledge and transformed it into practical, lived action. Vicki's work shows that creation of research knowledge depended on processes beyond those of rationality and logic. This is not to deny the value of scholarly analysis, interpretation and conceptualisation; nor is it to deny that scientific and propositional methods of thought can offer useful, if somewhat imperfect, intellectual instruments for creating meaning from data and experience (Magee, 1973). Rather, it is to claim, as does Chisholm (1990), that in action oriented research 'the integration of emotionality is not weakness, but enrichment' (p. 253). Indeed emotion may be the force which brings the action researcher to the research. Emotion may be the force which continues to find the personal commitment needed to complete the research. Emotion may be the force which, subsequently, causes the research to find a practical application in its relevant world. In her second project particularly, what Vicki came to 'know' about her pupils through her research affected her feeling. In turn, her reconstructed emotions pointed to new understandings of the children. There was, thus, a dialectic between head and heart as she progressed through her research. The development of emotion was related to the development of her thought; the development of thought was linked to the growth of feeling. 'Emotions are constituted in the ways in which we interpret and make sense of happenings and events in our environment, particularly our actions and the actions of others' (Crawford *et al.*, 1992, p. 111). Thus, this kind of 'passionate scholarship' (Chisholm, 1990, p. 253) may be a more appropriate stance within action research, replacing 'deceptive rational coolness in favour of explicit commitment' (*ibid.*). Vicki's was not a passion which overwhelms or 'overcomes' (Crawford *et al.*, 1992, p. 119). It was a passion which drove, motivated, directed. Far from worrying about the sadness, joy, commitment, frustration, concern that peppered the logic of Vicki's research process, we should count them favourably in the epistemological validity of the work. They were not only a vital part of the process of knowledge creation. They also gave us a more honest account of the human research experience.

Also, Vicki had a personal and professional concern to understand the perspectives and aspirations of those who made the communities of her research. She cared about her people. This care and concern fuelled the motivation which generated the multiple-perspective knowledge. Her drive to understand people through the research helped to create knowledge in which the communities could see themselves. It also extended Vicki's subjectivity into new, more complex understanding. It was knowledge, too, over which others had some sense of ownership and this communal involvement was inextricably linked to communal involvement in the research action.

Stenhouse (1975) pointed out that in the attempt to improve professional practice through the route of systematic enquiry, the practitioner's subjectivity is a necessary part of the knowledge base of action research. 'There is no escaping the fact that it is the teacher's subjective perception which is crucial for practice' (p. 157). This must, he suggested, be the basis for a new epistemology of teacher research; 'we are concerned with the development of a sensitive and self-critical subjective perspective and not with the aspiration to unattainable objectivity' (*ibid.*).

This subjective epistemology had a further dimension, for it proves impossible to separate the nature of the research knowledge from the procedures by which data were gathered and interpreted. Theories, insights, issues which emerged from analysis and interpretation were dependent upon the data which emerged. And the data were dependent upon, and a consequence of, the methods of collection. Vicki wrote in several places of the limitations and problematics of data gathering. She reflected upon the linguistic demands which questionnaire and interview placed upon the meanings which pupils could share. She pondered on the different insights which different pupils would give. She recognized the limitations and constraints that were placed on data by the geography and acoustics of the school. She realized all along that the researcher makes choices about data and method from the infinite possibilities that the field offers. And she recognized that insight derived from data and method became shaped through the agency of her personal perceptions and interpretations. Interpretations, insights, theories, were thus methodologically and personally situated. They could not have been otherwise. The epistemological validity of Vicki's work cannot, thus, be separated from the validity of the research process. The substantive and the methodological were the epistemological warp and weft of the research.

Thus, in several ways, Vicki offered her reader 'unalienated knowledge' (Stanley, 1990, p. 13). She made no pretence that the knowledge she produced had an existence independently of her creation of it. She acknowledged the epistemic effects of the research processes she adopted and she did not pretend to a detachment of self and subjectivity. Vicki made herself, her ideas, her feelings, her biographical predilections and her research processes visible. 'One of the preconditions of good research is that it should account for the conditions of its own production' (*ibid.*). We must admire and commend Vicki for the many ways in which she tried to do this.

On the other hand, there are procedural checks and balances for enhancing the validity of multiple perspective research which were not in evidence in Vicki's case story. Their absence, too, may have had an epistemological influence. Lather (1986, p. 271), for example, talks of 'face validity'. This involves a dialectic between the research and the field participants whose perspectives provide the logic of the data, and, thus, the research insights. Face validity involves 'recycling description, emerging analysis and conclusion back through at least a subsample of respondents' (*ibid.*). This dialectic may lead to modification or refinement of analysis, interpretations and theoretical insights. In this process lies the potential for respondents' reflections upon the researcher's insights to be treated, in themselves, as new forms of data. Theorizing becomes a more communal enterprise; participants engage in corporate theoretical reflection. Nothing in the data from Vicki's case story suggested that these processes took place in the development of research knowledge and understanding. Colleagues contributed to the collaborative data resource but not to collaborative theorizing. The research theory was principally of Vicki's making. Face validity may have been more in evidence during the professional development day as colleagues interacted with data and insights from the study; as their discussions, questions, debates shaped and stretched the logic of the data in new ways; as Vicki's theories were 'put under pressure' (Clarke *et al.*, 1993, p. 491). But this process of collaborative reflection and exchange did not form part of the epistemological basis of the written research report.

Enhancing face validity is problematic for the hard pressed, part-time award-seeking teacher action researcher even though it is an ideal towards which she may aspire. Award seeking teachers like Vicki often work to tight, short, timescales which award bearing institutions impose on them. Holly, P.J. (1984) pointed out that bureaucratic requirements of award-bearing systems often value administrative and examining procedures above the developmental needs of the schools and teachers who are being served by the research. Thus, teachers like Vicki may be caught in a dilemma between adopting more rigorous, but time consuming, and lengthier, validating procedures, or short cutting epistemological checks and balances to avoid the risk of missing submission deadlines. Regulations in my own academy allow flexibility in this such that submission dates can be negotiated in relation to the needs of the research. Even so, this did not dispel many of the practical difficulties which Vicki encountered in organizing her own, and her colleagues', time. There was also a continuing sense of encroachment on their goodwill and precious time resources. This caused worry and guilt. An academic insistence on rigorous face validity would add to these pressures, tensions and organizational difficulties. Procedures for enhancing face validity may, therefore, be a matter of practical expediency for the award-seeking teacher action researcher and for the award giving examiners. The academy may need to adjust its procedures to allow time for enhanced rigour, unless the sponsoring authorities give teachers such as Vicki more non-teaching time to do their research. This is unlikely to happen to any significant degree.

Unlike researchers on full-time projects and contracts, teacher action researchers tend not to have the luxury to 'enjoy the intellectual delights of rigorous thinking about minutiae' nor to 'devote long periods of time to it' (Bassey, 1986, p. 18). Theirs is the kind of research 'which people get on with and do quickly' (*ibid.*). Indeed, the pressures of the awarding system decree that it should be so. This is not to suggest that face validity is inappropriate for the teacher researcher, nor that it is unhelpful in shaping the research epistemology. Rather, it is to argue that the feasibility of procedures for enhancing epistemological validity may be contingent upon the working circumstances, style and time resources of the award-seeking teacher researcher. It is also to beg recognition that the epistemological positions reached be treated as pragmatic statements, or the best that could be shaped at the time, given the brief and possibly transitory nature of the work and the contextual constraints imposed upon it. The 'ideal' set of research procedures from which the teacher action researcher may draw may not fit adequately her time and working circumstances. Vicki's comments upon the choices facing her in the tape-slide work verify this.

Rorty's views about contingent epistemologies (Rorty, 1989) were helpful on this score and were ever so slightly more comforting. He suggested that truth can only reside in our language, 'since truth is a property of sentences' (p. 21). Our truths are represented by our vocabularies and discourses. And as we move through life, changing our understandings, so, too, do we develop new vocabularies or new ways of thinking. Thus, we should resist holding on to absolute views of truth. Rather, he exhorts us to think of truth as evolutionary, changing and related to the particular time and circumstances in which we find ourselves. We go through life adopting new ways of thinking and talking. We adopt new vocabularies and he suggests that we should 'try to get to the point where we no longer worship anything, where we treat nothing as quasi divinity, where we treat everything — our language, our conscience, our community — as a product of time and chance' (*ibid.*, p. 22).

Winter (1989) too reminded us of the provisional nature of our knowledge. Without provisionality and contingency, there would be no room for epistemological growth or creation through the research enterprise.

Yet these perspectives on contingency, provisionality and pragmatism do not adequately fit all that we saw of the epistemologies which Vicki utilized in her research. On the one hand, the truths of her research were contingent and provisional in that they were grounded in, and appropriate for, the particular time and circumstances of each particular study. They were all internally applicable to the contexts from which they evolved. On the other hand, the continuing usefulness and applicability of the humanities and the gender research suggested that the epistemologies had something more enduring about them than the fleeting and the contingent. Both continued to have value in a changing institutional context. The knowledge from the gender research transcended both time and place as Vicki considered applying it to her different institutional context some years on from its creation. This perhaps is one of the more cheerful epistemological paradoxes of particularistic case study research, for it can, at one and the same time, be accorded only provisional and contingent internal validity whilst having the potential for a more timeless and generalizable external validity.

The ideological dimensions of the gender epistemology seemed to be neither contingent, provisional nor lacking in divinity and worship. Whilst Vicki's gender knowledge and understanding of the school grew and changed through the research, her beliefs remained constant. Thus, the ideological epistemology of the research was transcendent and enduring, deeply rooted in Vicki's past self and holding the possibility of remaining a constant in her future self. Also, the fact that the knowledge and understanding informed practice suggests that people were willing to treat it as more than provisional. In the scale of eternity, the knowledge may, indeed, have a limited life span. We may never know. But the actions of those to whom it became useful indicated a willingness to treat it as absolute — if only for a while.

Willingness to endow the knowledge with certainty and confidence was a necessary prerequisite for applying it to professional decision-making in the practical world. Such certainty and confidence may be illusory (Smail, 1984) as, indeed, may be most of our consciousness (Bandler and Grinder, 1979). But the illusion of certainty and confidence may be necessary to guard against the paralysis of doubt and inaction, as Shakespeare seemed to understand all too well when he created Hamlet, the doubter and procrastinator par excellence. The action researcher cannot deliberate forever. So, Rorty's views about the shifting and contingent nature of truth may herald an intellectual, or epistemological provisionality that was not totally in evidence in Vicki's case story. Whilst Vicki's research epistemologies were essentially phenomenologically based, and, possibly, historically provisional, they were treated with a positivist respect in their application to practical action. There was no language of doubt surrounding Vicki's decision to construct the humanities policy, to understand and regard her handicapped pupils better than before, or to seek actively to improve gender perspectives and practices at Springfield and elsewhere. Her knowledge base changed in response to the logic of the data and to the contingencies of the historical moment but her beliefs and values endured as absolute and eternal.

Creation of the epistemological base of her research was, thus, a matter for the heart as well as the head and the genesis of ideas may be traceable into historical events that occurred way before the overt beginnings. These latent epistemological beginnings may have been as crucial to the research as the relatively contemporary database.

Past and present, passion and reason, will all be contained in knowing and understanding. Take away the many-sided subjectivities of Vicki's research epistemology and you take away the life force.

Chapter 9

Valuing Text

Some have argued that for teacher's work to be accorded the status of re-search, it has to be published in some form. Stenhouse (1975) defined research as systematic enquiry made public. Ebbutt (1982) suggested that for teacher enquiry to be considered seriously, not only should it be made public, but it should also be open to public critique. 'If action research is to be considered legitimately as research, the participants in it must, it seems to me, be pre-pared to produce written reports of their activities. Moreover these reports ought to be available to some form of public critique'.

Given this, it seems strange that relatively little time and attention is accorded in the action research literature to communication in comparison to other parts of the research process. Rob Walker suggested, for example, that 'Finding effective means of communication in applied research studies is an area that is undeveloped in relation to the effort that has gone into devising methods and techniques of data collection' (Walker, 1985, p. 164).

For teacher action researchers like Vicki, working for an award, the issue of publication is more complex than at first appears. As we have seen, Vicki's research served more than one audience and purpose. Her own learning was served; the requirements of the awarding academy were met; her school col-leagues benefited. Making her research public in one type of text did not fulfil all these purposes. The requirements of the academy were incompatible with the requirements of school colleagues.

There are tensions between presenting for an award, presenting for school colleagues, presenting for self. The academic award-giving world requires particular written textual forms for representing and communicating teachers' research findings. Yet these may, in Walker's terms, not be the most effective means of communication for the various audiences which the teacher researcher may wish to reach. The traditional written research report may be convenient for the award-giving institution and the examiners. It will even fit comfort-ably into the academic culture with its normative textual approaches to com-municating knowledge. Teacher researchers are socialized into these academic conventions. They learn about standard construction of bibliographies; pres-entation of data in supplementary appendices for validating the internal nature of the research; standardized bindings and lettering (the higher the award, the more standard becomes the binding); a one-and-a-half inch margin on one side and no more than half-an-inch on all the others; citation of relevant authorities. It is easy to see the sense, wisdom and necessity of some of these conventions for they help the reader to understand the researcher's sources upon which knowledge, understanding and argument are constructed. They clarify. They represent traditionally accepted textual requirements of the academy. Yet creating written texts to these norms for the purpose of seeking an award involves teachers in an 'academic learning' that may not be sufficient for promoting action and development in their schools or classrooms. For the school audience, Vicki needed other, and different, learning.

In controlling the award, the academy has the power, thus, to impose its own cultural expectations norms and practices on school oriented research. Holly, P.J. (1984) once asked whose needs were being served by these academic conventions; whether they bring benefit to school-based clients. Tight bibliographies, standard referencing and double-spaced black-bound texts may not be perceived as practically helpful by teachers, even though they serve the award-seeking purpose.

The teacher researcher becomes involved in a process of resocialization or acculturation. There is a bridge to cross from the school-based professional culture into the academically oriented culture of the awarding institution. This requires transformation of the teacher's ways of thinking, speaking and writing, for the discourses of the dominant academic culture, and the manner of conducting those discourses, may not match the discourses of the school (Gore, 1989a and 1989b). Thus, the cultural norms and discursive practices of the academy are reproduced within the awarding systems. When the teachers' ideas, talk and writing more closely match those of the academy they will be judged worthy of awards. As one Masters' degree teacher was heard to say, 'I knew I had made it as a successful researcher when I heard myself talking more and more like the course tutors'. Validation and awarding can be seen thus as a process of cultural reproduction in which the dominant culture maintains its power base over the language, thought and practices of teacher researchers, for better or worse.

Vicki's case story showed that the texts she produced for the awarding examiners and for assessment purposes were not read in school, full though they were of knowledge, insight, data that had potential developmental value for her school colleagues. Other award-seeking teacher researchers have reported similar problems with their formal texts in schools (Holly, P.J., 1984); texts not being read, texts not being put to practical, developmental use. This is ironic, given that school-based practitioner research is seen as a more effective force for change than less accessible and disconnected traditional educational research, for if the fruits of teacher research cannot be used because of the textual forms in which they are communicated, very little progress has been made.

Time may be a key problem, not just textual credibility. Vicki's texts may have had potential credibility of school colleagues because Vicki was known and trusted. Also, school colleagues had an identity, and thus, a potential interest in the studies. Yet in their award-bearing form, these texts had no operational validity because school colleagues could not find time to access the wisdom in them quickly and easily. As such, the knowledge from the research was inert professional knowledge. Only when Vicki transformed the texts into a genre that fitted the culture and needs of the school was this inertness swept aside. Dormant knowledge became live knowledge. The humanities research text gave rise to a school policy document. It was this text that colleagues used. The gender research text was translated into school-based processes and development processes. It was this text that school colleagues related to, responded to and used. These transformed texts created action in the school in a way that the standard academically oriented texts for examination failed to do.

Vicki displayed much wisdom in these textual matters and we can honour and value its qualities in a number of ways. We can consider not only the way in which Vicki constructed the academic research texts, but also the way she subsequently transformed and used them for the different professional purpose of practical school development. Vicki engaged in text construction, text transformation, text application.

Action research demands more than the production of knowledge and understanding. It requires communication and use. This involves the teacher researcher in making a wider range of judgments than the traditional researcher, for the action researcher not only conducts and communicates the research, but also seeks to operationalize it in the practical world. Judgments have to be formed on how the research will be done, how it will be shared with a range of others and how it can be related to practice.

We could commend Vicki's success in meeting these several textual challenges of knowledge production, knowledge communication and knowledge application. First, of the epistemology of the text we have already spoken in both the case story and the previous chapter. In addition, Winter's concept of 'plural structure' (1989, p. 62) is helpful here. He suggests that the research process and research epistemology should be reflected in the research report; that the nature of the research text be congruent with the nature of the research; that we 'consider an appropriate format, i.e., the nature of a "plural text", which can accommodate a plural structure of enquiry'.

Vicki's plural structure in the text was achieved by making explicit the multiple perspectives on which her three research studies drew. These were used to inform theory and insights, rather than being dominated by the monolithic perspective and control of the researcher. Vicki's written texts mirrored her methodology and mirrored the ways in which she constructed research knowledge. Alec's written comments on the humanities research, for example, confirmed that Vicki not only represented the multiple perspectives, but allowed these to shape and change her thinking and her personal theories. 'I liked the way (Vicki) resisted offering too much of her own thinking too early', Alex wrote, 'and the ways she genuinely sought and captured colleagues' opinions . . . It was also interesting to note how Vicki's views on the humanities teaching were challenged and clarified in this process and her assumptions on curriculum coherence and communication were broken'.

The plural nature of Vicki's texts evolved from an analysis and synthesis of the plural nature of her research experiences. There were multiple voices in the text because there were multiple voices in the research. The text gave the sense of self and others that the research was founded upon. Thus, there was an inevitable and inseparable link between the doing of the research and the construction of the research text. Perhaps, too, the strong personal voice that came through in her texts was a result of Vicki's developing confidence as she came to believe that her voice counted; that it was worth hearing.

In this plural structure, Vicki gave insight into her own learning in addition to representing the multiple voices of the research. In particular she gave textual accounts of her learning about research methodology. These reflections on personal learning in the research text are compatible with the professional developmental purpose of awarding bearing teacher action research and are, thus, an essential feature of plural structure. This issue is discussed more fully in chapter 10.

Vicki's own presence in her text is also congruent with her subjective epistemology. Teacher action research which has deeply personal starting points, motivations and consequences would not be well matched by texts that attempted cool depersonalization. Taking the 'I' out of the text gives a spurious sense of detachment and renders the researcher invisible. This is inconsistent with the 'first person' teacher action research; with research which studies the researcher's own practice (Kemmis, 1989). First person research demands first person text. A traditional, academic register with a third person rather than first person discursive stance would be inappropriate. It would also be dishonest for it would hide the convictions, emotions, beliefs, thoughts and judgment that helped to shape the research knowledge. To 'try to weed out the self . . . so that the flowers of pure reason may flourish' (Belenky *et al.*, 1986, p. 109) is to privilege erroneously the supreme role of logic in the shaping of theory. Reason cannot shape action research theory on its own. It can only play its part along with the emotive, motivational and historical qualities of the teacher researcher's being.

We have already seen much in the case story of Vicki's 'textual intelligence' or 'textual wisdom' in the business of knowledge dissemination and application and there is little, if anything, to add here to what had already been said. Her transformed texts created appropriate and helpful alternative genres for the school audiences and school purposes, giving rise to policy documents and staff development. In this, these texts carried a practical validity which the more conventional award-seeking texts alone did not. They generated debate, disagreement, policy. The policy generated practice.

None of this denies the worthwhileness of the more conventional award-seeking text for its contribution to the researcher's learning. Indeed, creation of this text may have helped development of the knowledge and understanding that gave rise to some of the action, since writing is cognition and a meaning making process. Hackman (1987) for example, reminds us that 'we often find out what we have to say only once we have started to say it' (p. 10) and Frank Smith (1982) gracefully suggests that 'Writing separates our ideas from ourselves in a way that is easiest for us to examine, explore and develop' (p. 15). The relationship between text creation and meaning making is often symbiotic. Assembling, selecting and discussing ideas and data in writing a research report is an act of cognitive organization and development. The research epistemology is, thus, shaped further beyond the glimmers of insights which emerge during the rushing and doing of the field work. At the point of the pen, theory becomes more explicit, better organized, different. Where action outcomes are determined subsequently from research theory, therefore, the role of the written text is crucial. If theories change when subjected to the sustained thinking of the pen, so, too, will the researcher's view of desired action.

This justification of the role of the text for the academy does not entirely solve all problems, however, for the research is not the same as the research text. The two may be confused. Vicki's case study showed that the research process was much more extensive than the research 'product' signified in the shape of her written text. The research reports may have been but the tip of a much larger, more comprehensive, research process.

Thinking, action and text creation cannot always be synchronized and do not always embody each other. The immediacy of the practical world of teaching may not always be able to wait upon the more measured, lengthier process of complex writing. The teacher action researcher may not always be able to afford the luxury of suspending action until her theory becomes shaped and developed through her writing. Thus, there may be equally strong links between data and action that are not mediated by written texts. There may be many action outcomes that precede the written text and that may never find a voice in print. Several such unwritten action outcomes were seen in Vicki's case story and were only made manifest through colleagues' accounts of the practical effects of Vicki's research.

Yet it is probably still the case that many institutions which foster teacher action research through their award structure focus predominantly on the 'end' stage of the research process in the form of the written research text. This is to do less than justice to the scope and quality of the teacher's research enterprise where much achievement takes place that may not be visible in the written report.

Validation by text alone may, therefore, disconnect itself from questions about the development of the research and the school. It also means that the teacher researcher's literacy skill is implicated, for her texts may carry only superficial and partial accounts of both knowledge and of action if she has had to struggle with the written word. In Vicki's case, it is true that all three written texts gave some insight into much of the action which was generated during the fieldwork processes. What they did not and could not, perhaps, do was give insights into the fullness of the action which happened in the process and which developed subsequently. In that sense, much of the action from the research may lie beyond the text. Capturing the detail, complexity, significance and essence of any research process places high literary demands on the most practised of researchers. It is exacting, and this has to be borne in mind when teacher action researchers are required to stand or fall by their textual products. Inadequate texts do not always signify inadequate action research (Dadds, 1994a).

Given, too, the vexations of post-structuralist and post-modernist views of text and language, (Bradbury, 1987; Byatt, 1991; Sturrock, 1979 and 1986; Lodge, 1988) in which meaning and interpretation dissipate like candy-floss between the signifier and the signified, it is hard to see how the academy's examiner can ever adequately receive the shifting sands of the teachers' meanings by sitting at a desk reading a research report. If meaning is individually constructed, so too is meaning-from-text. In addition, the examiners will be projecting their own meanings into the research report, or reading 'in front of the text' (Ricoeur, 1981) as well as reconstructing the writers meanings, or reading 'behind the text' (*ibid.*). Written texts cannot thus ever carry objectified meanings from the researcher to the examiner, for the constructivist influence of the reader is inevitable as his or her intellectual history interacts with the infinite possibilities which the words on the page offer. Harry's earlier comments illustrated this well, for it was clear that he was trying to make sense, and use of, Vicki's research report for his own professional purposes, as well as making the best attempt he could to understand Vicki's thinking. Sturrock (1979, p. 14) claimed that 'An author can have no special authority over what (he) has written, because (he) has committed it both to strangers and to the future. The meanings it will henceforth yield do not coincide with those (he) believed (he) had invested in it: they will depend on who reads it and in what circumstances. The circuit of the communication is all the less sure for no longer being immediate, as it is when meanings pass from speaker to hearer'. A good discussion with a researcher about his or her research report can be enriching and illuminating and can advance significantly the understandings generated by the written text alone. Academic practices which estrange the examiner from these enriching discussions also estrange him or her from layers and levels of understanding about the research. Some academic practices double the estrangement by doubling the 'objective' marking. Hence, two examiners who never meet, see, talk with the action researcher may be deprived of the understanding which lies beyond the text as they caste their detached, disconnected validation judgments.

Our postmodern linguistic condition suggests that 'autonomous text' (Ricoeur, 1981) is but a blunt instrument for seeking shared meanings even for the most skilful and developed writer. Nor does spoken 'text' solve the problem for meaning will be forever subjectivist, never absolute. But at least it allows meaning and subjectivities between participants to be negotiated and shaped through dialectical processes in a way which written text denies. Discussion is relational; it is 'connected' (Belenky *et al.*, 1986). The spoken 'research text' that evolved on Vicki's professional development day raised the opportunity for the enquiring community to move closer to common understanding. This was a wiser text for the school than the written report.

If we confine our view of 'text' to the more conventional academic research genre, therefore, we may ignore the appropriateness of other forms of communication, written or spoken, that may have greater potential for shaping and communicating meaning; for putting the action into action research; for acting as catalysts for institutional action and change.

Yet, as Walker (1985) suggests, it is no straightforward matter to change standard academic forms of reporting research nor to legitimize other audiences in the mysteries of the validation process. He writes of the historical and scientific expectation that research should be primarily communicated to the scientific peer group (p. 181). It is this 'invisible college', he argues, that scrutinizes and legitimizes research knowledge, and that perpetuates conventional views of what constitutes an appropriate research text. As Becher (1989) suggests, the pursuit of truth and knowledge is no puritanical affair. Rather, it is often characterized by power struggles and by defence of personal academic ambition. Traditions of thought, and traditions of academic conventions may be defended for reasons other than the sensible, rational or common sensical. To suggest, therefore, that the academic award giving audience be not the prime audience for teacher action research and that the conventional research report be not the only legitimate text type, is to risk entering into this traditional minefield, despite the logic of the argument.

> To write research studies for audiences other than for the invisible college might seem, from a professional point of view, self-evidently a good thing to do, but it should be realised that to attempt to do so is to enter long-standing and fiercely defended positions in the history and philosophy of science. (Walker, 1985, p. 181)

A non-written staff development, or INSET, presentation for example, could be one of the most effective 'texts' for bringing the school-based action into action research. Vicki's work on the professional development day was an 'enactive text', to borrow from Jerome Bruner, and included the use of 'iconic' forms of representation such as photographs and statistical charts and graphs drawn from the traditional research text. Such a text had much practical validity for the localized, if limited, audience which it served. It constituted a form of research reporting that was more valid at a practical level than Vicki's assessed research reports proved to be.

Alternative research texts require alternative validation processes. Reading a teacher's written research report may be the easiest and most convenient option for the academy, yet it may be a less than adequate validating procedure for accessing meanings and action beyond the text and for promoting and valuing the action in the action research. Validating norms, expectations and procedures may not match professional school improvement purposes. In this, the academy which fosters action research may still be at odds with itself, straddling uncomfortably the traditional research culture of academia and the action oriented world of the school; clinging onto the tradition of the written research text as a monolithic communication device; socialising teacher action researchers into the academic culture rather than looking towards the culture and practical world of the school to value and validate, alternative texts for alternative audiences.

If research is systematic enquiry made public, action research is systematic enquiry made public and practical. The tension inherent in creating texts that are public and action oriented for potentially competing and contradictory audiences is difficult to ignore.

We should, perhaps, ask whether the texts which the academy legitimizes are the kind that liberate the teacher action researcher to try to change her corner of the world in the best way she knows how. And we should admire

Vicki for finding practical textual solutions to this question. She cared enough about the people of her research to ensure that her work became practical, useable, relevant for them. No traditional research text was going to stand in the way of that; no unread essay, dissertation or over-burdened staff meeting. What people could not find time to read, what would not be compressed to the last five minutes, could be spoken, discussed, debated, transformed, made live. If we took away alternative textual ways through Vicki's action research we would take away the means by which her research was transformed into action research.

Chapter 10

Valuing Action

By its nature, definition and purpose, action research is oriented towards change, towards doing something useful with the knowledge gained through the research process. 'The action research paradigm is about actors trying to improve the phenomena of their surroundings' (Bassey, 1990b).

There is a long tradition supporting the concept of action oriented approaches to research. In this tradition, small groups and communities across the globe have sought, in various ways, to change their circumstances and lives. Knowledge and understanding generated by the enquiry process have been the foundation of action (for example, Elliott, 1981; Kemmis and McTaggart, 1981 and 1988; Winter, 1989; Dadds, 1986b; Oja and Smulyan, 1989; Hopkins, 1985; Hustler *et al.*, 1986; Nixon, 1981; Webb, 1990).

Elliott (1981) claimed that the validity of the theories which action research generates lies 'not so much on scientific tests of truth, as on their usefulness in helping people to act more intelligently and skilfully' (p. 1). He also suggested that since action research 'aims to feed practical judgment in concrete situations', validity of the theories which it generates can only lie within consequent action. The quality of argument, theorizing, understanding from the research is important in as much as it helps to shape action. Thus, the research links between data and action are as pertinent as the links between data and theory. This is not to deny the important relationship between data and theory. Rather, it is to suggest that the latter, in itself, holds little validity in action oriented research. Good arguments that gather dust may be less attractive than incomplete arguments that oil the wheels of purposeful action.

As we seek to value the action in action research, we must look further than end outcomes alone, for the journey from data into action may be far from simple or monolithic in its nature. It is certainly not always a singular line, as the action research spirals (Kemmis and MacTaggart, 1988; Elliott, 1981) in their 'iconic simplicity' (McTaggart and Singh, 1987) suggest. For example, data and action were inseparable in Vicki's blue-book method, as data gathering generated changes in consciousness and actions of field participants. Here, there was no tidy separation of data gathering from outcomes; no lengthy process of analysis and interpretation preceding change. New behaviours were stimulated by the research process rather than by some final, tangible research theory. As Vicki raised questions, colleagues' gender awarenesses became raised. This, in turn, changed thought and behaviour. And the personal reverberations from the seemingly incidental moments may have been as long-lasting and significant as the changes which emerged from the more formalized theories and events.

Also, action is not a value-neutral phenomenon, as we well know. So inherent in Elliott's claim that validity of theory lies in its capacity for helping the practitioner to act more intelligently and skilfully, lies a claim to the moral imperative. We have to ask whether any old action counts as a valid outcome in action research. The answer, clearly, is that it does not. This leads inexorably into the contradictions and dilemmas of value pluralism with which we have to grapple. It causes us to examine and debate the values we hold and that help to shape our judgments about the worthwhileness of actions in the worlds in which we live. An action research study which enabled a teacher to act more intelligently and skilfully in the daily use of inappropriate worksheets in the infant classroom, for example, would challenge the values of any early years educator committed to active learning. An action-research study leading to more 'effective' ways of exercising authoritarian teacher centred control over pupils would cause concern to educators who believed that schooling should foster independence, initiative, self-responsibility and a critical respect of authority. An action research study leading to more effective implementation of a Christian oriented curriculum in a multiethnic inter-city school would tax the values system of educators committed to child-oriented principles and ethnic respect. And improvement of a curriculum which was totally lacking in global and Third World perspectives in a society of plenty may be considered unacceptable. At the point of validation, values become explicit in the process of judging the worthwhileness of practical action.

There will forever be different and competing views about curriculum and what constitutes 'good practice'. People may not agree about whether infant children should be accorded the right to learn and express themselves through play and activity rather than sitting at worksheets; about whether children should be encouraged to learn self-responsibility, self-discipline and self-dependence rather than be led to believe in, and rely on, the uncontested knowledge of the adult; whether all children have the right to see their beliefs and traditions reflected in the life and culture of the school rather than learning within the ethnic framework of the dominant cultural group; whether rich societies have responsibilities for the starving and dispossessed. But on these issues, we cannot be 'neutral' (Zeichner, 1993, p. 201) in the validation process, especially where we fear that action research may be promoting a 'greater intentionality and power (which) . . . may help to . . . solidify and justify practices that are harmful to students' (p. 200).

In an education system in Britain which has become, and is still becoming, increasingly centralized, the questions and foci of the teacher research agenda are still of great concern, because values and practice are no longer the democratic matters they once were. The informed professional views of teachers are at risk and many are now working with a central curriculum which offends their beliefs about 'good practice' (Dadds, 1992a and 1993b). This curriculum is being reinforced — and enforced — through compulsory state inspection. Whatever the merits, or otherwise, of the central framework, the explication of values in the curriculum must still be a professional matter of concern for all educators. A plural debate is more urgent if democracy and diversity are to be sustained. Every small-scale action research study has a role to play, for the researcher's values may be at odds with the prevailing political values shaping the centralised curriculum. The research provides an opportunity to explicate alternative values through the questions the researcher raises. It also provides an opportunity to explore the relationship between those espoused values and the attendant practices in the classroom and school (McNiff, 1992, Whitehead, 1989); to challenge one's rhetoric, as well as testing one's values against the centralist agenda.

At Springfield, we saw some of the negative effects of central initiatives as a well respected insider development was arrested in the face of outsider imposition. There are similar stories to tell in which the development of democratizing internal educational practices have been threatened or disrupted by outsider directives (Dadds, 1994c and 1995). On the other hand, the outsider agenda may be helpful. We also saw Vicki skilfully planning to capitalize on the local authority agenda in order to make advances with the equal opportunities policy at Springfield and in her new post. The outsider agenda was congruent with the values and beliefs which Vicki held and she planned to use it to stimulate and enhance her research cause.

Thus, for the action researcher the question is not simply about how practice can be improved, but also whether the practice is worth improving; whether it is educationally worthwhile. Unless the ideological basis of the research focus be questioned and made explicit, therefore, action research may simply become a strategy for implementing, more effectively, and unreflectively, an uncritiqued agenda, as others have pointed out (for example, Elliott, 1991; Walker, 1994; Tripp, 1988).

Lather (1986) uses the term 'catalytic validity' (p. 272) to refer to the action oriented nature of newer forms of post-positivist research. These forms of research, she suggests, should be oriented towards cognitive emancipation in the course of social change and improvement. Catalytic validity, thus, 'represents the degree to which the research process reorients, focuses and energizes participants towards knowing reality in order to transform it' (*ibid.*). In Lather's view, too, not any old action will do. She suggests that the values-base from which catalytic validity may be judged lies in a commitment to improved social justice and to 'the struggle for a more equitable world' (*ibid.*). Zeichner (1993), likewise, nails his values to the church door. 'I am . . . committed to the joining of action research with the larger issue of building more humane and compassionate societies' (p. 203).

It takes little effort to borrow from Lather and Zeichner to give to educational action research, remembering in the process our prime commitment to improving learning opportunities for children. And we will not solve overnight, if ever, the problems and disagreements we will have in defining what constitutes 'a more equitable world', a 'humane and compassionate society' or worthwhile learning. Pluralistic cultures, including schools, will, perhaps, be forever ridden with unresolvable differences of values and definition. Improved worksheets may be better than not-improved worksheets even though many will consider them to be eminently inferior to play. But if worksheet-focussed teacher research failed to strike at the heart of under-standing the learning needs and rights of young children, the academy would inevitably face a contradiction between the teacher researcher's development and considerations for children.

Values are inherent in the research epistemology. As such, they must come 'under pressure' (Clarke *et al.*, 1993, p. 491) during the many processes of the research. This is no simple matter where the teacher researcher's basic ideological assumptions are at odds with those of the academy's examiner. These conflicts provide opportunities for debate and growth; for validation discourses which explore and try to connect perspectives and beliefs rather than separate and harshly judge.

The academy holds a powerful position over the teacher action-researcher in these ideological matters in the same way that central government control-ling systems do. The academy has powerful control over what legitimately counts as ideologically sound research and, by implication, ideologically sound practice. An enlighted academy will be in continual reflective mode, examin-ing the values assumptions embedded in its validating norms and procedures, submitting its practices to the same reflective critique which it will expect of teacher researchers. Here there is an opportunity for validation processes to strive towards the humanity, compassion and critique which action research itself is seeking to foster. Without this, any appeal to values analysis will be unsymmetrical if teachers' practices are rigorously subjected to critique and judgment whilst the other parts of the system remain unexamined.

We can think of the methodology, too, as a form of action. What ever the values base, the teacher researcher has responsibilities for the consequences of practical action where theory or method lead to changes for the communities of the school. This may not be so for non-action oriented researchers. Theirs may be the luxury of publishing and letting others be damned. But this can never be so for teacher action researchers. In their multiple roles as teachers, researchers and agents of change, the multiple ethical responsibilities are inex-tricably linked. What one does, and what one is, as an action researcher feeds into the heart of being the teacher and the school colleague. They cannot be separated. The actions of the researcher are the actions of the teacher and the actions of the colleague. As teaching is a moral act (Elliott, 1991), so too is teacher action research.

Action research has often been criticized for the quality of its theorizing (Nias, 1988). This may be a valid criticism in many cases. Yet there is a danger in privileging thought over action, for what is of greater significance than the quality of theorizing in improving the world of schooling is the quality of the action that emanates within, and from, the research.

As we seek to value the action in Vicki's case, we can consider these interrelated issues of the moral basis of research question, research process and research outcomes. In this, we could list again the many practical outcomes from each of the projects, but that would be to repeat what has already been summarized in the case story. And we must beware, in doing this analysis, of equating practical validity with practical outcomes. For example, Vicki's sec-ond project on the special educational needs of two of her pupils did not lead to the staff development outcomes to which she has initially aspired. Vicki considered it unwise to force her intended practical outcomes on an unreceptive school colleague. This decision to withhold dissemination of her study in the school was borne of a greater consideration for the well-being of her relationship with her colleague. Vicki made a professional prediction about the possible impact of dissemination, based on the best institutional and interpersonal knowledge she had at the time. The decision became a course of action in itself, a conscious choice, a deliberate, morally based professional judgment and an act of professional, practical wisdom. Clearly, therefore, this does not detract from the practical validity of the work at the institutional level. To act and be damned may not be a helpful nor professionally responsible principle for any teacher action researcher. Look before you leap may be a more appropriate guiding principle and one which matches more accurately the driving force behind the practical wisdom which Vicki employed.

Despite this conscious withholding of institutional action there were many other practical outcomes from the three projects which, in their motivations and their effect, served personal as well as altruistic purposes. All three projects were driven by Vicki's personal motivation to know, and understand, her situation more fully. And this personal motivation was matched by a desire to serve the community of the school, the pupils and colleagues, in some concurrent way. The humanities research was 'a chance to add to her own learning, and a chance to utilize that learning in the development of her professional tasks as Humanities Coordinator in the school'. Tracking the life of the research into the policy document and its long-term usage showed that these practical intentions had been achieved and surpassed. The second research project was also rooted in personal and altruistic origins designed to manage Vicki's sense of professional inadequacy at 'The realization that (her) knowledge and experience in dealing with handicapped children was very limited'. Classroom outcomes were infused with ethical and practical value. There was improved professional skill, 'Being more aware helped in the way I taught and handled the children', for example; and positive attitude changes, as Vicki's initial fear and apprehension turned to greater empathy and respect for the children. The quest to improve equality of educational opportunities in the third research study was likewise personally and altruistically motivated. Vicki's sense of self in the research focus was matched by her strong sense of the gendered community. The practical value of this third study was complex and multifaceted. In its various stages it touched the gendered consciousness of teachers, children, parents and academic readers.

But in pursuit of greater social justice in the gender research, the practical outcomes were not always comfortable and painless. There was concomitant personal uncertainty and threat; interpersonal disagreements; moments of social turbulence in the staff group, in the inferred marital and domestic effects and in the Barn Dance confrontations. The moral paradox of ideologically oriented change was evident. In the quest for an improved gendered world, the 'just war', was being fought. Existing gendered assumptions and daily practices came under scrutiny. The personal experience of challenge and change for those concerned was not always a comfortable matter.

We know that the personal process of change can be accompanied by feelings of guilt, anger, hostility , anxiety, depression and grief (Marris, 1974; Kanfer and Goldstein, 1980; Fullan, 1982; Dadds, 1990) as well as feelings of interest, excitement and achievement. In this, the ethical dilemmas of managing change through action research are evident, for the teacher researcher holds the emotional life of others in trust. There can be no guarantee that this will be smooth and harmonious, for herself and for those who the action affects. And if the struggle for the just cause in action research is not to be a perpetually painful moral paradox, regard and support may need to be given to these several and different felt experiences of personal change in the process (Dadds, 1993a and 1995). They need not be left to chance.

Humour was, as we saw, a valuable strategy for confronting difference and easing the demands of change. And it arose almost subliminally from the institutional sub-conscious. The introduction of the NOBBO board translated that humour into conscious and deliberate management. Also, there was evidence of interpersonal support for the gendered self-questioning that took place during the professional development day and an awareness that this collegial caring was an important contributing factor to the positive staff climate and ethos. These may have been natural human forces at work rather than planned and systematic management strategies. Whatever the case, Vicki's role as change agent in these processes was central. Consequently there were many and varied demands on Vicki's reflective skills which went beyond the need for reflection upon data. For the teacher researcher, the demands for reflection upon outcomes and upon possible consequences of action may be a far greater taxation on his or her professional skills than any demands that detached theorising may require.

The search for ethical consonance between research vision and research method is thus a challenge for all teacher action researchers. To be ethically consistent, a commitment to interpersonal care, regard and respect in the search for the just and humane world must drive the research question and inform the whole nature of the methodology. Vicki's ethical being was challenged on several occasions along the way and the decisions she took had consequences for children and adults. The actions and practices of her methodology were, thus, as important to people as the more formally recognized research outcomes. Vicki regarded children's and colleagues' feelings more highly than she valued her data. Human interest and well being, thus, informed methodology and its many integral actions.

It is of little moral use to argue for a more humane world through action research if a 'relational ethic' (Noddings, 1994) is absent from the many interactive processes of the research. But this is neither a simple nor problem-free challenge for the teacher researcher. This thorny and demanding ethical responsibility that falls on the teacher action researcher's shoulders arises from her close attachment to the people and circumstances of the research project. It may prove impossible — objectionable even — to separate off the feelings and responsibilities she has as a teacher towards pupils and colleagues, from the feelings she has as a teacher-researcher towards them. As we have said before, the researcher role is fused with the teacher role and, as such, carries all the attendant emotions, commitments and responsibilities of the teacher. The two selves of teacher and researcher are not different. They reside within the one, same person. Thus, to improve, or to damage, the institution as a researcher is to improve or damage it also as the teacher. In this, insider researchers share a common experience with insider evaluators for they have to live with the practical consequences of their own research action. Simons (1985) pointed out that 'Unlike the external evaluator who is not a club member bound by its rules and who is only a temporary intruder on a one-off mission, the internal evaluator is a permanent resident' (p. 3). The teacher action researcher is in a vulnerable ethical position. Data gathering and sharing can change people's consciousness, perceptions, attitudes and practices. These are complex processes to generate and manage, for it is not always clear, as Simon's points out, where they will lead. 'The information (the internal evaluator) proposes to gather will upset the existing distribution of institutional knowledge', she wrote 'and will remain within the school as a political resource of unpredictable consequence. Any mistakes made, any hostilities generated will have to be healed or lived with within the community' (p. 3).

Whilst Vicki could no more accurately predict the human consequences of her actions than anyone can, she brought a natural caring ethic to the judgments and choices she made. This caring ethic gave rise to ethical forethought and this was her gentle weapon against the potential ravages of unpredictable consequences.

'In every human encounter, there arises the possibility of a caring occasion' (Noddings, 1994, p. 176). Vicki showed this to be so for the many interpersonal processes of her action research. Practical impact of Vicki's research meant practical impact on people. Granted, some of the worthwhile practical outcomes were almost a feature of happy accident, rather than conscious design and considered judgment, such as the jesting over the blue book and the discourses between pupil and teacher by the computer. But other worthwhile practical outcomes evolved from careful thought and sound consideration of the needs of children and the institution in general.

Implicitly, therefore, we see a close link between the practical validity or worthwhileness of the research, and the quality and skills of Vicki's practical judgment. Had she judged moments badly, the practical validity of her work might have been negatively affected. For example, had she tried to impose the special needs study on an unwilling and unreceptive colleague, damage might have been done. Had she succumbed to the invitation to report her gender study at the tail end of that staff meeting, the research might never have seen the institutional light of day that it did and might never have attained the practical validity that it attained. Had she forced her questions upon her special needs children, distress may have been a consequence.

This suggests that Vicki's action research had no intrinsic practical validity. Its practical worthwhileness was only as good as the climate into which it seeded, and only as good as Vicki's judgment as she sowed her seeds. In judging practical validity, therefore, we are also judging the wisdom and actions of the teacher action researcher as an agent of change in the school context. The research has no objective, autonomous existence outside the people who create it. It is not a disembodied, disconnected artefact. It lives in, and through, human behaviours, thoughts, actions.

The relationship between data, theory and action in teacher action research is, thus, more complex than one might at first suppose. Theory from data alone will not automatically tell the teacher action researcher how to act, or how to apply and implement her research. However internally valid the research epistemology may be, it may not adequately account for the extraneous circumstances in the research environment that can make or break effective application. As we have seen, some of these extraneous features of theory may be personal and autobiographical in origin. But the institution, too, will have a biography, a history and ecology of its own that the wise teacher action researcher, as change agent, will try to account for as she seeks to link data to action. Such demands on institutional and interpersonal skill and wisdom are not necessarily required of the traditional, external researcher. But they are certainly central to the role of the insider teacher action researcher who, as action and change agent is, inevitably, also a moral agent. As such, teacher action research is morally and socially demanding. Action demands a personal and professional rigour that might pale the hardiest of traditional researchers. These ethical demands can be neither taken for granted, nor gainsaid. If the teacher action researcher judges implementation of action badly, the people she works most closely with and, probably, loves (Nias, 1989) might bear the negative consequences. There is not the benefit of geographical, psychological or interpersonal distance in the research situation to walk away or to close one's eyes, mind and conscience to these consequences.

In addition to developing substantive theories from research, therefore, the action researcher also needs some understanding of the nature of change. Without some working and workable personal theory of change, application of research into classroom or institutional practice may be a hazardous affair. Applying research thus requires as much professional reflection and judgment as does substantive theorizing.

Springfield may have been fortunate in having a teacher action researcher who was driven by a personal 'fire' and who had 'strong ideas put gently'. These were important forces that turned research into worthwhile action research. Similarly, Vicki was fortunate in working with a group of colleagues with open and interested minds and attitudes. Into this openness, her passions and theories could be planted and ideas could be translated into worthwhile action for children. The catalysis between the research, the researcher and the institution was, thus, more crucial in generating high practical value than either the link between data and theory or between data, theory and text. For practical, or action, validity to be optimized, therefore, teacher action researchers need the skills, maturity and wisdom to judge people, place, time and circumstances. The ability to shape theory and insight from data is only one part of their work, for they need to know how, when, and with whom, those theories and insights can be used to improve their corner of the world.

All of this further complicates Elliott's view (1981) that the validity of action research theories rests not so much in scientific tests for truth but rather in their ability to inform skilful and intelligent practice. In similar vein, Frank

Smith (1982) suggested that 'If you want to test whether something is part of your theory of the world, you have to put the theory into action' (p. 38). Yet practical theory can have no autonomous nature, purpose and quality of its own, independent of the theory user; it has no objective meaning and existence. On the contrary, interpretations of practical theory into action will be subjectivist. They will be rooted in the mind, heart and behaviours of the researcher and those in the research context.

In summary then we can see that practical validity centres around the frailties or triumphs of human action, not simply around the rigours, logic or construction of autonomous theory. Also practical validity or worthwhileness of the processes and outcomes from teacher action research cannot be divorced from consideration of ethical, or moral, validity of the work. They are inextricably bound. Not any old action will do when we seek to research and improve the world of schooling for children no more than any old research question will do to motivate the study. And not any old insensitive methodologies will do if the means of the action research are to be ethically consistent with the ends. Caring, sensitivity, regard, social justice and the search for a more compassionate world bind together research vision, research method and research outcome in good insider action research. They unite to make a total caring methodology. The good action researcher tries to make these qualities and values manifest in the many practices of her enquiry; in the questions she raises, the practices of her data gathering, the practical improvements she fosters as a result of the enquiry. As a researcher, she tries in the best way she can, as an imperfect human being, to be the living embodiment of the values which drive her research. Children and colleagues are not seen as the objects of research, nor even the subjects as in other traditions. In Vicki's kind of action research, children and colleagues are the outright beneficiaries. When the practical chips are down, human needs and interests are privileged over the pure pursuit of knowledge. There is opportunity for the more humane and compassionate society to be made manifest in the daily, lived experiences of the research methodology.

Chapter 11

Valuing Development

Since Stenhouse (1975) started teacher enquiry along the professional developmental path in Britain, the language of teacher action research has also been the language of teacher development. A generation of teacher educators in institutions of higher education have helped to develop that tradition in various award-bearing contexts (Nias, 1988). They have seen the potential value of teacher self-study through action research for teacher development. They have seized the developmental paradigm for their own work in helping and supporting teachers.

Valuing development through action research is, thus, important, even though we have to recognize its integral nature with practice, knowledge and curriculum. Stenhouse taught us to think of curriculum as a lived, growing and human entity — learning in motion. As the teacher researcher's knowledge and understanding grow through the enquiry process so, too, does her understanding of her curriculum. When she applies her new learning to her practice, the changes constitute curriculum development. Her development, her research and her practice become bound to each other. As we saw in the case study, there was much evidence of these integral moments of development. Research, learning and curriculum development could not always be separated into their constituent parts during the processes of Vicki's enquiry; for example, in dealing with a fit or discovering gender bias by the computer. This was also the case at staff and institutional level as teacher enquiry informed staff debate, staff self-analysis, staff analysis of curricular provision and practices in the humanities and in the gendered curriculum.

Since Stenhouse's contribution there has been accruing interest in seeking ways to build bridges between individual teacher development and school development (Dadds, 1986a; Holly, P.J., 1984 and 1991; Holly and Southworth, 1989; Hopkins, 1989; Lomax, 1986; Whitehead, 1989). To this end, action research became a distinct and identifiable school improvement methodology during the eighties in several institutions of higher education. The key qualities of enquiry, reflection, ownership of the research agenda which characterized individual teacher research were retained within the school improvement approach. The prime purposes of 'first person' teacher action research (Kemmis, 1989) were maintained. Teacher action research remained localised, focussed upon the developmental needs of teachers and individual schools, even though outcomes often proved to be of wider interest and benefit.

To apply a set of validity criteria that have evolved from other styles of research, in other contexts, and for other purposes is, thus, to detract from the possibility of evolving the most appropriate criteria which also honour the school and individual teacher developmental purposes. This means recognizing value in the research of teachers such as Vicki by virtue of its contribution to professional learning and growth. It also means recognizing the worthwhileness of the work as it contributes to school or institutional development, especially as many teachers feel a natural professional obligation to contribute their learning to developmental resources of their schools.

Many well evidenced claims have been made for the developmental potential of teacher action research and I did not really need Vicki's case story to convince me of the validity of Stenhouse's theory. For example, there has been a growing body of evidence in the Classroom Action Research Network publications (CARN Bulletins: Cambridge Institute of Education) and in other published work (for example Hustler *et al.*, 1986; Webb, 1990; Nixon, 1981; Oja, 1989; Mc Niff, 1993; Walker, 1993) that have laid testimony to the professional development which action research has offered the practitioner. These accounts have validated my own experience of working with teacher action researchers for several years, reassuring me of the developmental nature of action research.

Development is 'a transformational process' (McNiff, 1993, p. 1) and Vicki's case has helped to illuminate some of its complexities that I had not previously examined nor understood. Vicki has helped me to understand a little more fully what research-based professional development looks like in its many variations and, also, what it feels like at the level of personal experience. Also, Vicki has helped to illuminate the contextualized nature of professional development within the shifting ecology of the school culture and within the motivation and power of personal, historical and autobiographical agenda. The case story has served to demonstrate that professional development does not take place in a vacuum. Its contextual and cultural settings may have a profound influence on the direction it takes and the ultimate practical purposes it will service. Further, Vicki has demonstrated that the many aspects of development are holistically related, each affecting the other. We cannot talk of personal development separately from school developments. We cannot talk of personal development separately from the professional. Nor can we clearly separate out the cognitive from the affective nor the analytical from the ideological.

These several issues of multiple development, of personal and institutional contextualization and of holism will be considered in the rest of this chapter as we explore the developmental value of Vicki's action research.

Let us consider, first, the variety of Vicki's developmental transformations throughout her research. At a deeply personal level, we saw an apparently astonishing growth in self-confidence and self-esteem over the two years, as Vicki's contribution to staff discussions and policy decision was valued and used positively. From the tentative, uncertain and relatively withdrawn beginnings, Vicki emerged as a self-assured and psychologically safer person. We have hazarded an hypothesis about this, suggesting that transfer into the new culture of the course and the course group was a personally disempowering experience. What little confidence Vicki brought to the course may have been temporarily diminished by the way in which the course did not value well enough her existing professional and personal knowledge. But as new knowledge and new achievements developed through her own research, self-confidence grew. Not only did the vocabularies (Rorty, 1989) of the course match more closely with Vicki's, thus legitimizing her personal agenda but Vicki was developing new skill and understanding through her research. The personally focussed, self-chosen research brought Vicki's own identity into the centre of her work. In time the course culture started to confirm Vicki's sense of self-worth, of identity and, thus, of self-esteem. The changes in the nature of the course brought about changes in the teacher researcher.

Along this steady incline onto new plains of confidence and esteem, however, there were dips. In particular, there were differential and paradoxical experiences involved in her study of the handicapped pupils. There was much pride and growth at the gains she made in understanding. But this was accompanied by feelings of self-doubt and lowered self-esteem at her seeming inability to share the study institutionally. There was a different story to be told later in the case story. Here we saw the historical and developed state of the Springfield school culture confirming Vicki's sense of self and, thus, her confidence and self-esteem. The changes in the nature of the school context brought about changes in the teacher researcher's confidence and esteem. Finally, in her new post, the voice became hushed again and the development of Vicki's work went into hibernation. Her commitment remained intact, however, and did not atrophy through lack of institutional use.

Here then, we see time, circumstance and cultural context offering differential opportunities for Vicki's personal and professional voices to be developed and used. Where there was a cultural match with Vicki's work, in the course and the school, confidence and esteem were high. Where there was not, her sense of self was less well confirmed. Where the teacher researcher, thus, sees self mirrored in the values, attitudes, beliefs and discourses of her significant cultures, this may have a bearing on the extent of her professional development and the institutional life which her work will lead.

But let us not become too simplistic in assuming that development stops where the cultural context does not mirror and affirm self. This is only a partial explanation and let us be grateful that it is, because if it were not the individual would be conceptualized as little more than a passive being, with no agency. The individual would be conceptualized as a victim or beneficiary of structures over which she has no control and to which she can only respond in a structurally predetermined way. I should admit that this view of humanity is not to my theoretical, ideological, nor emotional liking. Nor, I suspect, would it be to Vicki's. Indeed, Vicki's story demands that we conceptualize free will, agency and self-determination into the structuring and developmental process. We had clear evidence that Vicki's professional knowledge, wisdom and commitment were kept alive through the medium of her research during the ups and downs she experienced on the course and in school. Vicki brought 'latent identities' (Becker and Geer, 1971) to her research, identities which were rooted in her past, in her passions and in her beliefs and which became 'manifest' (Becker and Geer, 1971) through the research in her school and on the course. But Vicki's identity did not disappear in response to negating circumstances. We saw, for example, how her gender beliefs and commitments were held in abeyance when she moved to a different school culture. This quality of her identity was sublimated, to be accessed and made manifest when time, circumstance and context changed. Agency lay dormant but not dead.

Confidence and self-belief are aspects of this essential agency. It may be that the practitioner needs to develop a belief in herself as change agent and needs confidence in her interpersonal skills and qualities before she can actively realize any institutional potential from her research.

Oja and Smulyan (1989) suggest that action research demands a high order, advanced stage of ego development in the practitioner for it to be conducted and used effectively and we saw this happening for Vicki. The qualities of sensitive, if enthusiastically driven, leadership, for example, which Vicki's course colleagues witnessed in the group work of term 4 suggest that Vicki was already emerging as a confident catalyst, or agent, of change. She rose within the group as the one with a helpful balance of drive, commitment, humour and empathy, a balance that was appropriate for stimulating and extending learning within the group. These developing personal qualities were equally important to her credibility as a change and professional development agent within the school. Her determination to share and activate her gender research in the school added fire to these personal and interpersonal qualities.

Intellect was also essential for Vicki's agency. She had also, as we saw from her reflections on the activists' charter, developed her own common sense theory of institutional change. For example, she believed that slow reform would, probably, be more effective than rapid revolution. Worthwhile change, as Fullan (1991) pointed out, takes time, though I doubt that Vicki needed to approach the change literature to work this out for herself. Her connected, lived experience was a better tutor. Without her personally constructed, good sense insights into the nature of change and her own context, it is doubtful that Vicki would have been able to apply her research to practise within the school; she may not have been an effective change agent. Her common sense theories, rooted in experience, serviced her agency.

But good sense insight alone is insufficient for managing the reality of change for self and others. Change as a subjective, personal process can be emotionally taxing at many levels (Fullan, 1991; Nias, 1987; Dadds, 1987b; Salzberger-Wittenberg et al., 1983; Smail, 1984). Even more taxing can be the challenge of accepting the turbulence and emotionality of others whilst trying to manage it for oneself. Ego maturity encompasses the growth of self which subsumes a growing awareness of, and regard for others. We spoke in the last chapter of the moral responsibility falling on the action researcher as she holds others' well being in trust during the many events of the process and we should not, therefore, underestimate the degree of personal, ego maturity required of Vicki in this. She needed to manage her own development whilst being sensitive to, and responsible for, that of others. We can infer the level of maturity which she brought to this complex challenge from the successes which others reported.

Ego maturity thus involves the 'development of more complex, differentiated and integrated understanding of self and others, away from manipulative, exploitative, self-protective attitudes towards self-respect, mutual respect and identity formation' (Oja, 1989, p. 151). It is not hard to find evidence in the case story of these matured qualities in Vicki. The multiple-perspective data, analysis, intepretation and consequent enriched understandings that we saw from all three research studies showed a tangible maturing of cognitive perspective. In addition, there was much evidence, especially in the second study, of concomitant maturing — blossoming even — of interpersonal attitude and regard for the others of her research. As Vicki's cognitive perspectives developed, so too did her attitudes and human empathies.

Oja's views on moral or ethical development of the action researcher are similarly helpful in accounting for Vicki's growth and maturity. Moral or ethical development is characterized as 'development towards principled moral judgments, away from unquestioned conformity to peer, social, and legal norms towards self-evaluated standards within a world view framework cherishing individual human rights and mutual interpersonal responsibilities' (*ibid*). Autonomous judgment is implicated and the locus of personal control resides not in external referents but in strongly internalized, inner referents. Aspects of Vicki's case clearly show this inner locus of control being shaped and operationalized. In particular, we can remember the way she felt about, and judged, the validity of her second research study. The research had, she knew, been of profound practical, professional and developmental value and she was able to set her own standards by which to judge the work. In his written feedback. Vicki's supervisor, Harry, reminded her of her summative declaration, 'I don't really care what is said about my research' and in a mid-course interview Vicki articulated this herself. She was clear about the contribution which the research had made to her learning and to her consequent work with the children. She did not need external course criteria to judge worthwhileness, for she had experienced it herself and evolved her own way of valuing the research. 'I think the process is equally as important, if not more important than the finished result', she commented. 'I got so involved in my last (research study) that when we had a supervision and we were getting pretty deep, I said to my supervisor, I don't really care what anybody thinks about my assignment, because I know what I've put into it and what I've learnt from it. I think you get to a stage where it's the learning process you go through (that's important)'. She was relying less on 'listening to the voice of others'; more on cultivating, valuing and trusting 'the inner voice' (Belenky *et al.*, 1986).

There was further evidence of Vicki's 'principled moral judgments' in both the substance and processes of her research. In the second study, she moved towards new moral perspectives that led to clearly explicated beliefs about provision for the handicapped. In the third research study, her autobiographically rooted principles provided the impetus for the research process and the motivation to pursue follow-up outcomes. This was explicit 'conviction-research', based upon principles of equity. It started from a principled basis in contrast to the study of the handicapped children which generated principled conviction in the doing of it.

Methodologies, too, demanded and received principled moral judgments as we have already discussed in the previous chapter. We can remember those ethically taxing moments, for example, when Vicki decided against probing deeper into her interviews with Darren and Caroline lest she touch potentially disturbing areas of their perceptions and experience. Likewise, we can remember how she over-gathered data on that same study to avoid the possibility of other pupils feeling excluded or rejected by the research process. Along with these examples, we could include the judgment she made not to share the study with her colleague because of the potential conflict and interpersonal disruption it may have generated. As we have previously said, these were all professional taxations on Vicki's capacity for moral and interpersonal judgment-making. They demanded ethical and interpersonal rigour which not all practitioner researchers will possess but which showed Vicki being guided by a 'framework cherishing individual human rights and mutual interpersonal responsibilities' (Oja, 1989, p. 151). When the methodological and ethical chips were down, Vicki consistently opted for actions oriented towards concern for others, rather than concern for self and the research. Also, each of her three research studies were altruistic in their focus and outcomes, even though they arose from personal interests, concerns, curiosities and passions. From the outset Vicki wanted her pupils and colleagues to benefit from the privileged professional development time she had been given for the Advanced Diploma course. 'You look at your needs and (colleagues') needs and you tackle it that way', she once explained to me as she recalled how she made decisions about her research. 'I've picked things at pretty high priority (in the school)'.

It is unnecessary and unhelpful to polarize altruism and self-interest, for here, in Vicki's work, we have seen the two qualities growing comfortably side-by-side, mutually compatible, symbiotic. Personal development, growth and actualization were related to the institutional development that was generated by the research. Vicki gained much from her research that added to her personal and professional development but her colleagues and pupils were beneficiaries in that process of personal change.

Thus, as we saw in discussing practical value, moral and ethical considerations were an integral part of research conceptualisation, research methods and processes and research outcomes. The research posed a series of moral challenges and generated a series of varied moral acts from Vicki all of which required high levels of ethical maturity.

Conceptual growth is also implicated, necessarily, in the action research process, as Oja (1989) suggests. We have seen, and said, repeatedly, that it is impossible to disembed Vicki's cognition and conceptualization from her feelings and from her personal, professional and autobiographical motivations. Principled moral and ego development touched the many parts of Vicki's being; her head, her heart, her care, her worry, her history. Cognition could

not be cut out, like the pound of flesh. And we saw how it developed organically through the many human, interactive processes of the research. In particular, conceptual growth evolved from the multiple perspective nature of
Vicki's enquiries, and from a consequent deepened understanding of the issues
that were of passionate concern to her 'self'. As her perceptions of, and attitudes towards pupils, colleagues, research methods and curriculum evolved,
so too, did her understandings.

Oja also characterizes conceptual growth as a move from cognitive sim-
plifications, 'away from thinking in terms of simple stereotypes and clichés'
(*ibid*, p. 151) towards complexity in which one sees a range of perspectives
beyond one's own, 'towards recognition of individual differences in attitudes,
interests and abilities' (*ibid*). As we have seen, the questions which were the
starting points for all three of Vicki's research studies gave rise to methodologies that drew upon and utilised others' views of the world, though Vicki's
starting points could hardly be described as either simple, stereotyped (perhaps with the exception of 'does he take sugar') nor cliché-ridden. The altruism
embedded in the personal starting points was indicative of moral conceptual
development and signified an already existing conceptual maturity. These mature starting points gave rise to further conceptual growth, leading to more
complex and more empathetic understanding of people, needs, curricular and
ideologies.

Conceptual growth can also be characterized as movement towards
'increased toleration for paradox, contradiction, and ambiguity' (*ibid*, p. 15),
qualities which Winter (1989) similarly sees as principles underpinning the
cognitive practices in action research, and which Piagetians have characterized
as 'acceptance of lack of closure' and a feature of formal operational thinking
(Dadds, 1978). These are, undeniably, cognitive features of most multiple
perspective research for this style of enquiry has the tendency to generate
more unresolvable and open-ended questions than it resolves, leaving new
areas of unknown at the researcher's feet in payment for closure on a few
others. Beyond the uncertainty which this creates, however, the action researcher needs to enter into some practical, action-oriented closure based
upon judgments made in the face of paradox and ambiguity. Such practical
closure, even though it may be pragmatic and somewhat arbitrary in time and
circumstance, 'contingent' even, (Rorty, 1989) is necessary if the researcher
is to act and to make practical decisions as a result of ambiguous, contradictory and paradoxical epistemologies. This demands strong conceptual and
emotional fibre, without which nothing would ever get done. The action
researcher cannot deliberate forever in the face of cognitive complexity.

Similarly, Elliott (1991, p. 74) points out that 'the process of analysis is
an endless one, but in action research it must be interrupted for the sake of
action'. Action researchers have to try to make practical sense of often incomplete, inconclusive and uncertain theories if they are to effect moral improvement to the world of schooling for children. They also have to behave as
though theories are absolute for a short while even though research action
steps out into a contingent and unpredictable world. Prediction from theory
is but a blunt instrument (Gleick, 1987), often overrated, and the action

researcher must try not to be too surprised or disappointed when apparently logical action plans take an unexpected turn. Who could have predicted, for example, that the strong impetus that fed into the draft gender policy would have much of the breath squeezed out of it in such a short time under the weight of Government educational reform?

Given this, it is clear that a further developmental dimension is implicated in action research which we could call agency maturity, for ego, moral and conceptual maturity in themselves are of little benefit to children if they do not manifest themselves in worthwhile practical action. Oja's ego maturity, moral/ethical development and conceptual growth, therefore, (1989) can be seen as the developmental bases of a further, higher order, development in action research which relates to application of understanding. The action researcher needs the maturity to turn knowledge, judgment and wisdom into action through her own sense of agency, for this is what improves education in some small way. This is what changes the world. And agency development requires a maturing insight and judgment about context and people. To act in the institution demands an understanding of the institution. It requires attention to, and sensitivity towards, the situation in which the research is located. It requires a commitment to improving that situation; a belief that the effort and energy which action requires, is worthwhile. It also requires courage.

Vicki's action or agency maturity was manifest in several ways. First, she came of her own accord to value the research for its practical institutional benefits. She had, for example, a keen sense of the awareness raising effect of the gender research process and the benefit of this for institutional development. She also understood the way in which her research with Darren and Caroline helped people to identify common concerns about the children in a way which had, perhaps, not previously been the case. Second, Vicki was aware of, and valued the link between the institutional awareness-raising which the gender research process fostered and the concomitant changes to gendered behaviour. The research affected professional cognition and, almost unconsciously, set new gendered norms in the school culture. A new set of values was offered which were made explicit through the research and which others adopted as yardsticks to evaluate, and modify, their own gendered behaviour. The values base of Vicki's gender research thus acted as a catalyst for others to enter into spontaneous self-enquiry and self-development. The research stimulated a spontaneous developmental combustion in the school, sparked off from Vicki at the centre. 'Whatever my research essay turns out like', Vicki asserted when she was in the midst of the research, 'I know that the actual gathering of data has affected everybody, because everybody is suddenly aware that I'm looking at gender issues. Because of that they're going to try not to do anything they feel is perhaps not quite right as far as gender is concerned. So they are more aware of it and I don't think that that can harm at all.' As well as showing how Vicki valued the practical benefit of her research, we also see here a further example of that institutional intelligence or 'situational understanding' (Elliott, 1991, p. 122) which we met earlier in the case story and which is of a similar order to the intelligence Vicki employed in making judgments about further dissemination of her work. It is one further example of Vicki's ability to read the text of the institution in many of its complexities, accounting for a range of individual differences in her colleagues, noticing and evaluating the impact of the research on attitudes, interaction, growth of ideas and practical change. It is one further example of her agency maturity.

This practical institutional maturity also entailed Vicki developing a range of personal, good sense theories-of-persons, theories which could help to explain and predict a complex range of human behaviour within a complex institutional setting. As we have already said, this advanced capacity to theorize about persons in an institutional context is necessary for the beneficial employment of teacher action research in school development processes. It draws upon the researcher's ability to construct common sense theories of mind, of feeling, of interaction and to use those to understand the complex workings of the institution. And for those theories to become practical, the researcher needs to draw upon her ability to predict behaviour and reactions in a range of institutional circumstances. In addition she also needs the ability and wisdom to speculate about the possible consequences of her own actions and their impact upon others; she needs some theory of self in relation to others.

These common sense theories of mind, behaviour, institution and self were employed by Vicki throughout the processes of the research studies, as she made those myriad decisions relating to children and colleagues which we have seen through her person-centred methodologies. These practical situational theories were also employed beyond the stages of field work in making decisions about sharing, dissemination and further practical application. Vicki showed herself, indeed, to have developed skills and knowledge of human agency (Giddens, 1982); the capability for employing regular wisdom in regular moral acts through her teaching and her research.

The challenges of the research also demanded the situational reflection-in-action which Schon (1983 and 1987) has shown us. Vicki's research processes posed a series of interactive problems which had to be solved in situ through the intelligent and sensitive application of personal and professional wisdom. The quality of Vicki's reflection in these research actions was, as such, crucial to the practical impact of the research on the institution in the short term and, probably, the longer term. They informed her agency.

Development is an elusive phenomon. Who can say that any behaviour or thought signifies development if we have no indication of its predecessors. Having spoken with conviction of Vicki's growth through the research at many levels and in many ways, one has to be tentative in the argument, for it is impossible to say whether these qualities that gave rise to the research and to the subsequent actions were ready formed, if latent, in Vicki, waiting to emerge in their fullness, or whether they were but glimmers, laying dormant like seeds of actualization, waiting for the right conditions to grow and develop into more substantial expression. If we think back to the focussed group project work in term 4 of the course, and if we remember the part Vicki played in that, and the qualities which her colleagues felt were vital to the group achievement, her leadership qualities were evident then. Thus, despite insecure course beginnings, which may, as we have said, been context-related, personal qualities of leadership, determination and commitment became manifest in the later part of the course. These qualities inspired trust, commitment and motivation in other course colleagues and were concomitantly reproduced by Vicki in her school context, making a similarly constructive contribution to professional and curriculum development. Did these qualities develop as a result of the course and the research or did they emerge from some existing, if latent, personal resources? Perhaps we will never know.

There is, of course, a sense in which it matters little whether these qualities were formed and dormant or whether they were nascent, embryonic. To the colleagues and children in the school what really mattered was that these qualities were made public and used. To myself as the course tutor too, it mattered little whether these qualities were latent or embryonic. It was, however, important that the work and the expectations of the course, in concert with the enabling culture and climate of the school, allowed these qualities to become manifest. The course and the school together created contexts and climates in which these qualities were given worth, were valued, and were employed in professionally purposeful ways. Vicki seemed to have little difficulty in taking a lead role in term 4, and the potential sense of self-worth that this fostered was reinforced by the feedback of tutor and course colleagues. The sense of self worth was, similarly, fed by the responsibilities endowed on Vicki in her school. These two professional cultures that Vicki moved in and out of, and in which her research was conceived, discussed, supported and developed, were mutually reinforcing. They provided complementary contexts in which Vicki's professional growth was almost guaranteed. The action research studies were the media through which this professional development was realized and through which curricular and institutional development became visible.

In the same way that the research raised aspects of Vicki's latent or embryonic identity to manifest level, the gender research brought latent institutional identity into the open. The staff development day continued subsequently to unlock a range of personal and professional responses that seemed ripe for development. This personal and professional 'capital' that was made explicit through the various processes and stages of Vicki's research fed curriculum and institutional development. Without this, the research would not have achieved the level of developmental validity that it did. Individual professional development became institutional development.

It would be overly simplistic to accredit developmental validity to Vicki alone, and to her endeavours and judgment, vital though they were. Vicki's endeavours were received and nurtured within an enabling school culture and managerial context. Developmental validity of the research, thus, takes on a complex hue when we try to locate its source, inspiration and agency. The research made a contribution to staff, curriculum and institutional development because of the complex catalysis between the course expectations and aspirations, the personality, commitment and endeavours of the teacher action researcher, and the particular cultural and historic moment of the school. Had Vicki been in a less enabling receiving school climate, however, her endeavours would have been no less valid. They may simply have been less effective in bringing about change, for although Vicki and her research were agents of change, other contributory forces necessary for ensuring action were, to an extent, beyond her control. Individual teacher action researchers cannot change the world that lies beyond their power and control unless that world decides that it will be so. Vicki had the will of that wider world on her side. Aspects of her research, as a consequence, found the developmental light of day on an institutional scale.

In summary, therefore, we can say that teacher action research of the kind that we have seen in Vicki's work holds extensive potential for both teacher professional development and institutional development. The nature, extent and quality of those developments will, in part, be determined by the culture of the course; by the extent to which the values, aspirations and processes promoted by the course culture are, or become, those with which the teacher can identify. But, more particularly, the culture and management of the school will have their effect. There needs to be some strong degree of match between the values and aspirations of the course and those of the school. In addition, the researcher will be a key determinant of the potential of those developments; her ego maturity, her moral and cognitive development; her sense of agency. The catalysis between the teacher researcher, the culture of the course and the culture of the school will determine the extent to which action research becomes a vehicle for school improvement.

Chapter 12

Valuing Collaboration

Individualism and self-interest are, ultimately, end games (Posch, 1994). They add little of honour, on their own, to the human condition though we may all experience them as part of our life force. Care, regard, compassion, community inoculate us from our natural inhumanity and our tendency towards selfishness and neglect of others. With human effort and determination, these benign qualities reproduce themselves, as do their violent counterparts (Miller, 1987). So ethical collaboration, predicated upon benign human means and ends, must be valued, though it be difficult to organize, complex to maintain, unpredictable in its effect; though honourable sharing and virtuous cooperation may be scorned as naivety by cynics.

The early British founders of the teacher action research movement wove a vision in which teacher action researchers would work harmoniously, collaboratively and professionally in the creation and development of practically-based educational theory (Nixon, 1981). More recently, Elliott (1991) suggested that collaborative approaches to teacher action research will rescue the profession from its inherently self-defeating, individualistic and insular 'craft culture'. In the process it will offer teachers a socially and intellectually powerful way of critiquing and resisting mechanistic, centralist views of education in Britain. Collaborative professional good sense will stem the tide of unhelpful authoritarian dogma. 'Out of the still smouldering embers of the traditional craft culture', Elliott claimed, 'the phoenix of a collaborative reflective practice arises to offer creative resistance to the hegemony of the technocrat' (p. 56).

Collaboration as a form of moral resistance features in Kemmis and McTaggart's vision (1988). They were less optimistic that action research would significantly affect macro-systems and they admitted that individuals and small groups may not be able to change the world at large. Yet through collaborative action research, people can change their own world, their own realities. This will impact on social and cultural processes and structures in a wider sphere beyond the action research group. 'Changing a whole society and culture is, on the face of it', they suggested, 'beyond the reach of individuals. In action research, groups work together to change THEIR language, THEIR modes of action, and THEIR social relationships and, thus, in their own ways, prefigure, foreshadow and provoke changes in the broader fabric of interactions which characterise our society and culture' (*ibid*, p. 17). And as Zeichner (1993) reminded us, 'You do not necessarily have to move out of the classroom to connect action research with the struggle for educational equity and justice' (p. 208). The challenge for a more equitable world, a more humane and compassionate society is on our doorstep.

One has to be hopeful, optimistic without relinquishing realism. When we consider Springfield, for example, we can see that Vicki's research stimulated collaborative processes that began to affect perceptions and attitudes beyond the staff group as well as within it though we have little data to confirm how far the collaborative reflection permeated into communities beyond. On the other hand, whilst the impact of those collaborative processes seemed strong and enduring within the school, there was little evidence that Vicki's action research created the kind, and scale, of resistance required to impede the oncoming motion of Government initiatives. When the law consigns your equal opportunities policy to the bottom of the pile, collaborative action research on a small and localized scale is unlikely to change that immediately. Hegemony rules. Nias, Southworth and Campbell (1992) have shown how 'it is much easier to call for whole school policies than to create the conditions in school for them to be realised' (p. 246). Their research reinforces what the Springfield story shows in terms of the 'inherent complexities, difficulties and fragility of the process of whole school curriculum development' (*ibid*). As if internal complexities were not enough for any school to bear, we have seen in Springfield the added demands and disadvantages of central initiatives creating their own discontinuities inside the school. Such conditions were hardly conducive for deep-seated, comprehensive and richly enduring change of the school's choosing.

Perhaps too, collaborative reflective practices are not yet sufficiently embedded in the craft culture of the teaching profession for them to offer the mass resistance of which Elliott dreamed and which might arrest the growth of unwanted centralist initiatives. On the other hand, it was heartening to see that the gender and humanities changes which Springield chose to adopt were not entirely fragile. In their localized and personalized way, they were surviving the ravages of mammoth Government directives. They lived on in the hearts, minds and practices of those whom Vicki's work had touched. 'We take the other person with us in ourselves' (McNiff, 1993, p. 64). Collaboration had, in some small way changed this small corner of the world, despite a potentially negating outside environment.

Collaboration, as we saw in chapter 8, is an epistemological necessity for the action researcher given the premise that knowledge is socially constructed. How else will the action researcher come to know the world of her research? How else will she understand the minds and hearts of those for whom she cares, those who she is driven to help? To understand social situations as a basis for changing and improving them, the researcher needs to understand the people in her research, their experiences, feelings, ideas, views of the world. She needs to understand the interpersonal, interactive and historical basis of the knowledge of which these social situations are constructed (Kemmis and McTaggart, 1988, p. 16). Her personal epistemologies are shaped and developed through others' multiple perspective data.

Further, Kemmis and McTaggart implied, decisions about change and improvement of social situations should be a collaborative matter. The action researcher cannot act unilaterally on others' behalf, cannot depend upon ego-centric perspectives and judgments. Power to construct and reconstruct social situations should reside within the participants. Change is a democractic, not individualistic, matter. 'In action research, the research process, like the educational action being studied, is regarded as socially constructed and as a matter for collective and collaborative decision making' (*ibid.*). Vicki did well to consult; to try to move forward with policy and practice on a negotiated and communal basis. Hers was the initiative. Theirs was the choice. The democratic ethic accords well with what we saw of the collaborative and collegial approaches to development through research at Springfield. Within the gender and humanities projects, Vicki acted as epistemological broker, mediating knowledge and consequent curricula recommendations through participant perspectives and involvement. Insights and practical action emerged from communal examination, debate and judgment.

Altruism need not be a one-way affair in action research. As the action researcher gives of herself to others in pursuit of school improvement, so, too, others may give of themselves to her as she pursues her research. They give their time, their thought, their insights, their experiences, despite con-straining timetables, demanding classes, impossible curricular, domestic res-ponsibilities. Without this giving, democratic methodologies would be denied the action researcher. Symbiosis is essential.

Nor was Vicki, through her constant caring ethic, confined to 'the care and empowerment of others while remaining selfless' (Belenky *et al.*, 1986, p. 46). The commitment which she gave to others' needs through her research were repaid to her many-fold. It was not, therefore, necessary to negate her own interests through the pursuit of others', for we saw how her own learn-ing and development flourished through her person oriented endeavours. There was much self-actualization through her collaborative commitments and Vicki gave her own development as serious consideration, as she did others'. The work was pursued for herself and it was pursued for children and colleagues. Thus, her research interests served her own learning agenda and they served the school community in the process. Benefits to self and community were integrated, compatible, inseparable.

The action researcher can be a beneficiary in other ways too, for collabor-ative processes can offer necessary 'support and challenge' (Dadds, 1990 and 1993a) for her development. Learning is a social experience. Insights, ideas, beliefs, attitudes evolve in the interactive cut and thrust of social intercourse. The social context has a profound influence; the company we keep is import-ant. Levels of kindness, generosity and care from the group or the critical friend can make or break the learner (Dadds, 1993a). A negating, hostile cli-mate can cause the learner to become defensive, to withdraw. Her learning suffers. An encouraging, self-affirming climate can stimulate openness and lead to continuing growth. Often, supportive groups are needed outside the researchers' school (Dadds, 1986b; Elliott, 1991) if the school culture is neither understanding of, nor predisposed towards, the nature and purpose of action research. Certainly some of Vicki's course colleagues relied on the Advanced

Diploma course group at the academy for the support, interest, challenge and collegiality that were, they felt, missing from the professional experience in their schools. These course members tended to be 'marginalized' teachers (Dadds, 1986a) who reported lack of interest in their research from their school colleagues — hostility even — and whose research necessarily followed an 'idiosyncratic' (*ibid.*) and classroom-oriented path. They researched away behind the safe, closed doors of their classrooms. They were privatized action researchers. Collaborative interest and public exposure were not for them. Some preferred it that way. Public and publicized research makes emotional demands which are not always easy to bear. Others are not always kind about the researcher's work; do not always interpret her motives benevolently; cannot celebrate her achievements generously. A harsh climate may require harsh emotional adjustments which are not entirely to the teacher's liking. She may need to become 'someone other' than the person she would like to be (Dadds, 1995) in order to cope. These disadvantaged action researchers cannot be judged negatively when constructive collaboration in the workplace is lacking. They may value collaborative approaches in principle but be denied them in practice. It may be sufficient, laudable even, that they make some small improvements to provision for each generation of children for whom they care as a result of their research. There will be many who benefit.

These problems of marginalization and cultural rift were identified by others in the early days of the British action research movement (for example, Elliott, 1991; Holly, 1986). Attempts to establish action research as a counter-culture within some schools met with misunderstanding, suspicion and hostility at various levels of the managerial hierarchy. Such responses were often effective in impeding the development of action research in the school and in consigning action researchers to a deviant sub-culture (Holly, 1991). School colleagues did not, therefore, form the supportive and challenging groups that were needed to foster teachers' learning through action research. The action-researching teacher had to look elsewhere. Solace, support and stimulus were usually found within the externally sponsored project or the award-bearing course at the academy.

Vicki, as we saw, was not working in those unfavourable and unsupportive circumstances. We saw her, for example, turn readily and successfully to colleagues, particularly to Christine, to test her ideas on methodology and dissemination. She was able to draw upon, and benefit from, Christine's knowledge of research. Christine was part of Vicki's 'collaborative resource' (Winter, 1989). Similarly, as Vicki gained research experience and expertise, she became a support and resource for others' learning. After the end of the course, for example, she told how one of her school colleagues, Tom, who had joined the next Advanced Diploma course, was already seeking her advice and support on constructing his own research project. Action research was, thus, sufficiently well institutionalized for the school group to become a source of support, challenge and critique. In addition, the learning climate in the school was, generally, helpful for Vicki's growth. Senior management offered opportunities and encouragement which confirmed Vicki's sense of self-worth.

Her colleagues' involvement in their own professional development set the learning norm. The collegial consideration, interest, humour, willingness kept Vicki buoyant in her research, kept her determined, kept her on her toes. The support may have had its hard-edge and was, most probably, accompanied by expectations that Vicki would make a valued contribution. But the support was positive and it fed Vicki's professional learning. It allowed her to develop her abilities as an agent of school change. It helped her to realize new capacities. She thus received much from her colleagues in return for much that she gave to them. Everyone benefitted from the collaboration. The action-research tradition at Springfield was constantly regenerated in this way by a succession of colleagues becoming involved in award-bearing research-based INSET and helping each other along.

Holly (1991) suggests that 'Action research within institutional development (is) becoming second nature to us now'. He infers that the evaluation movements of the last decade have nudged the culture of schools inexorably along a more reflective continuum. Asking evaluative questions of the curriculum, he infers, is now a more natural feature of the professional attitude to work and, as such, has created climates and cultures more conducive to the growth and use of action research for classroom and institutional improvement. He draws upon his own consultancy work with schools in the USA and UK. As such, his perspective is inevitably partial and cannot offer a wider analysis of the changing cultures of schools in all their complexity and differentiation. But he draws our attention to the macro-political movements that may affect the ways in which professionals work together in schools and develop their thinking about practice. Whole school self-evaluation in the past decade (Holly and Hopkins, 1988) has offered the potential for creating more collaborative, collegial and interactive staff groups. Similarly, there is evidence that developmental teacher appraisal can affect some school cultures, changing them into more reflective, open, sharing and mutually supportive ones (Bradley, 1989). Economic imperatives have also caused professionals to meet, talk and take decisions more collaboratively than ever before, for as schools have been forced to take control of their own budgets, time has been needed to discuss financial matters and the clustering of resources across schools (Morley, 1991).

Yet many have felt they are collaborating on the wrong projects in these market oriented times. Time for discussing budgets and the marketing of the school may be displacing valuable time for discussing teaching and learning. Practice seems to develop best when collaborative talk in the workplace focusses upon learning rather than extraneous matters; where 'teachers build up a shared language' (Smyth, 1991, p. 88) of practice. As we consider ethical collaboration, therefore, we need to consider educational worthwhileness. We need to ask whether it serves well the purpose of enhancing children's learning opportunities. We need, perhaps, a 'science of learning conversations' (Candy *et al.*, 1985, p. 115) to help us to understand where the collaborative professional talk leads and what ensues. We must ask whether, in the long term, collaborative cultures have the potential for allowing worthwhile action research to seed and develop, for some collaborative communities can be very effective in fostering abhorrent change. Some collaborative talk is wasted talk. Some is wicked.

When we reflect upon the value of collaboration in action research, therefore, we must recognize that not any old collaboration will do, no more than will any old epistemology or any old practice when we consider the value of knowledge and action. Wherever we choose to believe in the search for the common good, the struggle for justice and humanity, the enhancement of children's learning opportunities, we can also choose to realize these values in collaborative practices. Springfield and Vicki were fortunate. Their modes of collaboration which were manifest through the action research were benign and productive. This is not to suggest that collaboration was an entirely comfortable experience, for the case story suggests otherwise. There were challenges, disagreements, differences, heartaches and struggles to be faced along the collaborative road. Also, there may have been more subterranean discord in the school than my research accessed. This I do not know. Field participants often don the mantle of group loyalty in the face of questions from strangers, despite feelings to the contrary, for the research interview is often distorted by power relationships which threaten the ideal speech situation (Dadds, 1991). Researchers have to learn to live with these insecurities which validity and reliability impose. Yet it is clear that the Springfield modes of collaboration bore beneficent fruit. The democratic knowledge base was enriched. Vicki's learning and development flourished. Changes from the action research served the interests of professional colleagues and children. Many participated in realizing the collaboratively sought improvements.

Springfield teaches us that it makes sense to value collaboration. Cynics must take note. Vicki was fortunate in being able to draw from, feed into, and service the collaborative resource in her school. Not all action researchers are as fortunate, so let us not be discouraged from also seeing the value in the efforts of lone teacher action researchers (committed though we may be to the ideals of collaborative action research). Their efforts will improve the world in some small way where others are interested enough to listen. Government initiatives may, strangely, be helpful. Where centrally imposed change demands more whole school planning, thinking, evaluating, agreeing, we may see the continuing emergence of more collaborative school cultures — if teachers can survive the stress and ever demanding workload. Far from working against the interests of collaborative action research, this may help to provide the conditions in which reflection, critique and development emerge phoenix like, as Elliott (1991) dreamt they would. Collaborative action research may, indeed, become one of the dominant critical school improvement methodologies of the future. This could be one of the more entertaining political and educational paradoxes of our time. We wait.

Chapter 13

Final Reflections

So — after all the ponderings, evasions, moments of elation and anxiety, neglected friends and overgrown garden that make the part-time research process, one has to reflect upon the achievements and the validities of the work presented here. Although this was Vicki's story, and I have no wish to detract from its sovereignty, I am obliged to engage in some self reckoning in this first person action research; to offer some reflections on the worth-whileness of the project. I will try to do this briefly.

There is, at least, a tangible research text. Through the case story and the following discussions I have tried to construct a text that represents the processes and epistemologies of the research as well as I can. Always there are myriad other ways of telling the story in addition to the one the researcher chooses. But I hope, and believe, that the choices made in constructing this text have been adequate to preserve internal validities.

The case story has allowed the opportunity to represent the multiple perspectives embedded in the epistemology as well as finding a place for my own analytical and reflective voice. Interview transcripts were checked and cleared with field participants. Springfield colleagues cited in the text were sent their relevant parts of the case story through Jeff. He reported no dissension from my interpretations, though I realize that this may be partly due to field participants not having time to give firm textual agreement. I offered to visit the school and to discuss the text but this was difficult. Jeff had been Acting Head for over a term in the absence of Richard who had suffered a sustained illness. And the demands of the Education Reform Act were biting even harder. I decided, in the light of the pressures Jeff was describing, that pursuing such epistemological checks and balances would have been an egocentric act on my part. I accepted his validation and clearance by phone some weeks later.

Vicki was able to give these matters more attention. I left the final draft case story with her for two months and then discussed it with her over supper.

The experience of seeing herself in the case story had been a fascinating and compelling one, she told me. Never, she reported, had she had the feeling of someone 'knowing her' in the way that the case story seemed to do. She spoke of burying herself in the bedroom for long periods over the Christmas holidays to read what she saw as her biography. Also, she recognized Vicki-in-the-text as being her self, give or take the odd, over generous interpretation of her ability which she felt I had made.

Whilst receiving this confirmation of my interpretations with a good deal of relief, this was a strange moment for me, for I realized that the Vicki in the text had ceased to be the real-life Vicki. Internally valid though the case story was, Vicki-in-the-text had become a construction in my inner world. In my mind's-eye, the two appeared as Vicki spoke; I saw two different people and I felt differently towards them. I felt friendly, collegial and open towards Vicki sitting in the armchair and speaking her feelings. I felt possessive and secretive of Vicki in the case story. I had spent many a long private hour with Vicki-in-the-text, inspecting a short period of her professional history. I spent far less time with the real Vicki. The woman in the case story had much of my life devoted to the re-creation of character. The real Vicki had little of my own life and was in charge of her own character.

I still cannot explain the psychology of this adequately. I only know that there has been a mental and emotional separation of the one from the other, and I do not know whether or not time will foster a synthesis. Nor do I know in what way, if any, it matters to the epistemology of the case. It simply leaves me wondering what happens to our sense of reality when autonomous text separates itself from its origins in this way. 'There is', as Ted Hughes (1967) reminds us, 'the inner life which is the world of final reality'.

There have also been moments when, like Vicki, I have had to question the influence of 'self' on the interpretations I have offered. The multiple perspectives have provided checks and balances against any potentially rampant subjectivity. Yet I am well aware of the possible influence of my own professional commitment to action research on the epistemology of this text. This seems to me to be unavoidable. But I do not make methodological apologies for this. My interest in this project started from an existing belief in the value of action research through several previous years of working in this way. The project was designed to extend my understanding. In the process it might challenge that commitment but this was not the prime purpose. I met little in the research to undermine that commitment, even though I had to confront many of the problematics of action research through hard experience; though I saw at close quarters the taxations it placed on the energies and professionalism of the teachers.

I hope I have managed to be aware of my biases and to rely on my convictions being confirmed through others' realities rather than through any personal polemical fervour or unknown evangelical disposition. After all, I did not invent the humanities policy, nor Vicki's feelings for her handicapped pupils, nor the in-service staff development day and the gender policy. I did not invent her colleagues' validation of her work. All these existed outside my passions and convictions. Yet perception and pre-conception still decree, I realize, what we will see as we strive to look over and beyond our blinkers (Abercrombie, 1960) and it is, perhaps, no accident that the story told here is of relatively good news, despite the initial three cases being selected at random from the group of twenty-seven. Too many are pleased to tell bad news stories of the teaching profession in these destructive and derisive political times. There are more than enough pens busy disproving the case for valuing teachers' work through negating constructions of the education profession. So

I know I was driven partly by a desire to resurrect what has been so shamefully trampled underfoot. Objectivity is, thus, a fantasy.

This epistemological experience has also had its integral developmental and practical dimensions for me. Much of that has, I suspect, sped by ephemerally in the process of the research, never to be made fully visible in the textual product. But some conscious developmental and practical outcomes have been evident.

One of my initial purposes was to experience action research from the inside as a basis for supporting it from the outside for others' professional development. In my work as tutor to award-bearing action research-based courses, my felt credibility was, as I said at the outset, becoming an increasing problem. I was not teaching about action research from a basis of recent, relevant and lived first-hand personal knowledge. I was not living inside an action research project, nor had I done so since doing a classroom-based dissertation many years before.

The experience of doing this action research has worked to the effect I hoped it would in terms of shaping and transforming my second-hand knowledge into first-hand knowledge. This knowledge is no longer grounded in an unsatisfactory way in the literature and in the vicarious sharing of the teachers' action research experiences. It is also grounded more substantially in the demands, delights and heartaches of real experience with all its attendant challenges. Throughout the work I have come to see myself less as a disengaged academic separate from the teachers, and more as a fellow traveller; less a supposed authoritative leader, more a collaborator. My own experience of fitting no-budget research into an already full professional life helped me to identify with the teacher researchers' experiences more closely than I had ever done before.

This developed knowledge means that I am now more likely to teach from what I know personally, rather than from vicarious experience of others' personal knowledge; more likely to teach from the firmer inside rather than from the more tenuous outside. My understanding and my teaching are, thus, more closely connected to my own inner resources. I would like, ideally, to be recognized as one who has been there, rather than one who persuades the teachers that it is a good place for them to go. There is a greater confidence in personal knowledge as a resource for theorizing, teaching and acting.

Also, in studying and writing Vicki's case in close detail, I had a persisting sense of looking through a mirror, for many of my own feelings, thoughts, problems and aspirations as a researcher and learner were reflected in the case. Writing served to intensify identification with the teachers as I saw my own life reflected in theirs through the medium of Vicki's story.

My inner knowledge resource from which I draw for my teaching is, thus, radically changed and developed as a result. And if it has changed my professional knowledge and understanding, I believe it has also changed my attitude towards the teachers' experiences. For example, I feel more spontaneously sympathetic to their worries about meeting submission deadlines whilst wanting to purse quality in their research. I understand, more than I used to, the catalogue of methodological and circumstantial problems they share in persuading me to be empathetic to their needs. As a result, I am more likely to encourage them to accept these difficulties as characteristic features of small-scale action research rather than as indicators of the personal failure and inadequacy they often see them to be. I feel better resourced to understand when they complain about the encroachment of their research into their personal and family lives; more understanding of the practical and emotional challenges they meet in school; more genuinely engaged when they share their latest reflections about data, interpretations and implications. And when they persist in their work through all the attendant pressures, discouragements and elations to finish what they set out to do, driven by their care and concern to improve their work for children, I feel more pride for them, for I know better than before the shape and size of the personal investment that success has demanded.

There have been other practical spin-offs beyond the attitudinal and interactive. My teaching materials and methodologies have been influenced by the teachers' stories. For example, I understand more clearly that an award-bearing course on applied research or action research needs to attend to the management of change as seriously as it attends to research methods. The management of change IS part of action research methodology. Teachers may need as much support from the course and course tutors in this as in other parts of the research process. Also, my research has caused me to pause for further thought on the issue of alternative research texts especially in the light of the emotional struggles the individual may have in adopting a more public research stance. In addition, the data on alternative forms of presentation raised awareness of the extra technical challenges involved in presenting the outcomes of research in modes other than the written (Dadds, 1994b). It is unlikely for example, that the teacher action researcher will be as skilled in the use and presentation of audio-visual media as in the use and presentation of the written word, problematic though many find the latter. I understand this more clearly than before and realize that there are implications for the kinds of support and resources which the providing institution needs to offer. Also, I continued with a colleague to explore the practice and principles of the non-written enactive mode of research presentation; seeking alternative ways of validation through tutorial observation and discussion. Cost has to be borne in mind if off-site validation in the teacher's work place is preferred. In our current hard monetary context, the most appropriate procedures may prove to be too expensive. One has to juggle with these dilemmas and considerations in seeking an operational way of validating the problematics of action within an INSET and research paradigm devoted to educational change and development.

Of the implications beyond my own work, there is less to say, for the project was 'idiosyncratic' in its conceptualization, not institutional. But as time wore on, one or two colleagues began expressing some interest. This was partly as a result of my inability to keep my latest obsessions to myself. My excitements roused interest in a way which I found alarming and, to an extent, threatening, as these genuinely supportive colleagues discussed the evolving work a little more publicly than was comfortable for me. Whilst my vanity welcomed the interest and positive regard, the public exposure so early on in the project gave me intellectual palpitations. My ideas, methodology, insights, hypotheses felt precarious to say the least in those early stages. Self-confidence was, thus, concomitantly fragile. In addition, I was in the misty and uncertain methodological stages of the case study, stages which are characteristic of naturalistic research. Despite 'knowing' with my head that these uncertainties were to be expected, the fragile self-confidence prevailed. I made a conscious effort to retrieve the initial idiosyncratic underground position I had adopted. I wanted to retreat from exposure and possible peer judgment because my own psychological and emotional climate was not ripe for wider sharing.

This discomfort was to prove productive, however, for it caused me to review the rather naive assumptions I had made about the relative ease of linking individual teacher action research to institutional development. I had not previously thought seriously about the personal experience of public exposure within the institution. Only first-hand experience caused me to learn that this might be an exacting challenge for some of the teachers doing action research. One of the consequences of this personal learning was an increased regard for those teachers who offered their action research for school development purposes. I was suddenly made more aware of the demands on 'self' that this link might make and I rapidly learnt to respect the teachers' courage in contrast to my relative inhibition. In retrospect, I realize this marked something of an analytical turning point for it caused me to focus more on institutional dissemination of action research as a personal, emotional experience rather than simply a cognitive and mechanistic one. I also began to see that this involved much more complex learning for many teachers than I had previously thought. In time these insights provided the foundation for further reflection, research and writing (Dadds, 1994b, 1994c and 1995). Personal experience was thus a compelling resource in reflection, theorizing and the development of the research.

I have been presented with several opportunities since these insecure beginnings for sharing and debating this work in a range of contexts with colleagues interested in similar issues. The current state of the discourse about validity within the action research community suggests that the debate will continue for some time and I hope that I may play a part.

And what of the future? As the journey continues, a number of signposts reveal themselves. One points in the direction of teacher action research and academic validation practices. The principles and practices of democratic validation still continue to exercise the mind and here there are many questions still to consider. For example, how can multiple perspectives be incorporated into validation processes through spoken and written texts? Should they be? How do we deal with differences and disagreements? Who is the final arbiter? How do we balance the need for guidelines and criteria or qualities with the need for flexibility, creativity, innovation? Academic validation practices vary across institutions. Some work with liberal and creative procedures in a spirit of enquiry and innovation. Others are more constrained by the traditional ways of the academy. Some validation practices are interactive, critical, mutual, humane. Others are fixed, authoritarian, unexamined. Some practices seek to support, encourage, bestow, confirm. Others are alien, condescending, even harmful. We could learn much from revealing and analyzing academic practices together; challenge and support each other as we confront the assumptions underlying these practices; value our own development as we seek improved ways forward.

A second signpost points towards a thicket marked 'Paradigms of Thought'. Here there is much worry and fretting to be endured. There are different tongues to be understood here as we encounter bureaucratic and centralized forms of thought about teacher education in our current political context. These forms of thought and language are vastly different from those employed in making sense of Vicki's learning and development and they are achieving political supremacy in the analysis, description and monitoring of teacher professional competencies. There is anguish to rehearse in this thicket and a fear that the sound and power of these tongues will annul all others. For example, in a Government document I was shown recently on the 'Standards Methodology' (which 'is a theory of the assessment of occupational competence' and which is being piloted in teacher education through a Government-sponsored research and development project) the totality of human endeavour, commitment, and talent in the workplace is described in the algebraic equation, $S = C(PC \times RS)$. I have yet to figure out where the passion and life blood for educational improvement can be represented in these human mathematics and how such equations can help us to understand the complexity of professional growth.

This disjunction of vocabularies is of little consequence whilstever the paradigms of thought can exist productively side-by-side fulfilling, perhaps, different purposes. But power has a predictable way of spreading itself and there is already evidence of these bureaucratic discourses colonizing teacher education practices in alarming ways. Will our qualitative alternatives and developmental purposes remain safe in this alien mathematical territory?

So, the third and most compelling signpost points back towards the land of story, for it is over this horizon that further understanding is to be found. Whilst algebraic and bureaucratic paradigms of thought can only simplify, story can complicate. Whilst mathematics of human behaviour can only count, reduce and alienate, story can enrich, enliven, connect. What mathematics diminishes, story nurtures. What algebra renders invisible, story values. As mathematics standardizes, so story makes unique.

If we are to look deeper into this human mystery that drives benign professional endeavour, then we need rich descriptions and accounts not numbers and equations. We need detail, substance, expansion, explanation. There has to be scope for speaking of head and heart; for acknowledging past and present; for representing pain and pleasure, individuality and community. We need a language that allows us to view professionalism as part of the complexity of life; a vocabulary that speaks of our work as part of our being; a discourse that treasures human caring in the challenging task of education. This is the place for a language which renders strange and special that which is taken-for-ordinary; a canvass and colour to paint the many varied validities of committed professional growth that pass by unnoticed on the treadmill of life. We need an infinitely flexible research medium. We cannot dispense with story. We also need to treasure the generosity of teachers like Vicki as they narrate their lives and work in the cause of our professional development and their own.

There is a continuing need, then, to encourage and support storying in these algebraic times, for it is through these tales that we may come to understand why teachers like Vicki continue their voluntary development against almost impossible odds; why they give even more when already over-burdened by too much; why their history gains supremacy when the present is denying their value; why they learn to cultivate an inner voice when deafened by decree and direction from outside. It is through these stories that we may come to know a little more of the human secret which drives passionate en-quiry and binds it benevolently to school development. If we can understand a little more of this we may understand a little more of the life force which causes committed teachers to strive greedily and robustly for their generation of children. And if we can manage to apply this endless understanding to our practices as wisely as Vicki did then we, too, may be able to improve our small patch of the world in some small way through action research — and sleep a little more peacefully in our erstwhile troubled Protestant beds.

Chapter 14

Summary

Vicki, teacher action researcher is the heroine of the case story at the heart of the book. This chapter summarizes her story and the research within which it was situated. It can be read independently of chapters 1–13.

The first chapter of the book acts as an introduction to my own action research which gave rise to Vicki's story. As a teacher educator, I decided to undertake an action research project into my own work. I decided that I needed to study, and understand better, the learning of the teachers on the Advanced Diploma courses I tutored. The teachers undertook action research studies for assessment on the course and these studies became the main focus of my research. From the several cases researched, Vicki's story emerged as the one which I considered in greatest detail. I studied aspects of her learning through action research; some of the personal and professional changes she experienced; the impact of her research on her professional practices and those of school colleagues. Through the voices and perspectives of Vicki and several of her colleagues, I sought explanations for the emergence, growth and impact of her action research.

Understanding Vicki as a person was essential if the impact of her research and learning on her school was to be understood. Analysis of a range of data suggested that Vicki's hopes, motivations, biography, personal and interpersonal qualities were significant. They were related to her effectiveness as action researcher and agent of change in her school. They had a bearing on her choice of action research topics as well as on her effectiveness in changing practice in her school through them.

Chapter 2 reconstructs the images of Vicki from my own perceptions and from interviews with others who knew Vicki on the Advanced Diploma course. I also made use of small amounts of data from interviews with Sandra, a school colleague and two of Vicki's pupils. Data were also drawn from Vicki's writing and from her comments on the draft of the case story.

Perspectives on Vicki differed. All recognized her intellectual capabilities but different people seemed to bring out different parts of her persona. As tutor I remembered her as self-effacing; lacking in confidence; unsure. I was vexed that aspects of the course may have contributed to Vicki's apparent low self-esteem by failing to draw upon past experience as a resource for learning. Others saw Vicki differently.

In chapter 3 we see evidence of some of the changes which Vicki experienced as a result of her research and advanced studies.

Her Headteacher and a senior school colleague spoke of Vicki's increased participation in debate and decision-making in school. They spoke of her improved analytical and reflective approach to work. They gave testimony to her improved confidence in collegial interactions; her improved effectiveness in this.

Vicki was also aware of her development; of her greater willingness to risk and experiment with her practice. She spoke of a shift in focus from teaching to learning; from curriculum to children and of the way in which she now notices, observes, analyzes more than previously. She knew that she was becoming a more confident professional in school. She believed that this confidence had evolved from enhanced knowledge as well as from the experiences she had in the cut and thrust of group debates on the course. Knowledge and skill were being transferred to the school connext and were being used to good effect.

I drew upon my tutorial memories of Vicki on the course and easily found confirming evidence to support these other perspectives. I remembered the emergence of an energy and passion in Vicki in the second year of the course that surprised me. These qualities arose phoenix-like in the context of Vicki's small research study group on gender in education. This work led to Vicki's main area of research. This research and the attendant passions were to be seen later driving school development processes.

A course colleague recounted his experiences of Vicki's energy, passion and group leadership qualities during this period.

The following three chapters look at Vicki's action research projects. These chapters explore the origins and motivations of the research. They consider the links between the research and practical classroom and school developments. They also look at the personal experience of learning which the research signified for Vicki. Analysis was based upon Vicki's written research texts, upon interviews with Vicki, some of her school colleagues and a small number of children.

Chapter 4 looks at the first piece of research which grew from Vicki's felt need to develop herself as humanities coordinator, 'to work on (her) own knowledge within the subject'. But she also wanted to move beyond her own perspectives in developing policy. So she investigated colleagues' perspectives and practices too.

Her common sense knowledge and skill as small-scale researcher is examined. We see some of the methodological difficulties she had to face and overcome. We also see her reflecting critically upon her research process and raising some difficult methodological questions. In particular, she kept revisiting the problem of personal bias in insider, self-study research. This was a theme which recurred in her later research and which also became a key feature of the whole story.

Vicki spoke of the practical difficulties faced in data gathering and here we had authentic glimpses into some of the hazards and pitfalls of small-scale insider teacher research methodology. There is a key point here about the fortitude of teachers working without a supportive budget and within severe time constraints. Working against many odds, their methodological decisions are often expedient despite thoughtfulness. The interpersonal demands of insider research also emerges here as a key theme.

Those who read and examined Vicki's first research report praised its self-critique. There were a few problems with unexplicated meanings and with the logic of Vicki's thinking as she transformed tentative conclusions into certain action steps. But there was also respect for the scope and style of the research as well as for its effectiveness in informing practical developments.

Outcomes from this were varied. There is an account of Vicki's learning as researcher and also as Humanities Coordinator. There were changes to her own classroom practices and changes to the humanities policy. A year after the research there was also evidence that colleagues were using the agreed policy document to inform their teaching. The Headteacher's testimony confirmed the impact which Vicki's research had on policy and practice.

At this point, the Head spoke of some of the features of the school context and collegial group that enabled Vicki's research to become practically effective. These insights are developed progressively throughout this chapter as explanations are sought for the successes of Vicki's research.

Chapter 5 considers Vicki's second research project which was classroom, rather than institutionally, based. Vicki was to receive two children with special needs into her class. She recognized her own limited knowledge for responding to this as well as her own rather primitive stereotypes — she describes herself as of the 'does he take sugar' era. Her willingness and drive to learn are apparent so she decided to undertake two multiperspective child studies during the year.

We see her learning from some of the experiences of her first study in designing and conducting her research. She was not complacent, however, and there were problems and mistakes. Once more, her accounts show life as it really is for part-time teacher action researchers as they try to integrate data gathering into teaching and school processes — no easy task.

This second research project presented several new ethical challenges and we see Vicki balancing the needs of her research against the needs of the children. She used here knowledge, judgment and wisdom as teacher to help her. Consequently, the needs of the children were always at the forefront of her decisions. We see the inseparable nature of her two roles, the one of the teacher professional informing the other of the teacher researcher.

In constructing method and research text she moved into higher risk and experimental mode. There was concern for audience appeal and audience engagement as she decided that an accompanying tape slide sequence might enhance the interest and content of a written research text. Visual data might help the reader to empathize more closely with the struggles which these two children face daily. This decision proved to be demanding, time consuming and vexing but Vicki persevered. The midnight oil had to be burned as she integrated the periodic 'pings' into the audiotape to synchronize with the slide changes.

Despite Vicki's original intentions, she decided in the end not to share the finished research report (and the tape/slide sequence) with the teacher colleague who was to receive the two children next. Vicki had her reasons for this, reasons which showed her 'situational understanding'; which showed her making ethical judgments in the interest of sustaining professional relationships and which also showed the need for self-protection in a potentially critical public domain. Vicki's decision raised awareness of the personal difficulties which teacher action researchers have to face in sharing and disseminating their work within their school. There are levels of exposure which are not comfortable. I admit to having underestimated this concern in encouraging the teachers on the course to make good practical school use of the research. Vicki expressed guilt at not making greater whole school use of her research. She felt this guilt in the face of the pressure which she perceived the course exerted in this direction.

Vicki's second research report (and tape/slide sequence) was full of the language of feeling. It was not simply a cerebral, cognitively-based work. Vicki's emotions had been engaged in many ways and at many points of the research. It was the first written evidence of her passionate enquiry, of the engagement of many dimensions of her being with the research process. There was clear evidence of attitudinal development; of a greater understanding of children with special needs; of an enhanced regard for them and the difficulties which life presents; of the emotional struggles she encountered in learning how to deal with their difficulties. It had been a significant learning experience for her, one which influenced her feelings, ideas and practice.

Chapter 6 deals with Vicki's third, and longest, research study. In this, her previous public diffidence was displaced by confident openness and public determination. Here was her most passionate, committed research study to date — gender issues in education. This was the one most deeply rooted in her own gendered history; in her beneficial family experiences; in less beneficial professional and adult domestic experiences. As a woman, she suffered discrimination and the suffering was to stay with her. It was also to fuel the drive which propelled this research. She was concerned to change the gendered world of schooling in some small way. Her action research was a vehicle for such change.

From the start, this was an institutional enquiry based upon Vicki's personal interest. With the agreement of colleagues Vicki studied a range of gender practices and procedures in the school as well as researching issues through the literature and other research.

Her data gathering procedures were eclectic and, in part, original. She negotiated the use of a 'blue book' in which she recorded a range of school data as and when the opportunity arose. This became the source of much banter amongst colleagues when they saw it appearing. It raised colleagues' awareness of their gender behaviour, language and practices. Children, too, came to recognize Vicki's research intentions when the blue book appeared. It affected their gender awareness and discussions too. On occasions they turned the tables on Vicki, critiquing her unconscious lapses into stereotyped language. Nor were parents and governors exempt from the gendered spirit of Vicki's enquiry, even though some tended to be more entrenched in their perspectives than teacher colleagues appeared to be.

Vicki profoundly questioned the effect of her own biases and subjectivities on the research. Even though she tried to identify the source and influence of her own passions, convictions and pre-conceptions, she never felt that she had fully understood, nor overcome, them. Her written text betrayed her feelings and beliefs in places, as her gender bias and philosophy predominated over more detached analysis. Whilst Vicki continued to see this as a problem, I did not. There were multiple perspectives employed upon which Vicki drew successfully as she tried to analyze, and account for, unfair and unhelpful curriculum practices. These complemented her own declared beliefs and passions. The declaration of 'self' added to the honest and authentic qualities of the research.

Such was the collegial interest and involvement in the research that Vicki was asked to present her findings at a staff meeting. Time and the meeting however, ran on, leaving Vicki with a brief morsel at the end. True to her convictions, she refused to have something so important squeezed into such an inadequate space. Her refusal led to a request to present, and run, a school-based staff development event.

The story tells how Vicki approached this new leadership challenge. It tells of her thoughts, her feelings, the preparation, the activities, the supportive yet challenging response of the full staff group, the difficult and complex discourses which the day raised, the differences and disagreements, the sensitive areas of personal and professional terrain which colleagues were invited to tread. It tells of the qualities and skills which the work demanded of Vicki and of how dissemination of research lays new interpersonal challenges at the feet of the researcher. The ability to respond to these challenges cannot be taken for granted.

The story tells of the staff development event as a new kind of 'text' which Vicki had to create. This became a transformation of the previous, and conventional, written research text. It was better suited to the school development purposes which Vicki and her colleague were pursuing. It was transformed from a written mode to an 'enactive' one (to borrow from Bruner).

The story also elaborates on the features and qualities of the context which enabled this to be an effective event leading to the formulation of draft school policy. Vicki's personal qualities were, again, implicated: her ability to express 'strong ideas gently', to listen, to show regard; her willingness to share her work; her strong drive to improve things as a consequence of her endeavours; her passionate commitment to the topic, 'like a fire'. Help, encouragement and support from the Deputy contributed to Vicki's success as an agent of change. In her, Vicki had a good critical friend at a critical time of development. Interest and support from the staff and Head were also vital. There was also a positive professional development climate in the school. Almost all the teachers were engaged in further study at some level so professional learning was the norm, rather than the exception. In addition, the Head and Deputy were developing management structures and processes which encouraged targeted staff development. Whole school sharing and dissemination of individual teacher's learning was also fostered through formal processes. Individual professional capital was being drawn upon for institutional investment.

There were immediate practical outcomes from the staff development event. A working group was established which drew up a draft staff policy document. This work articulated principles and suggested practice. There was a review of the gendered nature of book resources; a reappraisal of the role models being offered to children in the history curriculum, in geography, science and in drama; reflections upon gender attitudes, beliefs and stereotypes; new awareness of gender behaviour and language patterns.

There is evidence in the story that Vicki's research changed the gendered culture of the school in numerous ways. But were the changes short lived? Eighteen months later, we heard of the heavy foot of the Education Reform Act arresting the growth of this collectively desired development. The policy document lay buried, metaphorically, under the weight of other policies required by Government reform. Vicki had also left the school to take a new post. Despite these two potential difficulties, the Deputy Head gave evidence of gender changes which continued as a result of Vicki's initiative and research. The Deputy had taken the baton from Vicki, trying to keep the issues and policy formulation alive. Other colleagues claimed that their gender consciousness and practices in school were irreversibly changed. Examples were given which impacted on children's experiences. There were still battles and differences within the school as well as with groups outside. Some pressures and influences outside school were contradicting the teachers' endeavours. Nor did the teachers' professional rhetoric always match unconscious and historically rooted personal behaviours. It was a difficult area to tackle. But there had been significant movement against this background of adversities. The changes had evolved an autonomous life, existing now independently of Vicki, their instigator.

Vicki left the changes from the research behind her. Her new school context was not conducive to a similar kind of development. Now we saw Vicki displaying her situational understanding in her new post and deciding this was neither the time nor the place, yet, to light her gender 'fire'. Whilst it was still glowing at Springfield it would not be appropriate to even lay the coals in her new school. She did, however, practise her beliefs in her own classroom.

The chapter summarizes Vicki's learning and development from her third research enterprise. In particular, witness is given to the confident and powerful professional who emerged from previously diffident positions. There was also an analysis and resumé of the institutional factors affecting the changes surrounding Vicki's research. The Deputy made special reference to Vicki's personal qualities once more as well as to her advantageous low position in the management hierarchy, for the staff were more open to 'one of us' fostering change at a time when too many of 'them' were imposing directives from above.

Time and change do not stand still. Nor are they always predictable. We hear of changing circumstances in Vicki's new school, a year from her appointment. School development plans had to be written. Equal opportunities had to be a compulsory element. 'A chink had appeared in the previous institutional wall Vicki felt she had seen in her new post. And she seemed fit to seize the day once more.'

The chapter and the case story end with brief accounts of the state of 'gender development' at Springfield and at the school to which Vicki moved. It is now some five years after the dissemination of her research. History keeps taking new turns.

Chapter 7 makes the transition from the case story into a theoretical analysis. Validity is the key analytical concept. The reasons are given for taking the analysis in this direction and the concept of 'worthwhileness' is chosen. Related issues of power, development and standards in action research are considered. The concept of 'democratic validation' is proposed and discussed, both at the level of principle and the more difficult practical application in the academy.

Five broad areas are offered which could be used for exploring validity in teacher action research. They refer to research knowledge, text, action, development and collaboration. These frame the discussion in the following chapters 8–12.

The reader is also invited to set consideration about action research validity against the broader notion of 'valuing' in order to bring notions of regard, respect and care into the debate.

The first broad area of validity to be explored is knowledge. Here, consideration is given to the nature of the knowledge which Vicki created through her research; to its originality in relation to the context; to its multi-perspective nature; to the contribution it makes to others' thinking. The personal biases of the researcher are seen as complex and problematic within the research methodology, as is the nature of knowledge itself. The tensions and dilemmas that exist between doubt and certainty are acknowledged.

There is a prominent epistemological relationship witnessed in the case story between the affective and the cognitive; between Vicki's emotions and ideas; between feelings and the development of thought. Far from worrying about this, it is argued that this relationship should be acknowledged and, perhaps, celebrated in action research. A case is made for the validity of passionate scholarship. The integration of emotion in the research process can be seen as enrichment rather than weakness.

In an ideal world the teacher action researcher could employ a range of checks and balance for enhancing epistemological validity. Meeting course submission deadlines does not provide an ideal world for teachers with little time for their research. This is acknowledged and discussed.

Whilst the knowledge generated by the research was, in several ways, provisional and problematic, Vicki's beliefs were not. Commitment to her three chosen areas of enquiry endured beyond the life of the projects. When the research texts were finished and laid aside, the commitment and action continued, for Vicki and for others.

Text validity is discussed in chapter 9. Here is an argument about whether research is worth its name if it is not made public. This leads to discussion about audiences and purposes for research texts. Different forms of presentation may be needed for different purposes. A traditional academic research text may not be the most appropriate or effective for school development purposes. Who in the staffroom is going to read a 12,000 word dissertation?

On the other hand, the enactive text of a staff development event may make the research more accessible for the school audience, even though it presents difficulties for the examiners. An enactive text may also be more effective in terms of putting the action into action research.

Much action from action research does not make an appearance in the texts which teachers submit for their awards. The logic of creating different texts in this way raises some unresolved questions. Who is the prime audience for the action research? Is it the school or is it the examiner in the academy? Should the hard-pressed teacher action researcher be required to create different texts for different audiences and purposes? How can the academy validate action which is not represented in written texts? Should the academy be rethinking its approach to validation in order to respond more seriously to the action focus of action research?

Leaving these unresolved questions in the air, chapter 10 moves on to consider practical or action validity.

'. . . the quality of argumentation and theorizing within the research is important only in as much as it helps to get things done . . .'. This chapter argues that good arguments which gather dust may be less helpful than shaky arguments which 'oil the wheels of purposeful action'. The purpose of action research is to improve education for children. The links between knowledge and practical outcomes therefore demands consideration by the academic awarding institution.

The moral basis of the action has to be considered seriously in the validation process. Not any old action will do. Action should honour improvement. Improvement implies values, and has an ethical orientation. The problematics of defining and agreeing values are recognised. The ethical responsibility of the teacher action researcher is acknowledged here as her responsibility for 'right' and 'just' processes and outcomes of action research is discussed. Such responsibility is seen to add to the skills and qualities demanded of the teacher action researcher. The case story is revisited for evidence of the ethical choices Vicki had to make at various points in her research and in the management of subsequent practical developments. Insider teacher research is seen to present unique ethical challenges which need managing wisely.

There is a further issue about practical validity which involves the management of change. If research is to be translated into action, then the researcher takes on an additional role as change agent. She is not only a producer of knowledge. She has to know how to work well with others if research findings are to be disseminated and used as a basis for practical decisions.

So, knowledge and theory from research are insufficient for school improvement. Theories need wise, skilful and caring people to implement them if they are to impact on practice. And those people need situational knowledge, understanding, wisdom and judgment if research is to become action research. Action research is seen as a potential total caring methodology.

Now we move on to developmental validity in chapter 11. This is closely allied to practical validity. The arguments here are rooted principally in Lawrence Stenhouse's work on the links between research, teacher development and curriculum development.

The prime purpose of the in-service provision which drives this action research is teacher professional development. To this end, it would be illogical not to validate action research in terms of its contribution to the teacher researcher's professional development. The case story is revisited for evidence of the many ways in which Vicki's professional development was witnessed. The development of the school is also considered.

Chapter 12 visits a well-rehearsed action research argument about the principle of collaboration. A collaborative, group approach is not always possible for award seeking teacher action researchers, even though it may be desirable. Many are bound to work in isolation in their schools. Their plight is acknowledged.

Yet there is convincing evidence in Vicki's story that collaboration, in its various forms, has many advantages. It benefits Vicki's research, her learning, her colleagues and children. The caring ethic which Vicki brings to others through her research is reciprocated in numbers of ways. Many are implicated in the caring and collaboration. Many benefit.

All these discussions imply a need to seek criteria standards and validation processes that are more congruent with the nature and purposes of teacher action research than are traditional practices in the academy.

Finally, chapter 13 engages in reflections upon the study, as a whole from my own perspective as an action researcher in the academy. There is a need for self-accounting; for a summary of the perceived value of my action research endeavours; for some final declaration of my interests, biases, motives. Also, there are new questions to confront from the fruits of the case story, new uncertainties to entertain, new mysteries to explore. The search for understanding through case story seems to have taken on a life of its own. A few beckoning fingers point to a few possible new destinations along this eternal route. The journey goes on.

Bibliography

ABERCROMBIE, M.L.J. (1960) *The Anatomy of Judgement*, London, Penguin.

ADELMAN, C., JENKINS, D. and KEMMIS, S. (1980) 'Re-thinking case study' in SIMONS, H. (Ed) *Towards a Science of the Singular*, Norwich, CARE.

ALLENDER, J.S. (1986) 'Educational research: A personal and social process', *Review of Educational Research*, **56**, 2, Summer.

ALTRICHTER, H. (1986) 'Visiting two worlds: An excursion into the methodological jungle including an optional evening's entertainment at the Rigour Club', *Cambridge Journal of Education*, **16**, 2.

ALTRICHTER, H., KEMMIS, S., McTAGGART, R. and ZUBER-SKERRITT, O. (1990) 'Defining, confining or refining action research', in ZUBER-SKERRITT, O. (Ed) *Action Research for Change and Development*, Brisbane, CALT.

ALTRICHTER, H. and POSCH, P. (1989) 'Does the grounded theory approach offer a guiding paradigm for teacher research?', *Cambridge Journal of Education*, **19**, 1.

BALL, S.J. (1990) *Foucault and Education: Disciplines and Knowledge*, London, Routledge.

BALL, S.J. and GOODSON, I.F. (1985) *Teachers Lives and Careers*, Lewes, Falmer Press.

BANDLER, R. and GRINDER, J. (1979) *Frogs into Princes: Neurolinguistic Programming*, Boston, MA, Real People Press.

BASSEY, M. (1986) 'Does action research require sophisticated research methods?' in HUSTLER, D. *et al.* (Eds) *Action Research in Classrooms and Schools*, London, Allen and Unwin.

BASSEY, M. (1990a) 'On the nature of research in education, part one', *Research Intelligence*, Summer.

BASSEY, M. (1990b) 'On the nature of research in education, part two', *Research Intelligence*, Autumn.

BAUME, D. and BAUME, C. (1986) 'Learner, know thyself: Self-assessment and self-determined assessment in education', *New Era*, **67**, 3.

BECHER, T. (1989) '*Academic Tribes and Territories*', Milton Keynes, Open University Press.

BECKER, H.S. and GEER, B. (1971) 'Latent culture: A note on the theory of latent social roles' in COSIN, B.R. *et al.* (Eds) *School and Society: A Sociological Reader*, London, R.K.P.

BELENKY, M.F., CLINCHY, B.M., GOLDBERGER, N.R. and TARULE, J.M. (1986) *Women's Ways of Knowing*, New York, Basic Books.

BERK, L. (1980) 'Education in lives: Biographic narrative in the study of educational outcomes', *The Journal of Curriculum Theorising*, **2**, 2, Summer.

BIOTT, C. (1988) 'The quest for authentic description: Shared reflections on teaching enquiry-based courses', in NIAS, J. and GROUNDWATER-SMITH, S. (Eds) *The Enquiring Teacher*, Lewes, Falmer Press.

BLAKE, D. (1986) 'Action research and INSET', *British Journal of In-Service Education*, **12**, 2.

BRADBURY, M. (1987) *Mensonge*, London, Arena.

BRADLEY, H. *et al.* (1989) *Evaluation of the School Teacher Appraisal Pilot Study*, Cambridge, Cambridge Institute of Education.

BRUNER, J. (1986) *Actual Minds, Possible Worlds*, Cambridge, Massachusetts, Harvard University Press.

BYATT, A.S. (1991) *Possession: A Romance*, London, Vintage.

CANDY, P., HARRI-AUGSTEIN, S. and THOMAS, L. (1985) 'Reflection and the self-organised learner: A model of learning conversations', in BOUD, D., KEOGH, R. and WALKER, D. (Eds) *Reflection: Turning Experience into Learning*, New York, Kogan Page.

CARR W. (1987) 'Critical theory and educational studies', *Journal of Philosophy of Education*, **21**, 2.

CARR W. (1988) 'Whatever happened to action research?', paper given at the annual meeting of the British Educational Research Association, Norwich, September.

CARR W. and KEMMIS, S. (1986) *Becoming Critical?*', Lewes, Falmer Press.

CHISHOLM, L. (1990) 'Action research: Some methodological and political considerations', *British Educational Research Journal*, **16**, 3.

CHRISTIE, F. (1985a) 'Language and context: The development of meaning', paper given to the fourteenth New Zealand Conference on Reading, Nelson, New Zealand, 28–31 August.

CHRISTIE, F. (1985b) *Language Education*, Geelong, Deakin University Press.

CHRISTIE, F. (1987) 'Genres as choice' in REID, I. (Ed) *The Place of Genre in Learning*, Geelong, Deakin University Press.

CLANDININ, D.J. and CONNELLY, F.M. (1990) 'Narrative, experience and the study of curriculum', *Cambridge Journal of Education*, **20**, 3.

CLARKE, J. *et al.* (1993) 'Ways of presenting and critiquing action research reports', *Educational Action Research*, **1**, 3.

COCHRAN-SMITH, M. and LYTLE, S. (1990) 'Research on teaching and teacher research: The issues that divide', *Educational Research*, March.

COLLIN, A. (1981) 'Mid-career change: Reflections upon the development of a piece of research and the part it has played in the development of the researcher', in REASON, P. and ROWAN, J. (Eds) *Human Inquiry*, Batley, John Wiley and Sons Ltd.

CONNELLY, F.M. and BEN-PERETZ, M. (1980) 'Teachers roles in the using and doing of research and curriculum development', *Journal of Curriculum Studies*, **12**, 2, pp. 95–107.

CRANDALL, D. (1987) 'External support for school improvement: Constructs from the International School Improvement Project' in HOPKINS, D. (Ed) *Improving the Quality of Schooling*, London, Falmer Press.

CRAWFORD, J., KIPPAX, S., ONYX, J., GAULT, U. and BENTON, P. (1992) *Emotion and Gender*, London, Sage.

DADDS, M. (1978) 'Group work in the classroom', unpublished MEd. dissertation, University of Nottingham.

DADDS, M. (1986a) 'The School, the teacher researcher and the in-service tutor', '*Classroom Action Research Network*', 7, pp. 96–107.

DADDS, M. (1986b) 'Group support for self-directed teacher reseach', *Forum*, 28, 2, pp. 43–6.

DADDS, M. (1987a) 'Helping the individual to help the school', paper presented to the BERA Conference on 'Teachers' Professional Learning', University of Lancaster, July.

DADDS, M. (1987b) 'Learning and teacher appraisal: The heart of the matter' in SOUTHWORTH, G.S. (Ed) *Readings in Primary Management*, London, Falmer Press.

DADDS, M. (1990) 'Teacher appraisal for teacher development', *Cambridge Institute Newsletter*, January.

DADDS, M. (1991) *Validity and Award Bearing Teacher Action Research*, Norwich, University of East Anglia Press.

DADDS, M. (1992a) 'Monty Python and the three wise men', *Cambridge Journal of Education*, 22, 2, pp. 129–41.

DADDS, M. (1992b) 'Thinking and being in teacher action research' in ELLIOTT, J. (Ed) *Reconstructing Teacher Education*, Lewes, Falmer Press.

DADDS, M. (1993a) 'The feeling of thinking in professional self-study', *Educational Action Research*, 1, 2.

DADDS, M. (1993b) 'The changing face of topic work in the primary curriculum', *The Curriculum Journal*, 4, 2.

DADDS, M. (1994a) Working towards the child's curriculum: Professionalism in adversity, paper presented to West Glamorgan headteachers' Conference, Newport, February.

DADDS, M. (1994b) 'Can INSET essays change the world for children?', in CONSTABLE, H. (Ed) *Change in Classroom Practice*, Lewes, Falmer Press.

DADDS, M. (1994c) 'Bridging the gap: Using the school-based project to link award-bearing INSET to school development', in BRADLEY, H. *et al.* (Eds) *Making INSET effective*, London, Fulton.

DADDS, M. (1995) 'Becoming someone other: Teacher professional development and the management of change through INSET', in SOUTHWORTH, G. (Ed) *Readings in Primary School Development*, London, Falmer Press.

DAY, C. (1985) 'Professional learning and researcher intervention: An action research perspective', *British Educational Research Journal*, 11, 2.

DAY, C. (1986) 'Sharing practice through consultancy: Individual and whole school staff development in the primary school', *C.A.R.N. Bulletin*, No.7, Cambridge Institute of Education.

EBBUTT, D. (1982) 'Educational action research: Some general concerns and specific quibbles', Cambridge Institute of Education, mimeo.

EISNER, E. (1982) 'Conceiving and representing: Implications for evaluation', in SMITH, N.L. (Ed) *Communication Strategies in Evaluation*, Beverley Hills, CA, Sage.

EISNER, E.W. (1990) 'The meaning of alternative paradigms for practice', in GUBA, E.G. (Ed) *The Paradigm Dialog*, Newbury Park, Sage.

ELLIOTT, J. (1980) 'Validating case studies', paper presented at the annual meeting of the British Educational Research Association, Cardiff.

ELLIOTT, J. (1981) *Action Research: A Framework for Self-evaluation in Schools*, Cambridge, Cambridge Institute of Education.

ELLIOTT, J. (1991) *Action Research for Educational Change*, Milton Keynes, Open University Press.

ELLIOTT, J. (1993) 'Frameworks and priorities for research in education: towards a strategy for the ESRC', *Research Intelligence*, BERA Newsletter, Spring.

ELLIOTT, J. (1994) 'Research on teachers' knowledge and action research', *Education Action Research*, **2**, 1.

EVANS, J. (1983) 'Criterion of validity in social research' in HAMMERSLEY, M. (Ed) *The Ethnography of Schooling*, Humberside, Nafferton.

EVANS, M. and HOPKINS, D. (1988) 'School climate and the psychological state of the individual teacher as factors affecting the utilisation of educational ideas following an in-service course', *British Educational Research Journal*, **14**, 3.

FEHER, F. (1987) 'The status of post-modernity', *Philosophy and Social Criticism*, **13**, 2.

FEKETE, J. (1988) *Life after Postmodernism*, Basingstoke, Macmillan.

FORD, J. (1975) *Paradigms and fairytales: An introduction to the Science of Meanings, 1 and 2*, London, RKP.

FOX, G.T. and STRONACH, J. (1985) 'Making research and evaluation educational by bracketing', *Cambridge Journal of Education*, **16**, 2.

FULLAN, M. (1982) *The Meaning of Educational Change*, Ontario, OISE Press.

FULLAN, M. (1991) *The New Meaning of Educational Change*, London, Cassell.

GADAMER, H.G. (1981) *Truth and Method*, London Sheed and Ward.

GIDDENS, A. (1982) *Profiles and Critiques in Social Theory*, London, Macmillan.

GLASER, B.G. and STRAUSS, A.L. (1967) *The Development of Grounded Theory*, New York, Aldine.

GLEICK, J. (1987) *Chaos: Making a New Science*, London, Cardinal.

GOODSON, I.F. (1991) 'Sponsoring the teacher's voice: Teachers' lives and teacher development', *Cambridge Journal of Education*, **21**, 1.

GORE, J. (1989a) 'The struggle for pedagogies: Critical and feminist discourses as regimes of truth', paper presented at the eleventh conference on Curriculum Theory and Classroom Practice, Ohio, October.

GORE, J. (1989b) 'Discourses of teacher empowerment: A post-structural critique', paper presented at the annual meeting of the Australian Association for Research in Education, Adelaide, November-December.

GROUNDWATER-SMITH, S. (1988) 'Credential bearing enquiry-based courses: Paradox or new challenge?', in NIAS, J. and GROUNDWATER-SMITH, S. (Eds) *The Enquiring Teacher*, London, Falmer Press.

GRUMET, M.R. (1980) 'Autobiography and reconceptualisation', *Journal of Curriculum Theorising*, **2**, 2, Summer.

GRUMET, M.R. (1990) 'Voice: The search for a feminist rhetoric for educational studies', *Cambridge Journal of Education*, **20**, 3.

GRUNDY, S. (1987) *'Curriculum: Product or Praxis'*, Lewes, Falmer Press.

GUBA, E.G. (1990) *The Paradigm Dialog*, Beverley Hills, CA, Sage.

GUBA, E.G. and LINCOLN, Y.S. (1985) *Naturalistic Inquiry*, Beverley Hills, CA, Sage.

HABERMAS, J. (1984) *The Theory of Communicative Action Volume One: Reason and Rationalisation of Society*, London, Heinemann.

HACKMAN, S. (1987) *Responding to Writing*, London, NATE.

HAMILTON, D. *et al.* (1977) *Beyond the Numbers Game*, London, Macmillan.

HARRIS, I.B. (1983) 'Forms of discourse and their possibilities for guiding practice: Towards an effective rhetoric', *Journal of Curriculum Studies*, **15**, 1, pp. 27–42.

HARRISON, R. (1962) 'Defenses and the need to know', *Human Relations Training News*, **6**, 4, Winter.

HALES, H.K. (1989) 'Chaos as orderly disorder: Shifting ground in contemporary literacy and science' *New Literary History*, **20**, 2.

HEANEY, S. (1991) *Seeing Things*, London, Faber.

HOLLY, M.L. (1984) *Keeping a Personal and Professional Diary*, Geelong, Deakin University Press.

HOLLY, P.J. (1984) 'Beyond the cult of the individual: Putting the partnership into in-service collaboration', in NIAS J. (Ed) *Teaching Enquiry Based Courses*, Cambridge, Cambridge Institute of Education.

HOLLY, P.J. (1986) 'Soaring like turkeys — the impossible dream', *School Organisation*, **6**, 3, pp. 346–64.

HOLLY, P.J. (1991) 'Action research within institutional development: It's becoming second nature to us now', unpublished paper, March.

HOLLY, P.J. and HOPKINS, D. (1988) 'Evaluation and school improvement', *Cambridge Journal of Education*, **18**, 2.

HOLLY, P.J. and SOUTHWORTH, G. (1989) *The Developing School*, Lewes, Falmer Press.

HOPKINS, D. (1985) *A Teachers Guide to Classroom Research*, Milton Keynes, Open University Press.

HOPKINS, D. (Ed) (1986a) *In-service Training and Educational Development: An International Survey?* London, Croom Helm.

HOPKINS, D. (1986b) 'Enhancing validity in action research', paper given at the 'Collaborative enquiry and information skills', London, July, British Library Research & Development Dept.

HOPKINS, D. (1989) 'Integrating teacher development and school improvement: A study in teacher personality and school climate', paper prepared for the 1990 ASCD Yearbook on Staff Development.

HOUSE, E.R. (1974) *The politics of educational innovation*, San Francisco, CA, McCutcheon.

HOUSE, E. (1980) *Evaluating with Validity*, Beverley Hills, CA, Sage.

HUGHES, T. (1967) *Poetry in the Making*, London, Faber.

HUSTLER, D. *et al.* (Ed) (1986) *Action Research in Classrooms and School*, London, Allen and Unwin.

JAMES, M. (1989) Negotiation and dialogue in student assessment and teacher appraisal in SIMONS, H. and ELLIOTT, J. (Eds) *Rethinking Appraisal and Assessment*, Milton Keynes, Open University Press.

JOHNSON, D.W. and JOHNSON, F.P. (1981) *Joining Together: Group Theory and Group Skills*, London, Prentice-Hall 4th edition.

KANFER, F.H and GOLDSTEIN, A.P. (1980) *Helping People Change*, New York, Pergamon.

KEMMIS, S. (1980) 'The imagination of the case and the invention of the study' in SIMONS, H. (Ed) *'Towards a Science of the Singular'*, CARE Occasional Publications No.10, Norwich, CARE.

KEMMIS, S. (1989) *Metatheory and Metapractice in Educational Theorising and Research*, Geelong, Deakin University Press.

KEMMIS, S. and McTAGGART, R. (1981) *The Action Research Planner*, Geelong, Deakin University Press.

KEMMIS, S. and McTAGGART, R. (1988) *The Action Research Planner* (3rd edition), Geelong, Deakin University Press.

KRALL, F.R. (1988) 'From the inside out — personal history as educational research', *Educational Theory*, **38**, 4.

Kress, G. (1988) *Communication and Culture*, Sydney, University of New South Wales Press.

KROKER, A. and COOK, D. (1986) *The Postmodern Scene*, New York, St. Peters Press.

LATHER, P. (1986) 'Research as praxis', *Harvard Educational Review*, **56**, 3, August.

LAWSON, H. (1985) *Reflexivity: The Post-modern Predicament*, La Salle, Open Court.

LODGE, D. (1988) *Nice Work*, Harmondsworth, Penguin.

LOMAX, P. (1986) 'Action researchers' action research: A symposium', *British Journal of In-service Education*, **13**, 1.

LOMAX, P. (1993) 'Standards, criteria and the problematic of action research within an award bearing course', *Educational Action Research*, **2**, 1.

LYOTARD, J.F. (1979) *The Postmodern Condition: A Report on Knowledge*, Minneapolis, MT, University of Minnesota.

MACDONALD, B. (1974) 'The portrayal of persons as evaluation data' in NORRIS N. (Ed) *Safari: Theory into Practice*, Papers 2, Norwich, CARE.

MACLURE, M. and STRONACH, I. (1989) 'Seeing through the self: Contemporary biography and some implications for educational research', paper given at the annual meeting of the American Educational Research Association, San Francisco, April.

McNIFF, J. (1988) *Action Research: Principles and Practice*, London, Macmillan.

McNIFF, J. (1992) *Creating A Good Social Order from Action Research*, Poole, Hyde.

McNIFF, J. (1993) *Teaching as Learning: An Action Research Approach*, London, Routledge.

McTAGGART, R. and SINGH, M. (1987) A Fourth Generation of Action Research: Notes on a Deakin Seminar, Geelong, Deakin University Press.

MAGEE, B. (1973) *Popper*, London, Fontana.

MARRIS, P. (1974) *Loss and Change*, London, RKP.

MARSHALL, J. (1981) 'Making sense as a personal process', in REASON, P. and ROWAN, J. (Eds) *Human Inquiry*, Bath, John Wiley and Sons Ltd.

MORLEY, G. (1991) 'Adapting to the INSET revolution', unpublished MA dissertation, CARE at Cambridge Institute of Education.

NIAS, J. (1987) *Seeing Anew: Teachers Theories of Action*, Geelong, Deakin University Press.

NIAS, J. (1988) 'Introduction' in NIAS, J. and GROUNDWATER-SMITH, S. (Eds) *The Enquiring Teacher*, London, Falmer Press.

NIAS, J. (1989) *Primary Teachers Talking*, London, RKP.

NIAS, J., SOUTHWORTH, G. and CAMPBELL, P. (1992) *Whole School Curriculum Development in the Primary School*, London, Falmer Press.

NIAS, J., SOUTHWORTH, G. and YEOMANS, R. (1989) *Staff Relationships in the Primary School*, London, Cassell.

NICHOLSON, C. (1989) 'Postmodernism, feminising and education: The need for solidarity', *Educational Theory*, **39**, 3, Summer.

NIXON, J. (Ed) (1981) *A Teachers Guide to Action Research*, London, Grant McIntyre.

NODDINGS, N. (1994) 'An ethic of caring and its implications for instructional arrangements', in STONE, L. (Ed) *The Education Feminism Reader*, New York, Routledge.

OJA, S.N. (1989) 'Teachers: Ages and stages of adult development', in HOLLY, M.L. and McLAUGHLIN, C.S. (Eds) *Perspectives on Teacher Prefessional Development*, Lewes, Falmer Press.

OJA, S.N. and SMULYAN, L. (1989) *Collaborative Action Research: A Developmental Approach*, London, Falmer Press.

OVENS, P. (1991) *A Tutor's Use of Action Research for Professional Development Within an In-service Course for Teachers*, Norwich, University of East Anglia Press.

PINAR, W. (1980) 'Life history and educational experience', *Journal of Curriculum Theorising*, **2**, 2, Summer.

PINAR, W.F. (1988), 'Autobiography and the architecture of self', *Journal of Curriculum Theorising*, **8**, 1.

POLANYI, M. (1958) *Personal Knowledge*, London, RKP.

POSCH, P. (1986) 'University support for independent learning — a new development in the in-service education of teachers', *Cambridge Journal of Education*, **16**, 1.

POSCH, P. (1994) 'Changes in the culture of teaching and learning and the implication for action research', paper presented to the Collaborative Action Research Network conference, Birmingham, April.

RICOEUR, P. (1981) 'Hermeneutics and the human sciences', translated and introduced by J.B. Thompson, Cambridge, Cambridge University Press.

RORTY, R. (1980) *Philosophy and the Mirror of Nature*, Princeton, NJ, Princeton University Press.

RORTY, R. (1989) *Contingency, Irony and Solidarity*, Cambridge, Cambridge University Press.

ROWLAND, S. 'My body of knowledge' in NIAS, J. and GROUNDWATER-SMITH, S. (1988) *The Enquiring Teacher*, London, Falmer Press.

RUDDUCK, J. (1994) *Developing a Gender Policy in Secondary Schools*, Buckingham, Open University Press.

RUDDUCK, J. and HOPKINS, D. (Ed) *Research as a Basis for Teaching: Readings from the Work of Lawrence Stenhouse*, London, Heinemann.

SALZBERGER-WITTENBERG, I., HENRY, G. and OSBORN, E. (1983) *The Emotional Experience of Learning and Teaching*, London, RKP.

SCHON, D. (1983) *The Reflective Practitioner*, New York, Basic Books.

SCHON, D.A. (1987) *Educating the Reflective Practitioner*, San Francisco, CA, Jossey-Bass.

SCHOOLS COUNCIL (1983) 'Teacher pupil interaction and the quality of learning', project directed by John Elliott, Cambridge Institute of Education.

SIMONS, H. (1985) 'Against the rules: Procedural problems in school self-evaluation', *Curriculum Perspectives*, **5**, 2, October.

SIMONS, H. (1987) *Getting to Know Schools in a Democracy: The Politics and Process of Evaluation*, Lewes, Falmer Press.

SMAIL, D. (1984) *Illusion and Reality: the Meaning of Anxiety*, London, Dent.

SMITH, F. (1982) *Writing and the Writer*, London, Lawrence Erlbaum.

SMITH, N.L. (Ed) (1981) *Metaphors for Evaluation*, London, Sage.

SMITH, N.L. (Ed) (1982) *Communication Strategies in Evaluation*, Beverly Hills, CA, Sage.

SMYTH, J. (1991) *Teachers as Collaborative Learners*, Buckingham, Open University Press.

SPENDER, S. (1946) 'The making of a poem' in VERNON, P.E. (Ed) *Creativity*, Harmondsworth, Penguin.

STAKE, R. (1975) *The Case Study Method in Social Enquiry*, Norwich CARE, University of East Anglia Press.

STANLEY, L. (Ed) (1990) *Feminist Praxis*, London, Routledge.

STEEDMAN, C. (1986) *Landscape for a Good Woman: A Story of Two Lives*, London, Virago.

STENHOUSE, L. (1975) *An Introduction to Curriculum Research and Development*, London, Heinemann.

STRONACH, I. (1989) 'Transition learning: A reflective approach to education and politics in a new age', unpublished PhD thesis, Norwich, CARE, University of East Anglia Press.

STURROCK, J. (1979) *Structuralism and Since*, Oxford, Oxford University Press.

STURROCK, J. (1986) *Structuralism*, London, Paladin.

TRIPP, D. (1988) 'On collaboration: Teachers, self-assessment and professional journals', *Cambridge Journal of Education*, **18**, 3.

WALKER, M. (1993) 'Developing the theory and practice of action research: A South African case', *Educational Action Research*, **1**, 1.

WALKER, M. (1994) Keynote presentation, CARN conference, Birmingham.

WALKER, R. (1980) 'Making sense and losing meaning' in SIMONS, H. (Ed) *Towards a Science of the Singular*, Norwich, CARE, University.

WALKER, R. (1981) 'On the uses of fiction in educational research' in SMETHERHAM D. (Ed) *Practising Evaluation*, Onffield, Nafferton Books.

WALKER, R. (1985) *Doing Research: A Handbook for Teachers*, London, Methuen.

WEBB, R. (1990) *Practitioner Research in the Primary School*, Lewes, Falmer Press.

WEINDLING, D. and EARLEY, P. (1986) 'How heads manage change', *School Organisation*, **6**, 3.

WEINER, G. (1994) *Feminisms in Education: An Introduction*, Buckingham, Open University Press.

WHITEHEAD, J. (1989) 'Creating a living educational theory from questions of the kind, How do I improve my practice?', *Cambridge Journal of Education*, **19**, 1.

WILLIAMSON, J. (1986) 'Teachers talking: A consideration of the use of seminars and group discussions in in-service education', *British Journal of In-service Education*, **12**, 2.

WINTER, R. (1987) *Action-research and the Nature of Social inquiry*, Aldershot, Avebury.

WINTER, R. (1988) 'Fictional — critical writing: An approach to case study research by practitioners and for in-service and pre-service work with teachers' in NIAS, J. and GROUNDWATER-SMITH, S. (Eds) *The Enquiring Teacher*, London, Falmer Press.

WINTER, R. (1989) *Learning from Experience: Principles and Practice in Action Research*, Lewes, Falmer Press.

WINTER, R. (1993) 'Action research, practice and theory', *Educational Action Research Journal*, **1**, 2.

WINTER, R. (1994) 'The relevance of feminist theories of knowledge for action research', *Education Action Research*, **2**, 3.

WOODS, P. (1985) 'New songs played skilfully: Creativity and technique in writing up qualitative research' in BURGESS, R. (Ed.) *Issues in Educational Research*, London, Falmer Press.

WOOLF, V. (1945) *A Room of One's Own*, Harmondsworth, Penguin.

ZEICHNER, K. (1993) 'Personal renewal and social reconstruction', *Educational Action Research Journal*, **1**, 2.

Index